The Meaning of Marriage:
A Couple's Devotional

The

Meaning of Marriage:

A COUPLE'S
DEVOTIONAL

A Year of
Daily Devotions

TIMOTHY KELLER
and KATHY KELLER

VIKING

VIKING

An imprint of Penguin Random House LLC
penguinrandomhouse.com

Based upon *The Meaning of Marriage*, originally published by Dutton,
an imprint of Penguin Random House LLC, New York, in 2011.

ISBN 9780525560777 (hardcover)
ISBN 9780525560784 (ebook)

Printed in the United States of America
1   3   5   7   9   10   8   6   4   2

Set in Warnock Pro Light
Designed by Cassandra Garruzzo

All Bible references are from the New International
Version (NIV), unless otherwise noted.

To our sons and to the remarkable women who married them—
David and Jen
Michael and Sara
Jonathan and Ann-Marie

INTRODUCTION

Several years ago Tim and I wrote a book, *The Meaning of Marriage: Facing the Complexities of Commitment with the Wisdom of God.* We discussed a number of issues related to knowing and loving your spouse in the context of a marriage grounded in the Christian faith. Many people have told us how much the book has helped them, and nothing makes us happier. It was the fruit of hard-won experience, and God promises that what he gives to one is meant for the benefit of all.

It is not necessary to have read that book in order to use this one. But it is worth recapping some of the basic themes of *The Meaning of Marriage.* The main problem every marriage faces is the self-centeredness in both spouse's hearts. Traditional cultures often dealt with this by browbeating people about their sin. Modern culture has virtually enshrined it, talking about "Me-Marriages" that last only as long as both parties feel the marriage is meeting their needs without too much exertion. The solution, however, is the gospel of Christ, for it both humbles us and exalts us at the same time.

An equally crucial theme is that the essence of your marriage is a covenant, a binding promise. A covenant is neither a cold contract nor merely an emotional pledge. It is giving your whole life to each other, not just physically but also legally, financially, emotionally, spiritually. The binding, legal commitment creates an unparalleled space for trust, vulnerability, and intimacy. Many modern people think the essence of marriage is a romantic feeling, but rather it is the marriage promise that keeps you together through the ups and downs of feeling, which over time provides a depth of love that could not be attained any other way.

We see marriage as friendship-with-a-mission. While ancient and traditional marriages gave priority to the roles of parents, and modern marriage elevates the desires of romantic lovers, we argued that, along with all the other factors, spouses need to be best friends. Friendship, however, needs to be *about* something, and in a Christian marriage it needs to be about spiritual growth and each spouse helping the other to grow into Christlikeness. If we aim at holiness for each other, happiness will come; if we aim primarily at just happiness, we will get neither.

Then, for these various tasks and responsibilities in marriage, we pointed to a "toolbox" of ways to know and love your spouse over the years, particularly as you both go through major life changes and sometimes we feel we are married to a stranger. What do we do? There are three basic things to do: speak the truth; show love—in the particular "currencies" or "love languages" that your spouse finds most valuable; and, finally, give grace through regular repentance, forgiveness, and reconciliation.

In Christian marriage, it is both a glory and a challenge to love someone of the other gender. Loving across the gender divide takes a great deal of patience, understanding, humility, and love. Today, of course, this is an area marked by controversy, but we tried as much as possible to follow the Scriptures here, which critique both overly rigid gender stereotypes as well as the modern denial of distinct gender roles.

In the last two chapters we turned to the subjects of singleness and sexuality. There we laid out something of the Christian ethic and understanding of sex, so revolutionary when it burst on the world scene, but so contested today.

So why this devotional? The purpose of this couple's devotional is to provide an opportunity for sustained and practical reflection on love and marriage within a Christian perspective. A book like *The Meaning of Marriage* can provide principles and insights, but it can also be hard to digest and apply to everyday life. In the book you hold, we both expanded on and broke down the themes and lessons into short meditations, looking at each concept in its various aspects and proposing application questions and practices.

This devotional pulls out passages from *The Meaning of Marriage* and provides an opportunity to think out the personal implications of one very specific aspect of Christian marriage each day.

On the first week of each month, we provide you with a Scripture text regarding love, sex, and marriage, followed by a meditation on an aspect of the biblical teaching. After that there is a reflection, which is a set of application questions, followed finally with a brief example of a prayer about the subject. While some of these biblical texts are referred to in *The Meaning of Marriage*, these studies are new and not found in the earlier book. The texts that are covered are listed on page xiv.

JANUARY	*Genesis 1 and 2*	Marriage and creation
FEBRUARY	*Genesis 2–3; Ephesians 5*	Marriage and redemption
MARCH	*Various*	The seventh commandment
APRIL	*Genesis 39 and various*	Preventing adultery
MAY	*Various*	Divorce
JUNE	*Proverbs and various*	Who we are to one another
JULY	*Various New Testament*	How to serve one another
AUGUST	*Various New Testament*	How to reconcile with one another
SEPTEMBER	*1 Corinthians 6*	The Christian sexual revolution: 1
OCTOBER	*1 Corinthians 7*	The Christian sexual revolution: 2
NOVEMBER	*The Song of Solomon -*	Love song: seeking one another
DECEMBER	*The Song of Solomon*	Love song: finding one another

On each day of the other three weeks of every month we begin with a quote from *The Meaning of Marriage* instead of a Bible verse, followed by a meditation and a reflection. Finally there is a "Thought for prayer" that gives some ideas for how you can pray the topic of the day into your heart and life.

This is a "couple's devotional," and it is designed for married couples to use. One way to do it is to read it aloud to each other. Then ask: "What helped you the most?" After that, answer the Reflection questions together. Finally pray together, using the "Thought for prayer" as a springboard for your own conversation with God. Another way to use this book, however, is to read it daily as an individual, write down your thoughts, and regularly meet with your spouse to discuss your insights and findings.

Keep in mind that the basic themes and lessons noted here

will be brought up numerous times, but each time they will be approached from a different perspective, or asking different practical questions.

The Meaning of Marriage was not written only for married couples. Its origin lay in a series of sermons to a congregation consisting overwhelmingly of single adults. This particular devotional, however, is meant for couples, though unmarried couples who are engaged or who are considering marriage could use it in the way we have prescribed. Some of the meditations near the end of the year should be especially applicable to them.

One very important caveat. Every Christian needs to be reading the Bible and praying daily. This book, while it can supplement that, should not be the only time one spends daily before God. As important as this subject is, marriage is not the only thing you should be talking to God about for an entire year! We would ask readers to consider also using either our Psalms or Proverbs devotionals along with this one, or some other aid to a daily time with God.

The Meaning of Marriage:
A Couple's Devotional

January 1

So God created mankind in his own image, in the image of God he created them. Male and female he created them. (Genesis 1:27)

INSTITUTED OF GOD. Today we think of marriage as a romantic relationship between two people on whom the marriage ceremony bestows some legal benefits. However, the Bible says marriage is the invention of God, and therefore it is woven into the very fabric of our human nature. The first mention of gender and marriage in the Bible occurs with the first mention of humanity itself. And while not all individuals must marry, the human race as a whole is built for it. No human society can thrive without healthy marriages.

Reflection: What links do you see between the health of people in general and the health of marriages?

Prayer: Lord, the strength of our marriages makes for well-being in society. Forgive me for thinking so narrowly and so selfishly about this. As we pursue happy marriages, help us to do it for your sake and for others' sake as well as for ourselves. Amen.

January 2

> The Lord God said, "It is not good for the man to be alone." (Genesis 2:18a)

THE NECESSITY OF FRIENDSHIP. Genesis shows us God creating everything "good." But the first thing declared *not* good is Adam's being alone. This means we have a God-created need that nothing but human love relationships can satisfy. Even Adam's unimpeded relationship with God and his home in paradise could not completely fulfill it. Loneliness, then, is not a sin, and this means two things. First, while it is not necessary to be married (e.g., Paul and Jesus), it *is* necessary for a thriving human life to have great friendships. Second, when God brings Eve to Adam it is clear she is not merely a sexual or business partner, but the friend for whom he has yearned.

Reflection: It is possible for spouses to give so much to co-parenting, romance, sexuality, and administering their affairs that they neglect their friendship. How can you avoid that?

Prayer: Lord Jesus, you are not only our true spouse (Ephesians 5:25–26) but also our greatest friend (John 15:12–15). Let our marriages be full of the truthfulness, affection, and faithful commitment of friendship. Amen.

That is why a man leaves his father and mother and is united to his wife, and they become one flesh. (Genesis 2:24)

LEAVING. Marriage entails *leaving*. It does not mean you reject or abandon your family of origin. Rather, it means that the needs and concerns of your present family take precedence over the desires and practices of your former family. You should work out new patterns of life together that fit your particular context, gifts, and needs. You have not "left" your former family if you automatically insist that everything in your marriage be done like you saw it done in your parents' marriage and family. In short, your spouse should have uncontested priority in your heart. The regard you have for your parents or even for your children should not rival that which you have for your spouse.

Reflection: Make a list of the ways that you can fail to "leave" and to transfer your supreme loyalty from all others to your spouse.

Prayer: Lord, take away our divided hearts. Let us love you more than all other beings in the universe. And when we marry, enable us to love each other more than any other person in the world. Amen.

Then the Lord God made a woman . . . and . . . brought her to the man. . . . That is why a man leaves his father and mother and is united to his wife, and they become one flesh. (Genesis 2:22, 24)

PROMISING. Genesis 2:22–25 is the first marriage ceremony, in which "God himself, like a father of the bride, leads the woman to the man."[1] The word "united" translates a Hebrew word meaning a binding covenantal relationship (Deuteronomy 10:20, 11:22–23). In our individualistic society, the legality of marriage seems inconsequential. It's said to be "just a piece of paper" and that what matters is that we love each other. Yet if you truly love each other, why not give yourselves to each other in every way—physically, emotionally, personally, legally, socially, and economically? That's what happens in a marriage covenant, and it is done through making a promise.

Reflection: Why are people hesitant to marry? What are the ways that our culture undermines this view of marriage as a covenant?

Prayer: Lord, we live in a commitment-fearing culture. We have been taught to always keep our relational options open, yet we don't want people to love *us* like that! Teach us how to be faithful friends and faithful spouses, in fair weather and foul, for better and for worse. You have been that to us. Amen.

That is why a man leaves his father and mother and is united to his wife, and they become one flesh. (Genesis 2:24)

CLEAVING. Older translations say that a man should "cleave unto his wife"—a term that means literally to be glued to something. Why is a binding covenant, created by solemn vows, so crucial to the biblical understanding of marriage? First, it is a crucial test. The willingness to enter a lifelong covenant is evidence that your love for each other has reached marriage-level proportions. Second, it is resource for strength. There will be hard times in any marriage, in which your patience and love will need the support of knowing you made a solemn promise. Last, it is instructive. The covenant teaches us that marriage is not ultimately about self-fulfillment but about self-giving.[2]

Reflection: "A wedding vow is confining in the short run but liberating in the long run." Do you agree? Why or why not?

Prayer: Lord, when our commitment to covenantal marriage weakens, help us remember your unwavering faithfulness to us, going even to the death of the cross. Amen.

> That is why a man leaves his father and mother and is united to his wife, and they become one flesh. (Genesis 2:24)

UNITING. A husband and wife become *one flesh*. "Flesh" in the Bible is often a synecdoche for the entire person (as in "I will pour out my Spirit upon all flesh," Acts 2:17). Just as male and female literally fit together as a whole in sex, so a husband and wife enter a deep personal union at all levels of their lives. They become physically, emotionally, socially, legally one. Sexual union, then, is a way to renew and deepen the covenant of marriage. It is an acting out, physically, of the inseparable oneness in all other areas created by the marriage covenant.

Reflection: How can sex be an ideal way to renew the marriage vow? How can married sex be practiced in such a way that fails to reflect the marriage vow? What can you do to avoid this?

Prayer: Lord, we have been taught that sex exists for self-fulfillment, not for self-giving. Help us to think about it differently. Show us how human sexuality should reflect your own love for us. Amen.

Male and female he created them. God blessed them and said to them, "Be fruitful and increase in number; fill the earth and subdue it." (Genesis 1:27–28)

PROCREATIVITY. Just as not all people must be married, so not all marriages will produce children. Nevertheless, God has designed marriage to be capable of creating and nurturing new life. Only male and female together, each doing something the other cannot, can produce new human beings. Then, as children grow in the presence of both mother and father, they are exposed to the unique glories and strengths of male and female humanity. Finally, the lifelong commitment of marriage gives children the necessary security and stability that they need to thrive. So God gives to marriage the procreativity that is a reflection of his own life-giving creativity.

Reflection: Think out the ways that every aspect of biblical marriage supports the reproduction and nurture of new human beings.

Prayer: Lord, you could have simply made new humans materialize by your power. Instead you made us your partners in bearing new human life into the world and nurturing them through committed love. Thank you for this great gift. Give more of us the wisdom and character we will need to use it well. Amen.

January 8

This book . . . is for those spouses who have discovered how challeng-ing day-to-day marriage is and who are searching for practical resources to survive the sometimes overwhelming "fiery trials" of matrimony and to grow through them. Our society's experience with marriage has given us the metaphor "the honeymoon is over." This is a book for those who have experienced this as a literal truth and may have fallen back to earth with a thud. (Hardcover, pp. 10–11; paper-back, p. 3)

DON'T BE NAÏVE OR CYNICAL. *The Meaning of Marriage* is a realistic book about marriage because the Bible is hyperrealis-tic about human beings. Marriage is a tremendous good. It was God's idea, and the human race as a whole could not do without it. However, because we are sinners, marriage is not easy. So the Bible aligns neither with sentimentality around marriage that may have existed in our imagined past nor with the cynicism about it that characterizes our own time. In the past marriage was an absolute necessity for everyone—single adults were almost social pariahs. Today marriage is seen as just one more lifestyle option.[3] Steering between these two distorted views is crucial if you are to either choose a marriage partner well or to live well with the spouse you have chosen.

Reflection: Considering these two distorted views—to which do you lean? Why? What effects has your inclination had on you?

Thought for prayer: Think of the Bible as a vast untapped resource for you as you live out your marriage. Ask God to reveal more and more of his wisdom regarding marriage to you from his Word.

[There is a] deep ambivalence with which Western culture views marriage. . . . [Objections include:] marriage was originally about property and is now in flux, marriage crushes individual identity and has been oppressive for women, marriage stifles passion and is ill-fitted to psychological reality, marriage is "just a piece of paper" that only serves to complicate love, and so on. But beneath these philosophical objections lies a snarl of conflicted personal emotions, born out of many negative experiences with marriage and family life. (Hardcover, p. 11; paperback, p. 4)

CONFLICTED OVER MARRIAGE. Our culture has a love-hate relationship with marriage. Mervyn Cadwallader argued that marriage was "a wretched institution." He wrote: "[M]arriage . . . spells the end of voluntary affection, of love freely given and joyously received. Beautiful romances are transmuted into dull marriages, and eventually the relationship becomes constricting, corrosive, grinding, and destructive. . . . The very idea of an irrevocable contract obliging the parties concerned to a lifetime of romantic effort is utterly absurd."[4] Yet Cadwallader admits he keeps trying for a good marriage (he was married three times) and that most people will still try it, too. But if the very idea of marriage is absurd, why *do* we keep trying? There may never have been a society as deeply conflicted about marriage as is ours.

Reflection: How fair are each of the objections to marriage listed in the quotes above? Why do you think many people believe this about marriage? Why, on the other hand, do you think many people still desire marriage?

Thought for prayer: Pray that the attitude of your hearts toward your marriage would not be overly shaped by its difficulties, but more by the promises and instructions of the Bible.

[The *Meaning of Marriage*'s] primary goal is to give both married and unmarried people a vision for what marriage is according to the Bible. That will help married people correct mistaken views that might be harming their marriage, and it will help single people stop destructively over-desiring marriage or destructively dismissing marriage altogether. Also, a Bible-based marriage book will help each reader have a better idea of whom he or she should consider as a prospective mate. (Hardcover, p. 12; paperback, pp. 4–5)

MARRIAGE IS NOT ENOUGH. In the book *Mere Christianity*, C. S. Lewis says that when we first "fall in love" that "the longings which arise in us . . . are longings which no marriage . . . can really satisfy." He adds that he is not talking of "unsuccessful marriages" but "of the best possible ones." If Lewis is right—and we believe he is—then how you respond to this fact of human existence will determine the course not only of your marriage but also of the rest of your life. You have three options. One is to blame the spouse and look for another. The second is to become cynical and disillusioned about marriage. The third is to realize, "If I find in myself a desire which no experience in this world can satisfy, the most probable explanation is that I was made for another world."[5]

Reflection: If you were to realize and embrace Lewis's third option, what would it mean for your attitude toward marriage if you are in a difficult one? For your attitude toward marriage if you are a single person assessing prospective spouses?

Thought for prayer: Pray that you would be able to embrace the third option, in order to avoid romanticism or cynicism about marriage, and also in order to learn to love God more than anything else.

Marriage did not evolve in the late Bronze Age as a way to determine property rights. At the climax of the Genesis account of creation we see God bringing a woman and a man together to unite them in marriage. The Bible begins with a wedding (of Adam and Eve) and ends in the book of Revelation with a wedding (of Christ and the church). Marriage is God's idea. (Hardcover, p. 13; paperback, p. 6)

MADE FOR MARRIAGE. God created us *for* certain things. He made us to worship him (Exodus 20:2–3). He made us for labor—to create and cultivate (Genesis 2:15). History shows that to ignore or try to avoid these things leads to dire consequences. God also, when he created us in his image, made us male and female (Genesis 1:27) and gave us the gift of marriage (Genesis 2:21–25). This means that, while not all marry (1 Corinthians 7), the human race as a whole cannot do without it. It also means that what we do sexually either reflects and images God and participates in his ways and work, or it rejects them. We can't make marriage to suit us. Rather, God made us for it.

Reflection: Our culture is the first to see marriage as something we can design as we wish, rather than an institution that we receive and submit to. To what degree have you been influenced by our culture's view? What effect has that had on how you live out your marriage?

Thought for prayer: Pray for our society, that we might not harm ourselves by marring the institution of marriage. Pray for ourselves, that we can receive marriage from God as a gift.

January 12

If God invented marriage, then those who enter it should make every effort to understand and submit to his purposes for it. We do this in many other aspects of our lives. Think of buying a car: If you purchase a vehicle, a machine well beyond your own ability to create, you will certainly take up the owner's manual and abide by what the designer says the car needs by way of treatment and maintenance. To ignore it would be to court disaster. (Hardcover, p. 13; paperback, p. 6)

REGULATED BY GOD. Many argue that marriage has been evolving for centuries and so we can make it whatever we want it to be. But what God creates he also regulates—the Bible shows us how marriage should be conducted and so it critiques all cultural distortions of it. Genesis is a sustained critique of ancient polygamy and the misery it brought, especially to women. Yet the binding, covenantal nature of marriage in the Bible also opposes the modern idea of marriage as a merely transactional, provisional relationship between individuals. If we honor God by mutually loving and serving our spouse rather than ourselves—as the Bible prescribes—we transcend these historic distortions of marriage.

Reflection: Think of the lack of mutuality in many traditional forms of marriage as well as the highly negotiated, transitory nature of many modern relationships. How does each of these undermine the biblical idea of love as unselfish service to another?

Thought for prayer: Pray that you would be able to reject all of these cultural idolatries as you live out your own marriage.

It is hard to get a good perspective on marriage. We all see it through the inevitably distorted lenses of our own experience. If you came from an unusually stable home, where your parents had a great marriage, that may have "made it look easy" to you, and so when you get to your own marriage you may be shocked by how much it takes to forge a lasting relationship. On the other hand, if you have experienced a bad marriage or a divorce, either as a child or an adult, your view of marriage may be overly wary and pessimistic. You may be *too* expectant of relationship problems and, when they appear, be too ready to say, "Yup, here it goes," and to give up. (Hardcover, pp. 14–15; paperback, pp. 7–8)

FREE FROM THE PAST. One place we can get a distorted view of marriage is from our culture. The other place we can get one is from our family background. It is understandable but mistaken to look to our parents' marital relationship as the final word on what marriage really is like. That makes no more sense than letting your encounters with one or two doctors determine your view of the entire medical profession. Instead, consider that while you've seen firsthand part of what marriage is all about—some of the joys or many of the difficulties—only the Bible can give you the fullness of God's perspective. The Bible's wisdom and promises regarding marriage can free you from your own past.

Reflection: If you had no idea of marriage apart from your parents' marriage, what would your view be? How has your view of marriage been shaped by their marriage or the marriages of the people who raised you?

Thought for prayer: Thank God for what you have learned about marriage from your parents or those who have raised you, and ask him to supplement and fill out that knowledge from his Word.

In other words, any kind of background experience of marriage may make you ill equipped for [doing] it yourself. So where can you go for a comprehensive view of marriage? There are many good "how-to" volumes usually written by counselors that can be very helpful. In a few years, however, marriage manuals look dated. In the Bible you have teaching that has been tested by millions of people over centuries and in multiple cultures. Do we have any other resource on marriage like that? (Hardcover, pp. 14–15; paperback, p. 8)

LEARNING FROM THE WHOLE BIBLE. We have been calling ourselves to look to the Bible for our views of marriage, but where? We must not think that the Bible only gives us information about marriage when speaking directly about it in places like Genesis 2, 1 Corinthians 7, or Ephesians 5. For example, virtually the entire book of Proverbs is crucial for marital wisdom, because it discusses at length subjects such as money, emotions, the use and abuse of our tongues, sexuality, decision-making, and the deadly sins of pride, anger, envy, sloth, gluttony, greed, and lust. See also the many biblical texts on repentance, forgiveness, and reconciliation (e.g., Matthew 18:15–35; Ephesians 4:25–32). All these topics, drawn from the entire Bible, are necessary to master if your marriage is to grow and thrive.

Reflection: If marital thriving is dependent on your grasp of the whole Bible, how could you plan to know it better than you do now? Consider ways of reading whole books of the Bible (such as Proverbs or Ephesians) looking specifically for marital wisdom.

Thought for prayer: Ask God for help in not merely knowing the Bible in general, but being shaped by it in the way you think and act in the areas of sex, love, and marriage.

January 15

According to the Bible, God devised marriage to reflect his saving love for us in Christ, to refine our character, to create stable human community for the birth and nurture of children, and to accomplish all this by bringing the complementary sexes into an enduring whole-life union. (Hardcover, p. 9; paperback, p. 16)

HAPPINESS AS A BY-PRODUCT. We live in an individualistic culture in which marriage is seen as a means for personal happiness. The Bible says married love is an image of our union with Christ, which comes only because he emptied himself of his glory for us (Philippians 2:1–11) and because we have in turn humbled ourselves in repentance and service to him. Marriage can reflect the saving love of God and shape our character into his likeness. And there is a great happiness that is a by-product of giving sacrificial love both to Christ and to our spouse.

Reflection: The quote lists four reasons God created marriage. How does each support the others? Are each of these reasons equally important?

Thought for prayer: Ask God to show you all the ways that your marriage is strengthening your character. Thank him for them, even for those ways that have been difficult.

The Bible's teaching on marriage does not . . . reflect the perspective of any one culture or time. The teachings of Scripture challenge our contemporary Western culture's narrative of individual freedom as the only way to be happy. At the same time, it critiques how traditional cultures perceive the unmarried adult to be less than a fully formed human being. (Hardcover, p. 16; paperback, p. 10)

NEITHER LEFT NOR RIGHT. Progressive Western culture is suspicious of marriage, seeing it as inherently incompatible with individual freedom. It accepts marriage only if it is stripped down to be just a romantic, emotional relationship that lasts as long as it brings happiness and fulfillment to both parties. On the other hand, non-Western, traditional societies are suspicious of singleness. They valorize marriage and consider the long-term single adult deficient. The Christian view does not fit on this "left-to-right" spectrum. Our primary identity is in Christ and our primary family consists of our brothers and sisters in Christ (Mark 3:31–35). This frees us to give ourselves to each other in marriage *or* to remain single, as God calls us.

Reflection: By which of these two cultural views of marriage— progressive or traditional—have you been most influenced? How has that influence affected how you approach marriage yourself?

Thought for prayer: Ask God to make your church one that welcomes and supports both married couples and singles. Or ask God to help you find a congregation that does.

The Biblical authors' teaching constantly challenged their own cultures' beliefs—they were not simply a product of ancient mores and practices. We cannot, therefore, write off the Biblical view of marriage as one-dimensionally regressive or culturally obsolete. (Hardcover, p. 17; paperback, p. 10)

NEITHER ANCIENT NOR MODERN. Ancient Near-Eastern cultures supported polygamy. But Genesis shows the misery of multiple-spouse marriages. Roman culture dictated that while a wife could not have sex with anyone but her spouse, every husband was free to have sex with many others. The New Testament put an end to that double standard and introduced mutual consent in marital sex (1 Corinthians 7:2–5). What the Bible says about sex and marriage is not the product of any human culture. Rather it critiques every human culture with divine revelation of what God wants marriage to be.

Reflection: Since the biblical teaching is subversive toward every culture, in what ways does it critique and undermine the dominant beliefs in our culture about sex, romance, and marriage?

Thought for prayer: Ask God to help you receive the Bible's teaching on sex and marriage as his wise Word, even though our culture and our own inward feelings and sensibilities may resist it.

January 18

Unless you're able to look at marriage through the lens of Scripture instead of through your own fears or romanticism, through your particular experience, or through your culture's narrow perspectives, you won't be able to make intelligent decisions about your own marital future. (Hardcover, p. 17; paperback, p. 10)

NEITHER FEARFUL NOR GULLIBLE. Many today fear that marriage requires more self-discipline than any human being can really muster. Others believe that everyone has a soul mate just waiting for us and, if we can just find him or her, everything in marriage will go smoothly. Our culture is just as schizophrenic as we are. Some books, movies, and talk-show experts lead us to believe that the perfect romance will heal everything wrong with us, while other strong cultural voices tell us not to give up our independence to anyone. If, however, we look to the love of God for our highest fulfillment rather than to either romantic love *or* personal freedom, then we will be neither too optimistic nor pessimistic about marriage. We will see marriage for what it is—a good gift from God. It is neither an absolute necessity for a fulfilled human life nor an impossible dream.

Reflection: Do you tend to be too romantic and desperate for marriage or too fearful and pessimistic about marriage? Why? How has this affected your courtship and marriage so far?

Thought for prayer: Remember St. Augustine's famous statement that our souls are restless until they find their great rest in God. Ask the Lord to help you to find your satisfaction in him so you don't look to marriage for what only he can give you.

January 19

Marriage is glorious but hard. It's a burning joy and strength, and yet it is also blood, sweat, and tears, humbling defeats and exhausting victories. No marriage I know more than a few weeks old could be described as a fairy tale come true. Therefore, it is not surprising that the only phrase in Paul's famous discourse on marriage in Ephesians 5 that many couples can relate to is verse 32 [". . . and the two will become one flesh. This is a profound mystery."]. Sometimes you fall into bed, after a long, hard day of trying to understand each other, and you can only sigh: "This is all a profound mystery!" At times, your marriage seems to be an unsolvable puzzle, a maze in which you feel lost. (Hardcover, p. 21; paperback, pp. 13–14)

BOTH HARD AND WONDERFUL. Here are two facts about marriage: it is exceedingly hard and uniquely wonderful. That sounds contradictory, but it is not. Think of the endless, excruciating hours of practice it takes to become a premier athlete, musician, scholar, or writer. The long, strenuous hours of labor gives those who endure them the ability, power, insight, and skill to create beauty. Marriage is hard, but so wonderful that the hardness and difficulty are absolutely worth it.

Reflection: Make two lists. What are the hardest things about marriage? What are the most wonderful things? How do the hard things actually lead to the wonderful things?

Thought for prayer: Ask God to help you to grow through trials and difficulties into someone who can love another person wisely and well.

There's no relationship between human beings that is greater or more important than marriage. In the Bible's account, God himself officiates at the first wedding (Genesis 2:22–25). And when the man sees the woman, he breaks into poetry and exclaims, "At last!" Everything in the text proclaims that marriage, next to our relationship to God, is the most profound relationship there is. And that is why, like knowing God himself, coming to know and love your spouse is difficult and painful yet rewarding and wondrous. (Hardcover, pp. 21–22; paperback, p. 14)

LOSING INDEPENDENCE AND FINDING FREEDOM. The Bible likens our relationship to God to a marriage, and with good reason. Christ lost his glory and power in order to come to earth and die for us. We must give up our rights to self-determination in order to unite with him in love. In the same way, spouses give up their freedom and independence in order to know the deeper freedom of mutual love and sacrificial service to one another. Once we are saved in Christ, then our knowledge and love of him progresses mainly through failures, repentance, and forgiveness. Failures are the way to learn and grow. Similarly, spouses find their love deepening as they fail, repent, and forgive each other.

Reflection: List other ways that our relationship with God is like the relationship of marriage. How does seeing these analogies help us with both relationships?

Thought for prayer: Ask God to help you more willingly surrender the freedom of independence in order to know the freedom of mutual love.

[There is] an increasing wariness and pessimism about marriage in our culture, and this is especially true of younger adults. They believe their chances of having a good marriage are not great, and, even if a marriage is stable, there is in their view the horrifying prospect that it will become sexually boring. (Hardcover, p. 22; paperback, pp. 14–15)

ARRANGED MARRIAGES? Some countries still include the practice of arranged marriage, where one's spouse is chosen for you. Divorce rates for such marriages are actually lower than for other types of marriage in the society.[6] The premise of such unions is that you can grow to love someone with whom you are not initially passionate. My own grandmother's marriage was arranged and in describing it she told me that feelings of love follow actions of love as long as you are both seeking to love the other person. The Bible does not favor arranged marriages, but neither does it require strong sexual chemistry as a prerequisite. Modern people commonly assume that we have to have overwhelming, passionate feelings to begin a marriage, and that they can recede completely against our will. No wonder we are afraid.

Reflection: The Bible doesn't prescribe any one way to find a mate. What are the disadvantages of arranged marriages? What are the advantages?

Thought for prayer: Ask God to help Christian couples to put more stock in character and compassion than chemistry.

> Driving this practice [of cohabitation] are several widespread beliefs. One is the assumption that most marriages are unhappy. . . . Living together before marriage, many argue, improves your chances of making a good marriage choice. It helps you discover whether you are compatible before you take the plunge. . . . The problem with these beliefs and assumptions, however, is that every one of them is almost completely wrong. . . . "[A] substantial body of evidence indicates that those who live together before marriage are more likely to break up after marriage." (Hardcover, p. 23; paperback, pp. 15–16)

LIVING TOGETHER? Many couples think it common sense to live together before marriage in order to determine whether their romantic feelings will endure and if they are compatible. However, the majority of studies show that cohabiting couples are more likely to divorce should they marry, and they experience much more instability and dissatisfaction in general than married people. Why? One reason is that cohabitation fails to make committed trust the heart of the love relationship. To say "I love you but I don't want to marry" is a contradiction. What you mean is, "I want to receive things from you, but I don't love you enough to trust my whole life to you."

Reflection: What are some of the reasons that cohabitation can set a couple up for trouble later, even if they marry? What are the advantages to living together only after you have married?

Thought for prayer: Ask God to help the people of our society not fear marriage. Give them the strength to believe that marriage can offer them so much more than fleeting passion or convenience.

[I]ndividuals who were continuously married had 75 percent more wealth at retirement than those who never married or who divorced and did not remarry. . . . [M]arried people experience greater physical and mental health . . . marriage provides a profound "shock absorber" that helps you navigate disappointments, illnesses, and other difficulties. . . . Studies show that spouses hold one another to greater levels of personal responsibility and self-discipline than friends or other family members can. . . . Married people make each other practice saving, investment, and delayed gratification. Nothing can mature character like marriage. (Hardcover, p. 24; paperback, pp. 16–17)

POWER FOR CHANGE. There are many reasons why marriage can refine and change us for the good in ways that no other relationship can. Some are listed above. It provides support in suffering, accountability for behavior change, and incentive to learn long-term thinking rather than impulsiveness. Perhaps the biggest resource for personal transformation is that your spouse can see (and feel) your faults more than anyone else, even more than your parents or your siblings. And so it is possible to see ourselves more accurately through the eyes of our spouse than we have before. That makes change possible—but only if we learn to speak the truth in love to one another. If we refuse to speak truthfully in marriage we can get a *more* distorted picture of ourselves than we had before.

Reflection: How does failing to speak the truth in love in a marriage distort each spouse's view of him- or herself? How does speaking the truth without love distort? How does loving but hiding the truth distort?

Thought for prayer: Ask God to help you speak the truth in love to one another. Especially ask for the graciousness and wisdom it takes to say hard things in a way that the listener can still accept.

[T]he number of married people who say they are "*very* happy" in their marriages is high—about 61–62 percent—and there has been little decrease in this figure during the last decade. Most striking of all, longitudinal studies demonstrate that two-thirds of those unhappy marriages out there will become happy within five years if people stay married and do not get divorced.... [One researcher wrote:] "the benefits of divorce have been oversold." (Hardcover, p. 26; paperback, pp. 18–19)

NOT SO FAST. The Bible recognizes that in a sinful world, divorce may be right (Matthew 19:8), and no one should make excuses for an adulterer, a deserter, or an abuser. It is never loving to allow someone to sin against you. Nevertheless, the Bible indicates that divorce is to be a last resort. We are all quick to believe that the fault for any marriage problem lies mainly in the *other*, not us. If we refuse efforts to reconcile, if we flee too quickly from the marriage rather than recognizing our own flaws and growing past them, we may only take the seeds of a new failure into the next marriage. Longitudinal studies and anecdotal experience confirm this biblical wisdom.[7]

Reflection: Can you name what looked like an intractable problem in your marriage (or someone else's)? What helped you or the couple move forward?

Thought for prayer: Ask God to give you patience with your spouse, and to see your own faults and sins more clearly. Understanding your role in any relationship's problems is essential to getting beyond it.

During the last two decades, the great preponderance of research evidence shows that people who are married consistently show much higher degrees of satisfaction with their lives than those who are single, divorced, or living with a partner. It also reveals that most people are happy in their marriages, and most of those who are not and who don't get divorced eventually become happy. (Hardcover, p. 26; paperback, p. 19)

THE GOODNESS OF MARRIAGE. The percentage of American adults who have never been married is greater than ever and fewer never-married adults say they would like to be married.[8] Marriage rates have also fallen dramatically in most European nations over the last ten years because younger adults value their independence but still want intimacy.[9] Yet even under present cultural conditions, most marriages are happy and married people live more satisfied lives than unmarried people. This runs counter to the intuitions of younger adults, but it should not surprise us. Marriage is good for most of the population because it was invented by God for human well-being. That will always be the case.

Reflection: Do the findings mentioned in the quote above surprise you? Why is married life so satisfying for people?

Thought for prayer: Ask God to use his loving power over history to change social conditions, changing people's fear and indifference toward marriage.

[C]hildren who grow up in married, two-parent families have two to three times more positive life outcomes than those who do not. The overwhelming verdict, then, is that being married and growing up with parents who are married are enormous boosts to our well-being. (Hardcover, p. 26; paperback, p. 19)

THE IRREPLACEABILITY OF MARRIAGE. A survey asked people which of the following statements came closer to their own views: "Society is better off if people make marriage and having children a priority, or society is just as well off if people have priorities other than marriage and children." In 2014 fully two-thirds of those in their twenties chose the second.[10] Yet no society has ever come up with any better way to nurture children into healthy adults other than through married, two-parent families.[11] The Bible, of course, told us all this long ago, namely, that marriage is not exclusively about the fulfillment of the couple, but also about the creation of a new, enduring community for the nurture of new human life.

Reflection: Why do you think most young people agreed with the second statement? What beliefs lie behind it? Do you share those views?

Thought for prayer: Ask God to use his loving power over history to strengthen families for the sake of the happiness and well-being of the next generation of children.

Paradoxically, it may be that the pessimism [about marriage] comes from a new kind of unrealistic idealism about marriage, born of a significant shift in our culture's understanding of the purpose of marriage.... [T]he earlier "ideal of marriage as a permanent contractual union designed for the sake of mutual love, procreation, and protection is slowly giving way to a new reality of marriage as a 'terminal sexual contract' designed for the gratification of the individual parties." (Hardcover, p. 27; paperback, p. 20)

THE PRESSURE OF MODERN MARRIAGE. In previous times, the essence of marriage was seen as the covenant. Tension and disappointment was expected, but the contract was there when our emotions were unreliable. Jane Eyre gives the old view of vows and promises: "If at my individual convenience I might break them, what would be their worth? . . . [On them] I plant my foot."[12] Modern marriage, however, is conditional and based on mutual gratification. That puts huge pressure on each spouse to stay attractive and low maintenance at all times to the other partner. Who can do that over the years? So the supposedly more liberating modern model of marriage might be dooming itself.

Reflection: Which of the two views described in the quote above is closer to your personal belief about the nature of marriage? Discuss how the older, more restrictive view can be more liberating.

Thought for prayer: Ask God to help you to see that, just as his service leads to freedom, so marriage vows and promises are ways to liberation.

The [older, Western view of marriage was] that the purpose of marriage was to create a framework for lifelong devotion and love between a husband and a wife. It was a solemn bond, designed to help each party subordinate individual impulses and interests in favor of the relationship. . . . Marriage created character by bringing male and female into a binding partnership . . . creating the only kind of social stability in which children could grow and thrive. (Hardcover, p. 27; paperback, pp. 20–21)

MARRIAGE AND CHRISTLIKENESS. Marriage is uniquely character forming. One reason (as we saw previously) is because no one can see your sins like your spouse. Your spouse will become a mirror in which you can see yourself more clearly than ever—if you have the courage to look. But there is a second reason. Marriage presents you with more opportunities for voluntary self-sacrifice than even parenting does. (The sacrifices you make for your children do not feel as *voluntary.*) Over and over every day marriage provides occasions in which you can respond to your spouse graciously rather than with irritation, humbly rather than with arrogance. This gives you many opportunities to grow into Christlikeness—if you have the courage to use them.

Reflection: What other reasons can you think of that make marriage uniquely character forming? How has it helped you in particular?

Thought for prayer: Ask God to shape you into Christlikeness through your marriage.

[In the new view] marriage was redefined as finding emotional and sexual fulfillment and self-actualization. . . . [So] married persons married for themselves, not to fulfill responsibilities to God or society. . . . [This] privatized marriage, taking it out of the public sphere, and redefined its purpose as individual gratification, not any "broader good" such as reflecting God's nature, producing character, or raising children. Slowly, but surely, this newer understanding of marriage has displaced the older ones in Western culture. (Hardcover, p. 28; paperback, pp. 21–22)

MARRIAGE AND SOCIAL JUSTICE. Modern young people are intensely committed to public good—to social justice, to improving society, to making the world a better place for all people to live. So it is ironic that they think of marriage as something strictly for their private happiness. In the past, people got married and had children with a weighty sense that this was a crucial good for society. While their marriages were often less than satisfying, people stayed married out of a sense of duty. The private-happiness view of marriage also puts far greater pressure on us to feel passionately in love all the time, while the older view did not. It is time to think again of marriage as, as least in large part, a public institution, and not just a lifestyle option.

Reflection: Do you think of your marriage as a "public good"? How does it function as such?

Thought for prayer: Ask God to strengthen your society and nation by strengthening your country's marriages.

[Many speak of marrying] the "perfect soul mate," someone very "compatible." But what does that mean? . . . The first [factor] is physical attractiveness and sexual chemistry. . . . "We had settled into a routine where we only had sex once a week or so, maybe even less. There was no variety, and no real mental or emotional rewards. There was none of the urgency or tension that makes sex so great—that sense of wanting to impress or entice someone." (Hardcover, p. 30; paperback, pp. 23–24)

SEX OVER THE LONG TERM. Many believe that what makes sex so great is "the desire to impress or entice someone." This definition excludes the idea that sex can be enduringly wonderful over the long term in marriage. How could you "impress" someone who has been married to you for twenty years? How do you "entice" someone who has promised to be with you no matter what? And how do you do either when both of your bodies are aging and becoming inexorably less attractive? The deeper way to impress someone is with your character and to attract someone is with your delight in him or her. That sustains and grows sexual desire through the years. And that does not depend on what is now called "chemistry."

Reflection: What do you think the term "sexual chemistry" means today? In what ways is it helpful for married couples? In what ways is it unhelpful?

Thought for prayer: Ask God to show you ways to sustain the romantic aspect of your relationship over the years.

However, sexual attractiveness was not the number one factor that men named when surveyed. . . . "More than a few of the men expressed resentment at women who try to change them. . . . Some of the men described marital compatibility as finding a woman who will 'fit into their life.' 'If you are truly compatible, then you don't have to change,' one man commented." (Hardcover, pp. 30–31; paperback, p. 24)

THE REALISM OF BIBLICAL MARRIAGE. When marriage was seen as a public good, it was expected that being married would change the participants. Now that marriage is seen as primarily about private, individual happiness, it follows that many would insist their partner not demand any major alterations. But living in close quarters with *any* one is an infringement on one's independence, and so any marriage must require massive changes to one's life as well as the self-control and discipline to maintain them. Raising children takes the requirements for change to another level. Here, then, is another way in which more modern views of marriage may not fit reality as well as the Bible's vision and prescription for it.

Reflection: What are changes that marriage has required of you? What changes would your spouse still like to see?

Thought for prayer: Ask God to make you more open to—and able to make—the changes that your marriage requires of you.

So God created mankind in his own image, in the image of God he created them; male and female he created them. . . . The LORD God said, "It is not good for the man to be alone. I will make a helper suitable for him." (Genesis 1:27, 2:18)

IRREPLACEABILITY. Human beings have always existed in two forms—male and female. This is seen in the word "helper" (Hebrew, *'ezer*). It implies the woman has supplementary and complementary strengths that the man does not have, and vice versa. The new unity that solves Adam's "aloneness" comes about not through the addition of an animal or another male but a female. Each gender has abilities and unique beauties that the other cannot reproduce, so we need each other. As you could not have an entirely male or female society or church without impoverishment, neither can you have such a marriage. The historic Christian position has been that marriage includes the full range of human excellence, which is only available if we have both genders present.

Reflection: Gender differences express themselves differently in every marriage. How have they done so in your marriage?

Prayer: Lord, help us so that we neither acquiesce in the peculiar sins of our genders, nor be resentful or unappreciative of their differences. Amen.

But for Adam no suitable helper was found. So the LORD God caused the man to fall into a deep sleep; and while he was sleeping, he took one of the man's ribs and then closed up the place with flesh. Then the LORD God made a woman from the rib he had taken out of the man, and he brought her to the man. The man said, "This is now bone of my bones and flesh of my flesh; she shall be called 'woman,' for she was taken out of man." (Genesis 2: 20–23)

DIVERSITY. God takes a rib out of Adam's side. This signifies that the woman will have qualities that are identical to the man's but also some that are now missing from him. Thus God describes her as "suitable" (Hebrew, *kenegdo*), a word that means "like-opposite". Men and women are both like and unlike, equal yet profoundly different. Marriage is therefore complementary companionship, a unity achieved across difference. Ephesians 5, in which the husband-wife relationship is likened to the union of Christ and the church, shows us that such unity between deeply diverse parties is always hard won. We should not be surprised that gender differences are both glorious and difficult.

Reflection: In what ways have gender difference made your marriage hard? How has it made it richer?

Prayer: Lord Jesus, we praise you that you left heaven and your glory and rejoiced to unite with us human beings. Teach us what we must do to live in harmony and interdependence with each other. Amen.

Adam and his wife were both naked, and they felt no shame. (Genesis 2:25)

TRANSPARENCY. Marriage was designed for truth as well as love. Adam and Eve had a perfect relationship. "Nakedness-without-shame" meant total transparency and total vulnerability to one another. They had nothing to hide. They were absolutely open to each other, and neither partner abused the privilege. Their relationship had "no alloy of greed, distrust, or dishonor."[13] It had an "openness and a unity, not masked by guilt, not disordered by lust, not hampered by shame."[14] Because we are now sinners, the ideal of perfect openness and affirmation is not possible. Yet the gospel gives us the tools (Ephesians 4:15)—the inner security and fullness of love—we need to make progress toward it.

Reflection: Discuss with your spouse the reasons that openness and transparency require both truth and love. What happens when you speak the truth but your spouse doesn't fully trust you? Is it still possible to speak truthfully and have your message received the way it is intended?

Prayer: Lord, you made yourself vulnerable to us and we humans rejected you—yet you loved us and opened our eyes to love you. Help us to take the same risks of love in order to love each other well. Amen.

To the woman he said, "I will make your pains in childbearing very severe; with painful labor you will give birth to children. Your desire will be for your husband, and he will rule over you." To Adam he said . . . "Cursed is the ground because of you; through painful toil you will eat food from it all the days of your life. By the sweat of your brow you will eat your food until you return to the ground, since from it you were taken; for dust you are and to dust you will return." (Genesis 3:16–17, 19)

HUMILITY. When Adam and Eve sinned, the curse of sin descended. The human family, both in its procreative and economic function, was now deeply disordered. Much ink has been spilled over exactly what each of the statements above mean. Let us notice that sin affects the woman and the man differently. This is another indication that the genders are somewhat distinct in both their strengths and weaknesses. Here it appears their idols and frustrations are different. Our shelves are filled with "how-to" books for building a wonderful marriage, but this passage calls us to humility. Even inside a Christian marriage, we must expect obsessiveness, fear, guilt, addiction, and oppression. We cannot avoid it. But we can understand why we have those feelings and emotions and work to overcome them.

Reflection: Why do you think the woman's relationship to her children and husband are mentioned and the man's relationship to his work is mentioned? What does that say about our characteristic sins?

Prayer: Lord, in our marriage help keep us from either hopeless cynicism or naïve romanticism. Amen.

"For this reason a man will leave his father and mother and be united to his wife, and the two will become one flesh." This is a profound mystery—but I am talking about Christ and the church. (Ephesians 5:31–32)

RECONCILIATION. In marriage, God gives us a powerful sign of our salvation. Christ's loving sacrifice—and our surrender to him—reconciles God and humanity, bringing two alienated, different persons into a covenantal unity. Marriage mirrors the gospel when, through mutual self-giving, the estranging effects of sin are overcome and a union brought about of the very different—male and female. Sex, then, is no mere physical appetite. In marriage it is a sign of our union with Christ and can even be called participation with God in his restoration of the world. "[H]e made known to us the mystery of his will according to his good pleasure, which he purposed in Christ, to be put into effect when the times reach their fulfillment—to bring unity to all things in heaven and on earth under Christ" (Ephesians 1:9–10).

Reflection: When you experience alienation in your marriage, what bridges the gap? How can you do better at that bridging?

Prayer: Father, help us to see that when we are distant and alienated, there is no resolution other than the same, humble self-giving that your Son did in order to reconcile with us. Amen.

"For this reason a man will leave his father and mother and be united to his wife, and the two will become one flesh." This is a profound mystery—but I am talking about Christ and the church. (Ephesians 5:31–32)

EXCLUSIVITY. There is no way to know Christ without exclusive, lifelong commitment to him. Christ literally gave up everything in order to reconcile and unite with us. And there is no way to know Christ at all unless he is our *only* Savior and Lord. The first two of the Ten Commandments make that point clearly. This means, obviously, that we must be sexually faithful to our spouse. But further, it means no marriage can work if our careers or even our children vie with our spouse for first place in our hearts. Only through exclusive, whole-life commitment to Christ can we have a relationship with him. The same goes for our spouse.

Reflection: Ask your spouse to tell you frankly what things compete with him or her for first place in your life.

Prayer: Lord Jesus, thank you for counting equality with the Father as something you were willing to part with in order to gain us (Philippians 2:4–11). Let our relationship to each other show the same exclusive love. Amen.

"For this reason a man will leave his father and mother and be united to his wife, and the two will become one flesh." This is a profound mystery—but I am talking about Christ and the church. (Ephesians 5:31–32)

TRANSFORMATION. Salvation in Christ transforms us. No one can come into an intimate relationship with the Lord and Savior of the world and remain as they are. Although we are saved by faith, not by our moral efforts, nevertheless "faith without works [i.e., a changed life of love and holiness] is dead" (James 2:17). We may say we have faith, but if we don't change, we demonstrate that the faith is illusory. In the same way, if we marry someone and then refuse to make major changes in order to serve their needs better, then we may say we love them, but we don't. In a good marriage we know the other loves us despite our flaws, yet that should motivate us to change in order to better love them. The connection between Ephesians 5 and Genesis shows us this—the gospel explains marriage, and marriage explains the gospel.

Reflection: Think of more ways in which marriage teaches us about our relationship to Christ, and vice versa.

Prayer: (Each pray:) Lord, I confess I have neither changed my character enough in response to your love or to my spouse's love and need. Strengthen my desire and give me the power to do so. Amen.

Many of the males in the research were adamant that their relationship with a woman should not curtail their freedom at all. The report concluded, "Cohabitation gives men regular access to the domestic and sexual ministrations of a girlfriend while allowing them . . . to lead a more independent life and continue to look around for a better partner." (Hardcover, p. 31; paperback, p. 25)

LIVING TOGETHER. In ancient Rome, husbands were expected to have sex with other women, while wives were forbidden to do so. Christianity ended that double standard. Some have argued that the contemporary popularity of cohabitation similarly privileges men. Women are generally more desirous of putting aside their independence and being married than men are, so any society that makes living together without marriage socially acceptable is tilting the culture toward male interests over female.[15] It puts men in a place of real power whenever a couple cohabits rather than marrying. The woman dares not be too insistent on them making decisions mutually, and he is free to be constantly comparing her with other prospective partners. Could it be that, again, Christian sexual ethics are better for women?

Reflection: What do you think—is cohabitation better for men than women?

Thought for prayer: Pray that, for the good of society and of children, that the institution of marriage be strengthened in our culture.

Part of the traditional understanding of marriage was that it "civilized" men. Men have been perceived as being more independent and less willing and able than women to enter into relationships that require mutual communication, support, and teamwork. So one of the classic purposes of marriage was very definitely to "change" men and be a "school" in which they learned how to conduct new, more interdependent relationships. (Hardcover, p. 31; paperback, p. 25)

GENDER DIFFERENCES. It is unfair to talk of men needing to be "civilized" by women, but gender differences are real. Women consistently see themselves as more agreeable, friendly, and sensitive to feelings, while men see themselves as more assertive and open to new ideas. These differences persist across times and cultures.[16] What does that mean? It means that men and women need each other. Each of these strengths comes with attached weaknesses. While the Bible does not define these differences, which may take different shapes in different cultures, its insistence on gender diversity in marriage assumes them. So, especially in marriage, men and women should listen to one another, call one another to change, and heed one another's call.

Reflection: Marriage requires intimate interdependence and some argue that women, in general, come into marriage with greater skills in that area. Do you agree?

Thought for prayer: Pray that gender differences in your marriage would be more a basis for growth than for conflict.

[A scholar] argued that marriage was traditionally a place where males *became* truly masculine: "For most of Western history, the primary and most valued characteristic of manhood was self-mastery. . . . A man who indulged in excessive eating, drinking, sleeping or sex—who failed to 'rule himself'—was considered unfit to rule his household, much less a polity. . . . [S]exual restraint rather than sexual prowess was once the measure of a man." (Hardcover, p. 32; paperback, p. 26)

MALE SELF-CONTROL. Since, by all accounts, men naturally tend to be more aggressive, it is not surprising that many struggle with control of both their anger and their sexual desires. Marriage not only demands both kinds of self-discipline from men, but it also helps achieve them. Men who grew up in intact families are less likely to cheat on their spouse in their own marriages.[17] Traditionally, this kind of self-control was considered the very essence of masculinity. So-called leaders who cannot even master themselves are disasters. And a wife will not be able to trust and respect a man who cannot submit his impulses to his promises and his commitments. "Real men" are strong enough to control themselves.

Reflection: In what ways have you seen a wife's love and respect for her husband increase with his growth in self-control?

Thought for prayer: If you are a man, think of the areas of your life that require self-control and pray for it. If you are a woman, pray for the man in your life to grow in self-control.

[I]f your desire is for a spouse who will not demand a lot of change from you, then you are also looking for a spouse who is . . . very "low maintenance" without much in the way of personal problems. . . . You are searching, therefore, for an ideal person—happy, healthy, interesting, content with life. Never before in history has there been a society filled with people so idealistic in what they are seeking in a spouse. (Hardcover, pp. 32–33; paperback, pp. 26–27)

FINISHING SCHOOL? A recent article explains "How Millennials Are Redefining Marriage."[18] Traditionally, the writer says, people were willing to take marriage vows earlier "and figure it out." That meant discovering one another's strengths and weaknesses, callings and mission in life—but doing it together, after marriage, not individually before. Today young adults wait longer to marry, so that all by themselves they can figure out who they want to be, without input from anyone as empowered as a spouse in their lives. Then they want a marriage partner who also is fully formed—economically, psychologically, and socially—and who merely affirms the identity and trajectory they have already set for themselves. This "partnership of finished products" doesn't create anything like the same kind of bond. And needless to say, it is unrealistic. You will continue to change after marriage.

Reflection: Some have said that marriage today is like "finishing school" while in the past it was more analogous to high school and college. Do you agree? How has your spouse helped shape the person you are today?

Thought for prayer: Ask God to help both you and your generation not to fear marriage, but to give themselves to their spouses in trust and love.

Older views of marriage are considered to be traditional and oppressive, while the newer view of the "Me-Marriage" seems so liberating. And yet it is the newer view that has led to a steep decline in marriage and to an oppressive sense of hopelessness with regard to it. To conduct a Me-Marriage requires two completely well-adjusted, happy individuals, with very little in the way of emotional neediness of their own or character flaws that need a lot of work. The problem is—there is almost no one like that out there to marry! The new conception of marriage-as-self-realization has put us in a position of wanting too much out of marriage and yet not nearly enough—at the same time. (Hardcover, p. 34; paperback, p. 28)

WHY NOT TO POSTPONE MARRIAGE. One psychologist says postponing marriage until later in life, until you have an established identity and you know who you are, is a wiser way to go.[19] Certainly two people may be too young to marry, but that is because they lack the necessary character for mutually submitting their selfish desires for the good of the other. That takes humility, grace, self-control, and inner security. But waiting to "find oneself" before marriage assumes that self-knowledge is mainly a solitary process of discovering one's deepest desires. It is not. When we look inside our hearts we will see inner desires that contradict each other. We need intimate companionship to discern the bad from the good from the best within. There's no better place for that than marriage.

Reflection: Jesus said we must "lose" ourselves in service to him in order to "find" our true selves. That's the primary way to find your true identity—in Christ. Is there an analogy in marriage? Can we find ourselves as we serve our spouses?

Thought for prayer: Ask God to teach you more about your strengths and weaknesses, your gifts and callings, through your marriage.

They do not see marriage as two flawed people coming together to create a space of stability, love, and consolation—a "haven in a heartless world," as Christopher Lasch describes it. . . . A marriage based not on self-denial but on self-fulfillment will require a low- or no-maintenance partner who meets your needs while making almost no claims on you. Simply put—today people are asking far too much in the marriage partner. (Hardcover, p. 35; paperback, p. 30)

HOW VOWS HELP. Marriage in the past was about duty as well as desire. It was recognized that when flawed people (and there aren't any other kind) got married, there would be difficult times in which the parties would want to give up. That's what the wedding vows were for—they were "Ulysses pacts." In Greek mythology, Ulysses knew that when his ship approached the island of the Sirens, their song would drive him to be incapable of reasonable thinking. So he had himself tied to the mast and told his men (who were told to put wax in their ears) to ignore his ravings until they passed the island and he came to his senses. Wedding vows often serve the same purpose during times of conflict in marriage. They are ways of tying oneself to the marriage so you stick with it during times in which your thinking is confused.

Reflection: In what ways is this Ulysses story helpful as a metaphor for wedding vows? In what ways does it *not* apply to marriages? Do you remember your wedding vows?

Thought for prayer: Ask God to help you "come to your senses" quickly after times of anger, self-pity, and discouragement that can put pressure on your marriage.

Those dreaming of the perfect match are outnumbered by those who don't really want [marriage] at all, though perhaps they can't admit it. After all, our culture makes individual freedom, autonomy, and fulfillment the very highest values, and thoughtful people know down deep that any love relationship at all means the loss of all three. . . . Yet it is hard to admit to the world or to yourself that you don't want to be married. [So you find flaws in all prospective partners.] . . . That will keep marriage away. (Hardcover, p. 36; paperback, p. 30)

FREEDOM. Many complain that the legal bond of marriage creates the "requirement to hold a lifelong relationship," but today many do "not want to give into those kinds of pressures" and so want to live together without a marriage license that compromises their freedom. They see their relationship as "their own"—not society's—and as one based on "love and commitment, and not in need of external validation."[20] But the legal vows were not made to "validate" love but to deepen and strengthen it. And there is nothing more liberating than to know there is someone who has solemnly promised to be *there* for you through thick and thin.

Reflection: How does the modern idea of freedom clash with the ideals of marriage?

Thought for prayer: In the "Collect for Peace" in *The Book of Common Prayer*, God's service is said to be "perfect freedom." Ask God to help you experience the "freedom of service" in your marriage.

[Especially for men, a] pornographic media culture may contribute to unrealistic expectations of what their future soul mate should look like. Influenced by the sexy images of young women on MTV, the Internet, and on the runway in televised Victoria's Secret specials, men may be putting off marriage to their current girlfriend in the hopes that they will eventually find a combination "soul mate/babe." (Hardcover, p. 33; paperback, p. 27)

IMAGE VS. CHARACTER. In 1858, when Lincoln and Douglas debated each other while running for the U.S. Senate, the national newspapers ran pages and pages of their arguments.[21] Yet if either had walked down the main street in any U.S. town they'd not have been recognized. Photographs existed but could not be disseminated. What mattered publicly was not their appearance but their ideas. Today we have moved from a text-based culture to an image-based culture, one in which looks and impressions matter the most. Among other things, this means that pornography flourishes as never before. But it also means that aging people and overweight people—especially women—can easily come to hate themselves. Beauty is idolized and this puts pressure on marriages and on marriage seekers. The Bible puts the emphasis elsewhere—on beliefs and character.

Reflection: How does beauty idolatry distort the judgment of those looking to get married? How does it hurt existing marriages?

Thought for prayer: Meditate on 1 Peter 3:4: "Your beauty should not come from outward adornment such as braided hair or gold jewelry or fine clothes, but from the inner disposition of your heart, the unfading beauty of a gentle and quiet spirit, which is precious in God's sight."

February 16

Women have been just as affected by our consumer culture. Both men and women today see marriage not as a way of creating character and community but as a way to reach personal life goals. They are all looking for a marriage partner who will "fulfill their emotional, sexual, and spiritual desires." And that creates an extreme idealism that in turn leads to deep pessimism that you will ever find the right person to marry. This is the reason so many put off marriage and look right past great prospective spouses that simply are "not good enough." (Hardcover, pp. 33–34; paperback, p. 28)

WET CEMENT—OR NOT. "Women have more choice than ever before. They are choosing to focus on their careers for a longer period of time and using egg freezing and other technology to 'buy time,'" says a psychologist.[22] She goes on to say that women now look for a partner who will not try to change them, but will affirm who they already are. It is indeed true that the older we get the more set in our ways we become . . . less "wet cement." But when we come to see ourselves through the eyes of our spouse we recognize that we are both better and worse than we thought. We are liberated from denial and blindness. In a good marriage we will *want* to be different. Why put off marriage until it is harder to change?

Reflection: List some ways in which it is shortsighted to put off marriage "in general" until you can become set in your ways.

Thought for prayer: Help your spouse to see him- or herself better through your marriage. Ask God to keep you from being too critical or not critical enough, and to do all out of love.

C. S. Lewis put it vividly: "Love anything, and your heart will certainly be wrung and possibly broken. If you want to make sure of keeping it intact, you must give your heart to no one, not even to an animal. Wrap it carefully round with hobbies and little luxuries; avoid all entanglements; lock it up safe in the casket or coffin of your selfishness. But in that casket—safe, dark, motionless, airless—it will change. It will not be broken; it will become unbreakable, impenetrable, irredeemable. The alternative to tragedy, or at least to the risk of tragedy, is damnation."[23] (Hardcover, p. 36; paperback, p. 31)

THE CASKET OF SELFISHNESS. Lewis's quote shows us the horns of the dilemma presented by love. If we love anyone, we are sure to be disappointed and even hurt. This haunts young adults today and makes them wary of marriage. However, the alternative has just as many risks. The opposite of love is not hate, but fear (1 John 4:18), because love is self-opening. Love is committing yourself to the good of someone else, and that makes you vulnerable. The only way to protect yourself from hurt in relationships is to withdraw from them. But that kind of self-protectiveness will be a coffin for your ability to love; it will make you hardened and lonely. Such withdrawal can even happen within marriage, but it should be avoided at all costs.

Reflection: Have you seen Lewis's vivid statement play out in real life? How is experiencing tragedy better than not experiencing tragedy?

Thought for prayer: Meditate on I John 4:18: "Perfect love casts out fear." Ask that God give you enough of his perfect love that your fear and anxiety in relationships diminishes.

[People] say over and over, "Love *shouldn't* be this hard; it should come naturally." In response, I always say something like, "Why believe that? Would someone who wants to play professional baseball say, 'It shouldn't be so hard to hit a fastball'? Would someone who wants to write the greatest American novel of her generation say, 'It shouldn't be hard to create believable characters and compelling narrative'?" The understandable retort is, "But this is not baseball or literature. This is *love*. Love should just come naturally if two people are compatible, if they are truly soul mates." (Hardcover, p. 37; paperback, p. 32)

NO ONE IS TALENTED IN MARRIAGE. The illustrations that liken baseball or fiction writing to marriage are a bit of a stretch. Those kinds of work require practice and hard work, but they also assume natural talent. Some people are just far better athletes or writers than the rest of us. That is not true of marriage. No one is just "gifted" at marriage the way some young athletes have impressive natural abilities. The difficulty of marriage is due to our character and especially to our selfishness. No amount of natural "chemistry" will eradicate it. We can hide our selfishness from others and even, to a degree, from ourselves. But in marriage both you and your spouse can see it clearly. It takes great effort to overcome our natural *lack* of talent for marriage.

Reflection: Can you think of a time in which you were blaming your spouse for a conflict—when it was really your selfishness?

Thought for prayer: Ask God to make you honest about the level of your own selfishness. Ask him to save you from self-justification.

Stanley Hauerwas has famously made this point: "Destructive to marriage is the self-fulfillment ethic that assumes marriage and the family are primarily institutions of personal fulfillment, necessary for us to become 'whole' and happy. The assumption is that there is someone just right for us to marry and that if we look closely enough we will find the right person. This moral assumption overlooks a crucial aspect to marriage. It fails to appreciate the fact that we always marry the wrong person."[24] (Hardcover, pp. 37–38; paperback, p. 32)

WE MARRY A SINNER. Stanley Hauerwas famously says that "we always marry the wrong person" as a way to get your attention. He doesn't mean that there cannot be two people so incompatible in temperament or culture or age or in some other way that they should not be married. He is trying to dispel the myth that if you choose the right person the marriage will be free from sharp conflicts. If the Bible is right that all human beings are sinners, then no two sinners are ever naturally compatible. "There's no need for red-hot pokers," says one of Jean-Paul Sartre's characters when they get to hell. "Hell is other people."[25] Sinful people will always be rubbing each other the wrong way and blaming the other person.

Reflection: What is your definition of sin? Think of the ways that sin complicates and hurts all relationships.

Thought for prayer: Ask God for the wisdom to see those conflicts that come from genuine differences of temperament with your spouse—which should be accepted—and those that stem from flaws in your character—which should not.

[Hauerwas goes on to explain what he means about always marrying the wrong person.] "We never know whom we marry; we just think we do. Or even if we first marry the right person, just give it a while and he or she will change. For marriage, being [the enormous thing it is] means we are not the same person after we have entered it. The primary problem is . . . learning how to love and care for the stranger to whom you find yourself married."[26] (Hardcover, p. 38; paperback, pp. 32–33)

WE MARRY A CHANGER. Here we have a second reason that "we never marry the right person." The first reason is sin, and the second is change. Many counsel that we wait on marriage until "we know who we are," but even that is constantly in flux. Marriage itself changes us drastically, bringing out the best and worst in us. Aging bodies, babies and children, work and career— all change who we are, and that means recalibrating the marriage relationship. What we need, then, is not the perfect mate who never changes (there is no such person), but wisdom, the ability to repent, and a sustained commitment to your wedding promises.

Reflection: How have you changed in your marriage? How well have you navigated the changes?

Thought for prayer: Ask God to help you both accept the inevitable changes in each other, even as he aids you in remaining unchangeably committed to one another.

[T]here are good reasons not to marry someone who is a great deal older or younger, or someone with whom you do not share a common language, and so on. . . . Some people are really, *really* the wrong people to marry. But everyone else is still incompatible. . . . Over the years you will go through seasons in which you have to learn to love a person who you didn't marry, who is something of a stranger. The journey may eventually take you into a strong, tender, joyful marriage. But it is not because you married the perfectly compatible person. (Hardcover, pp. 38–39; paperback, pp. 33–34)

WE MARRY A SUFFERER. There are several ways your spouse can become a stranger to you. One way is this—trials and pressures can bring out weaknesses in character, just like a stress test in a doctor's office can reveal irregularities in your heart function. No one can live a life without suffering. Bad things will happen to your spouse, and it is very disappointing to see him or her as less mature, or strong, or wise than you thought he or she was. But at that time you should use the gospel to remind you that God sees *you* all the way to the bottom, sees all kinds of flaws that you yourself will not see until years from now, but he loves you anyway. So love your spouse as God in Christ loves you.

Reflection: What are some other ways your spouse can "feel like a stranger" to you? When that has happened, how well have you handled it?

Thought for prayer: Ask God to empower you with a sense of the reality of his love in order to love your spouse despite his or her flaws.

[T]he first reason that no two people are compatible for marriage . . . [is] that marriage profoundly changes us. But there is another reason. Any two people who enter into marriage are spiritually broken by sin, which among other things means to be self-centered—living life *incurvatus in se*. As author Denis de Rougemont said, "Why should neurotic, selfish, immature people suddenly become angels when they fall in love?"[27] (Hardcover, p. 40; paperback, p. 35)

WE MARRY A SELFISH PERSON: 1. Perhaps the greatest barrier to a happy marriage is the self-centeredness of both spouses. But nothing can be done about it if the partners are in denial about the reality or severity of the problem. Jonathan Edwards lists several marks of self-centered persons. They are dogmatic and always sure of every point of their beliefs. They are fault-finding, prone to self-pity, and never satisfied. They need a lot of praise and are easily offended. They tend to talk a lot about themselves and are poor listeners. Christians should do self-examination (2 Corinthians 13:5), not in order to beat ourselves up, but in order to, first, deepen our appreciation of God's patience and grace, and second, to take concrete action toward becoming more Christlike in our character.

Reflection: There are four marks of self-centeredness listed above. Honestly assess the degree to which they apply to you. What can you do about them?

Thought for prayer: Ask God to replace your restless efforts to steal love and acceptance from others with a Christ-centeredness and a resting in his love for you.

That is why a good marriage is *more* painfully hard to achieve than athletic or artistic prowess. Raw, natural talent does not enable you to play baseball as a pro or write great literature without enduring discipline and enormous work. Why would it be easy to live lovingly and well with another human being in light of what is profoundly wrong within our human nature? Indeed, many people who have mastered athletics and art have failed miserably at marriage. (Hardcover, pp. 40–41; paperback, pp. 35–36)

WE MARRY A SELFISH PERSON: 2. In yesterday's daily devotion we read that at the heart of our fallen human nature is self-centeredness, a problem that undermines the happiness of our marriage. Here are several more marks of self-centered persons from Jonathan Edwards. They are willful, always insisting on their own way. They are ungenerous with praise and encouragement, tending instead to be scornful. They are slow to admit when they are in the wrong, and repentance is always traumatic, never a relief. Finally, they either enjoy confrontation too much or else refuse to ever do it. (Both are results of thinking more of one's own interests than the good of the other.) The more self-centered you are, the less aware you are of it; the less self-centered you are, the more you sense it in yourself.

Reflection: Again, there are four marks of self-centeredness listed above. Honestly assess the degree to which they apply to you. What can you do about them?

Thought for prayer: Ask God to speak to you not only about your sin, to see yourself more clearly, but about his love for you, so you can repent and change in joy and relief.

Ernest Becker believed that modern culture had produced a desire for what he called "apocalyptic romance." At one time we expected marriage and family to provide love, support, and security. But for meaning in life, hope for the future, moral compass, and self-identity we looked to God and the afterlife. Today, however, our culture has taught us that no one can be sure of those things, not even whether they exist. Therefore, Becker argued, something has to fill the gap, and often that something is romantic love. We look to sex and romance to give us what we used to get from faith in God. (Hardcover, p. 41; paperback, p. 36)

MARRIAGE NO SUBSTITUTE FOR GOD. Both Ernest Becker and St. Augustine argued that, if the supreme love and hope of our lives is not a real God but is instead something else, then that thing will become elevated to a kind of pseudo-god. So as God recedes from our lives, we put far more pressure on sex, romance, and marriage to be transcendent, fulfilling experiences. No wonder modern people think it unreasonable to expect singles to refrain from sex if they are not married. No wonder that people put off marriage as they hunt for the absolutely perfect soul mate. Sex and romance are now called on to deliver a transcendent experience they were never created to provide. Marriage was never meant to satisfy us like communion with God, nor is it capable of doing so.

Reflection: What are some of the bad effects of this idolization of marriage: For singles? For married people? In your life specifically?

Thought for prayer: Admit to God that his love for you is too abstract and his fellowship with you is too weak and this makes you put pressure on other things to make you happy, including your marriage.

[Ernest Becker writes:] "The love partner becomes the divine ideal within which to fulfill one's life. All spiritual and moral needs now become focused in one individual. . . . In one word, the love object is God. . . . Man reached for a 'thou' when the world-view of the great religious community overseen by God died. . . . After all, what is it that we want when we elevate the love partner to the position of God? We want redemption—nothing less."[28] (Hardcover, p. 41; paperback, pp. 36–37)

MARRIAGE NO SUBSTITUTE FOR REDEMPTION. Without God in our lives, we will turn something else into a source of redemption, and one of the most usual candidates for that sort of "god-making" is the romantic partner or spouse. When Becker uses the word "redemption" for this, is he exaggerating? We don't think so. We all share a sense that we have not lived as we should and that we are not the persons we ought to be. We can look to our partner to assure us and the world that we are indeed worthy of love. This not only puts enormous pressure on our spouse to always be affirming, but it also puts too much power in their hands to define our very being. That should belong only to God.

Reflection: Think of some other ways in which in our culture we might be prone to look to our spouse for a kind of "redemption." Do you think women and men pursue that differently?

Thought for prayer: Meditate on John 19:30, where the dying Jesus said, "It is finished!" Thank God for a complete, finished redemption in Christ, and ask him for help to rest in that, and not seek any further salvation in anyone or anything else.

Disenchantment, the "end of the honeymoon," is common and has been for centuries. . . . But the depth of the disillusionment people experience in our time is something new, as is the speed with which marriages spiral down. In our day, something has intensified this natural experience and turned it toxic. It is the illusion that if we find our one true soul mate, everything wrong with us will be healed; but that makes the lover into God, and no human being can live up to that. (Hardcover, p. 42; paperback, pp. 37–38)

HARD OR EASY? My (Tim's) grandmother, who was born around the turn of the nineteenth century, told me that marriage had been more rewarding than she had been led to expect by her family and friends. Today, as God has receded in the culture, the pressure on marriage to be a fully rewarding, self-enhancing enterprise has grown. Now couples become disenchanted because marriage is harder than they had been led to expect. Both the older and modern cultures are wrong. Marriage is more like our walk with God. It is often confusing and difficult but the rewards infinitely dwarf the costs.

Reflection: Would it be fair to say that there was an incident or time that "ended the honeymoon" era of your marriage? If so, what was it, and did it end up being a means of growth? Or not?

Thought for prayer: Ask God to help you rest and hope in him so that you can avoid either naïveté *or* cynicism in every area of your life.

There are few if any serious, sustained arguments being made today that society can do without marriage. Even today's critics of monogamy must grant that, at least pragmatically, we can't really live without it. One of the reasons for this is the growing body of empirical research. . . . Evidence continues to mount up that marriage—indeed traditional, exclusively monogamous marriage—brings enormous benefits of all kinds to adults, and even more to children and society at large. (Hardcover, pp. 43–44; paperback, p. 39)

THE PARADOX. As we have seen, young adults today marry both much later and much less frequently. Fully two-thirds of Americans in their twenties say that society is just as well off if people don't put a priority on marrying and having children as if they do.[29] This is a marked change in attitude from every previous generation. It also contradicts all the empirical studies that show that traditional marriage has enormous benefits for adults and children. So why do younger adults have a view of marriage that flies in the face of both science and tradition? The answer probably has to do with the paradox that we have been exploring, namely, because of the vacuum in our lives created by the decline of religion, people need marriage too much and therefore fear marriage too much, at the same time.

Reflection: If many common views of marriage are mistaken, could we see them begin to change?

Thought for prayer: Pray not for yourself but for our society. Ask God to change hearts so that people would not miss out on the richness and joys of marriage due to inordinate fears.

There is a profound longing we feel for marriage. We hear it in Adam's "At last!" cry at the sight of Eve, the indelible sense that locked within marriage is some inexpressible treasure. And that is right. The problem is not with marriage itself. According to Genesis 1 and 2, we were made for marriage, and marriage was made for us. Genesis 3 tells us that marriage, along with every other aspect of human life, has been broken because of sin. (Hardcover, p. 44; paperback, p. 40)

BITTERSWEETNESS. There is an irreducible bittersweetness about marriage. We know intuitively that marriage has the ability to satisfy, deepen, and enrich us in ways that no other human relationship can do. The Bible explains this powerful sensibility by telling us it is a divine invention, instituted directly by him to reflect his own character and saving love. And yet, even those in the happiest marriages can look back on a long string of missed opportunities and unfulfilled aspirations for loving our spouse well. Here's the wonderful consolation. Eternity will finally end the bittersweetness, because "Heaven Is a World of Love," in which our ability to love, clogged and diminished here on earth, will be healed completely.[30] Rest in that certain hope.

Reflection: How can the knowledge of our future—a future of perfect love—help you now in the marriage? How can it mitigate the regret of never getting marriage right? How can it make you less afraid of failure in your marriage?

Thought for prayer: Ask God to use the Christian future hope in your heart, both to encourage you when you fall short in your marriage, and also to provoke you to keep trying.

"Have no other gods before me. . . . You shall not commit adultery."
(Exodus 20: 3, 14)

A SIN AGAINST GOD. The Bible says that committing adultery against your spouse is also spiritual adultery—unfaithfulness to God (Psalm 51:4). Thomas Watson wrote that adultery dishonors all three persons of the Trinity, because it is ingratitude toward the Father who gave you all you have, it despises the work of the Son who died to save you from sin, and it defiles the temple of the Holy Spirit, your body (1 Corinthians 6:19).[31] Why meditate this week on something so unpleasant? First, understanding the reasons behind the wrongness of adultery will reveal much about God and our own hearts. Second, there are marriages that have been repaired after adultery, but an ounce of prevention is more valuable than a ton of cure.

Reflection: As difficult as this subject is, reflect on ways that you can guard against adultery.

Prayer: Lord, the Bible is filled with prayerful pleas to help us "keep our way pure." I make the same prayer now. Show me how I must think and behave to stay faithful to my spouse. Amen.

March 2

> This is what the LORD says: "For three sins of Israel, even for four, I will not relent. They sell the innocent for silver, and the needy for a pair of sandals. They trample on the heads of the poor as on the dust of the ground and deny justice to the oppressed. Father and son use the same girl and so profane my holy name." (Amos 2:6–7)

A SIN OF INJUSTICE. Progressive, liberal people see sexual norms as fluid and not to be rigidly enforced, yet they rightly are greatly concerned for racial and economic justice. On the other hand, traditional, conservative people can be strict and even prudish about sexual morality, but often notice little and say less about the poor. The moral vision of the Bible does not fit into such reductionistic categories. God puts *both* trampling on the poor and sex outside marriage on the same level (see Amos 2:7). Why? They *both* "profane my holy name." They both offend and grieve God, because he is both just and pure and he calls us to be like him (Leviticus 11:44; 1 Peter 1:16). They are also both forms of exploitative injustice, as we will see.

Reflection: Why do you think that today the schools of thought and political parties choose to be concerned *either* about social morality *or* personal sexual morality—but not both?

Prayer: Lord, let our moral sense and conscience be molded not by popular opinion or changing cultural trends but by your Word, under the influence of your Spirit. Amen.

> Wisdom will save you also from the adulterous woman, from the wayward woman with her seductive words. . . . Surely her house leads down to death and her paths to the spirits of the dead. None who go to her return, or attain the paths of life. (Proverbs 2:16, 18–19)

ADULTERY AND DEATH. This passage says that adultery can start with "seductive words." The Hebrew means flattering speech. Before we commit adultery we first indulge the ego boost of having an attractive person's attention. But the adulterer "strays into [death's] territory and finds himself among its citizens before ever he quits this earth."[32] Death is a state of irreversible disintegration, and adultery can lead to not just the crumbling of your marriage, but to alienation from children, friends, and family; to the dissolution of your joy and peace and any self-respect; and often to enormous legal and personal conflict. Together, they indeed lead to disintegration.

Reflection: Reflect on other bad things that can happen when you give in and listen to "smooth words."

Prayer: Lord, there are many ways that we can stray into the territory of death even while still alive, and paths to that place always begin with disobedience to and distrust of you. Keep us in the paths of life. Amen.

March 4

> For this command is a lamp, this teaching is a light, and correction and instruction are the way to life, keeping you from your neighbor's wife, from the smooth talk of a wayward woman. Do not lust in your heart after her beauty or let her captivate you with her eyes. (Proverbs 6:23–25)

ADULTERY AND THE EMPTY HEART. Verse 25 tells us not to "lust in your heart after . . . beauty." To lust is to crave as an empty stomach craves food to fill it. Lust, then, is imagining that someone's beauty will bolster your flagging self-esteem. If our ego is like an empty stomach we will not be able to resist, we will be "captivated." And yet this biblical text assumes that we can control what happens in our hearts. Tell yourself that lust desires to take, while love wants to give. Remember that lust is something you are doing for yourself—because of how it will build you up. Love, however, is a desire to serve someone else. If you are tempted to commit adultery, there is some kind of emptiness that you must turn to God to fill. Mere stoic self-control won't be enough.

Reflection: In light of this, what is the appeal of pornography? How can it be resisted?

Prayer: Lord, "You have made us for yourself and our hearts are restless until they find their rest in you." (Augustine, *Confessions* 1:1). Let us rest in your love so that we do not lust after the beauty of anything else. Amen.

> But a man who commits adultery has no sense; whoever does so destroys himself. Blows and disgrace are his lot, and his shame will never be wiped away. (Proverbs 6:32–33)

A SIN AGAINST THE SELF. Both David (Psalm 51:4) and Joseph (see April 4) say that the sin of adultery is primarily against God, who forbids it. And certainly it also does injustice—even violence—to your spouse if you are married (see May 3). Yet this text points out that you are sinning against yourself as well. Sex should be a way to give yourself wholly to someone, a commitment apparatus. If you have sex with a spouse and with someone else you are destroying your ability to commit. People who lie and break promises destroy their ability to trust others and to entrust themselves to others. The result is loneliness as well as an indelible sense of shame. When we violate the law of our Creator we also violate our nature as designed by God.

Reflection: It has been said that the more you lie the more you distrust what anyone else says. Why would that be? It is also said that those who lie tend to be lied to. Do you agree?

Prayer: Lord, help us remember that when we break your laws, we also break ourselves; when we violate your Word, we also violate ourselves. Help us to remember that sin is first of all an offense and grief to your holy, good heart. But it is also stupid. Amen.

If a man is found sleeping with another man's wife, both the man who slept with her and the woman must die. You must purge the evil from Israel. (Deuteronomy 22:22)

ADULTERY AND EQUALITY. To modern ears this sounds terribly harsh, and we must keep in mind since New Testament times sexual immorality is met with moral exhortation and church discipline, not civil punishments (1 Corinthians 5:1ff.). But this text still reveals much. In the Old Testament theft was never punished by death but by restitution. So it is clear that, unlike in other ancient cultures, husbands did not own their wives as property. Not only that, we see no double standard—both the man and woman are punished equally for adultery. In this apparently "regressive" text, then, we see God revealing a way to understand marriage in which men and women are equals, and are equally, solemnly bound to keep their promises.

Reflection: Think of some ways that double standards for husbands and wives still exist in our day and time. Do they affect you in your marriage? What can you do about that?

Prayer: Lord, keep us from our hearts' natural tendency to manipulate or use one another for our own ends. Renew our minds (Romans 12:2) to treat each other with the deepest mutual respect and love. Amen.

"You have heard that it was said, 'You shall not commit adultery.' But I tell you that anyone who looks at a woman lustfully has already committed adultery with her in his heart." (Matthew 5:27–28)

ADULTERY AND FAITHFULNESS. Often husbands who stray sexually are regarded more leniently than wives. The background to such a double standard is the belief in the "husband's right to have sole sexual possession of his wife."[33] The Old Testament undermined that view, and now Jesus cancels it entirely. He says that the husband who allows himself to desire sex with any other woman has already broken his vow to his wife and committed adultery "in his heart." Speaking to a culture that saw adultery as mainly a matter of *theft* of a man's property, Jesus insisted instead that it was high treason, a lack of *faithfulness* to your spouse and to your God.

Reflection: In ancient times adultery was seen as theft. Today it's often seen as no big deal. Why? What background beliefs shape popular views of adultery today?

Prayer: Lord, do whatever it takes to keep us faithful—keeping all our promises to you and to each other. Amen.

There is a profound longing we feel for marriage. We hear it in Adam's "At last!" cry at the sight of Eve, the indelible sense that locked within marriage is some inexpressible treasure. And that is right. The problem is not with marriage itself. According to Genesis 1 and 2, we were made for marriage, and marriage was made for us. Genesis 3 tells us that marriage, along with every other aspect of human life, has been broken because of sin. (Hardcover, p. 44; paperback, p. 40)

THE HEART OF A GOOD MARRIAGE. The approach/avoidance feelings many people have about marriage are understandable. The longing for loving union is powerful; so is the fear of being hurt at one's most vulnerable core. The solution to our ambivalence is mutual repentance. Martin Luther wrote: "All of life is repentance." He didn't mean we should adopt a self-hating posture, but rather, knowing the Father's welcome because of the atonement of Christ for our sins, we can repent freely, often, and joyfully, both to God and to others. Repentance is at the heart of life and especially of marriage. If two people are able and willing to repent, they can entrust themselves to each other in marriage without fear.

Reflection: Are you confident that your spouse will welcome you freely when you repent? Do you make it safe for your spouse to repent to you? Discuss your answers with each other.

Thought for prayer: Repentance requires both the humility that comes from knowing you are a sinner and the confidence that comes from an assurance of God's unconditional love. Ask God to strengthen both in you, so you can repent joyfully and readily.

If our views of marriage are too romantic and idealistic, we underestimate the influence of sin on human life. If they are too pessimistic and cynical, we misunderstand marriage's divine origin. If we somehow manage, as our modern culture has, to do both at once, we are doubly burdened by a distorted vision. Yet the trouble is not within the institution of marriage but within ourselves. (Hardcover, p. 44; paperback, p. 40)

NO MARRIAGE IS AN ISLAND. Christians work hard to not adopt "the spirit of the age," which is always at odds with God's Holy Spirit. The more overt features of immorality and exploitation are fairly easy to avoid. But the world's more subtle distortions creep in through advertisements, self-help programs, movies, TV and magazines, talk shows, and a hundred other ways. As we breathe in this alien vision of what a good life looks like—freedom from all constraint, trusting our feelings above all—it will affect every part of our life, and nowhere more than in a marriage. The antidote is "life together."[34] It means reading Scripture and praying regularly, both individually and with others. It means accountability and discernment through friendship. It takes a Christian village to guard a Christian marriage.

Reflection: Can you think of ways that cultural beliefs that are antithetical to the teaching of the Bible may have affected your thinking about marriage? Who, within the Christian community, could help you with that?

Thought for prayer: Ask God to show you the reasons that you do not have stronger fellowship with other Christian believers—whether they are busyness, fear, pride, or something else. Then ask God to help you shed them.

Paul declared that marriage is a "great mystery." . . . [T]he Greek word Paul used, *mysterion*, has a lexical range that also includes the idea of a "secret." In the Bible, this word is used to mean not some esoteric knowledge known only to insiders but rather some wondrous, unlooked-for truth that God is revealing through his Spirit. Elsewhere, Paul uses the term to refer to other revelations of God's saving purposes in the gospel. But in Ephesians 5 he applies this rich term, surprisingly, to marriage. (Hardcover, p. 45; paperback, pp. 40–41)

MARRIAGE HAS DEPTHS. Marriage is no mere human institution, invented for social and political convenience. It is a vehicle of God's grace, supplying our need ("it is not good to be alone") and at the same time, revealing God's passionate love for his people. As with all true wonders, there are layers upon layers to discover within marriage. It has unique, inherent powers to show you to yourself, to heal your deepest wounds, and to transform your character. When we are in conflict with our spouse and tempted to give up, we have forgotten that, despite his or her weaknesses (and yours!), marriage has its own powers. Give it time to do its work.

Reflection: Have you ever (I certainly have) been so angry you just wanted to walk out and end the marriage? What stopped you? Were you aware of evil both within and without prompting you to do or say something horrible? How can you protect yourself against future attacks?

Thought for prayer: Thank God for his uniquely rich gift of marriage to the human race and to you. Ask him also for enough patience with it so it can do all its good work in you.

But what *is* the secret of marriage? Paul immediately adds, "I am talking about Christ and the church," referring to what he said earlier in [Ephesians] verse 25: "Husbands, love your wives as just as Christ loved the church and gave himself up for her." In short, the "secret" is not simply the fact of marriage per se. It is the message that what husbands should do for their wives is what Jesus did to bring us into union with himself. (Hardcover, p. 45; paperback, p. 41)

FREEING MARRIAGE FROM THE CULTURE. Marriage is so much more than a sexual relationship with legal benefits. The Bible says that it is a place where we get a foretaste of the full union we will someday have with Christ as his bride. This is indeed a profound mystery. In the Roman world sexual relationships were determined by the social order (in which men ruled women, and the rich exploited the poor.)[35] Today sex also is made to serve the modern, market-driven culture's agenda of individual self-actualization through relationships conducted on a cost-benefit basis. The original Christian sexual revolution was to connect sex not to the social order but to God's way of redemption and communion with him. Marriage becomes both a signpost and participation in Christ's unconditional self-giving.

Reflection: Married couples—in what ways does your marriage reveal glimpses of future glory?

Thought for prayer: Think of the ways that marriage is making you more ready for heaven and future glory. Then thank and praise him for them.

[Jesus] willingly went to the cross and paid the penalty for our sins, removing our guilt and condemnation, so that we could be united with him (Romans 6:5) and take on his nature (2 Peter 1:4). He gave up his glory and power and became a servant. He died to his own interests and looked to our needs and interests instead (Romans 15:1–3). Jesus's sacrificial service to us has brought us into a deep union with him and he with us. And *that*, Paul says, is the key not only to understanding marriage but to living it. (Hardcover, pp. 45–46; paperback, pp. 41–42)

REAL MASCULINITY. One writer said that the essence of masculinity was a sacrificial protectiveness that permits life to grow and thrive. To begin with, men must sacrifice their cherished independence in order to become husbands. Then they must sacrifice much of their pride to respect their wives, listen to them, and serve them. Because so much of this is against male tendencies and patterns, it requires the strength to be weak. Christ sacrifices to win his bride, the Church, the Second Adam's Second Eve,[36] who bears his fruit into the world. In order to save and protect his bride, Jesus spared no effort and no cost. He should be the model and hero for all husbands to imitate.

Reflection: Husbands, in what ways do you inconvenience yourself in order to see your wife grow in Christ? Wives, do you appreciate and take advantage of your husband's sacrifice in order to be a better Bride of Christ and a better wife?

Thought for prayer: Remember that Jesus was no weakling (see him throwing the money changers from the temple—John 2:13–19), yet was the gentlest servant of all (Matthew 11:28–29). If you are a husband pray for the same spirit. Pray that God would form more Christlike husbands in your church and community.

In Philippians 2, Paul tells us that the Son of God did not exploit his equality with the Father, but his greatness was revealed in his willingness to become the Father's servant. He went to the Cross; but the Father raised him from the dead. "This shows us what God is like. . . . The Father, the Son, and the Holy Spirit do not manipulate each other for their own ends. . . . There is no conquest of unity by diversity or diversity by unity. The three are one and the one is three."[37] (Hardcover, p. 46; paperback, p. 42)

THE TRINITY AND MARRIAGE. The inner workings of the Trinity will always be a source of great awe and wonder before which we bow in worship. In the Bible we only get a few glimpses of the Son being sent to earth where he submits to the Father, and of the Father loving and glorifying the Son, and of the Spirit illuminating the work of both in orchestrating our salvation. (Study John 16–17 for the most sustained description of this in the Scripture.) Yet even in those few glimpses we see at the heart of the Godhead the desire to lift up the other, to defer, to honor, and to work in such perfect harmony and delight that the word "dance" is not too strong an image for it.[38]

Reflection: If lifting up the other for praise and honor is at the center of the Godhead, to what degree does your marriage right now reflect that?

Thought for prayer: First think of several specific ways that you could be lifting up and showing your spouse more honor and respect. Then pray that God would give you the focus and ability to perform them.

[Paul] is able to tie the original statement about marriage in Genesis 2 to Jesus and the church. As one commentator put it, "Paul saw that when God designed the original marriage He already had Christ and the church in mind. This is one of God's great purposes in marriage: to picture the relationship between Christ and His redeemed people forever!" . . . This is the secret—that the gospel of Jesus and marriage explain one another. That when God invented marriage, he already had the saving work of Jesus in mind. (Hardcover, pp. 46–47; paperback, pp. 42–43)

REPAIRING THE WORLD. All that God has created and achieved in history has been working toward one single goal—the redemption and sanctification of his people. In assuming the role of servant-leader or suitable helper, husbands and wives are caught up into the great dance that is restoring the universe (see yesterday's devotional).[39] The requirements of marriage make us more servant-hearted like Jesus, whose very nature is to give up power and privilege to serve others.[40] Thus marriage works at two levels. Marriage makes us into the kind of people who serve others and can repair the world in general. But it also teaches us to love and serve our spouses in particular. That can make us something beautiful—"radiant" and "unstained" (Ephesians 5:27).

Reflection: List the aspects of marriage that reveal something about God's relationship to his people. Try to have at least ten examples. There are many more.

Thought for prayer: Thank God that, in his love for us, he does not leave us as we are, but finds ways to wake us up and move us to make changes we need to make for his sake, our sakes, and for the sakes of all those around us.

If God had the gospel of Jesus's salvation in mind when he established marriage, then marriage only "works" to the degree that it approximates the pattern of God's self-giving love in Christ. What Paul is saying not only answers the objection that marriage is oppressive and restrictive, but it also addresses the sense that the demands of marriage are overwhelming. There is so much to do that we don't know where to start. Start here, Paul says. Do for your spouse what God did for you in Jesus, and the rest will follow. . . . [T]he gospel of Jesus and marriage explain one another. (Hardcover, pp. 46–47; paperback, pp. 42–43)

THE LIBERTY OF OBEDIENCE. Seen through the lens of dos and don'ts, the obligations of marriage can appear oppressive. But to see it as the joy of offering obedience to *him* rather than to a list of rules is liberating. When we first fall in love we almost ache to find ways of pleasing the other. We alter behavior and give up things—all for the pleasure of giving pleasure to the one we love. We don't see such changes as "sacrifices," though they are. Now think of Jesus and all he has done for us. Change your life first for him and then for each other. Sacrifice and submission allow us to participate in a cosmic dance that pulses with joy. All the powers of heaven rejoice to see a married couple following in the footsteps of Jesus.

Reflection: What are the changes you should make in yourself for the sake of your marriage that you are reluctant to do? How can the concepts in today's devotional help you make them?

Thought for prayer: Meditate on Hebrews 12:2, how Jesus endured the pain of the Cross for us "for the joy set before him"—the joy of pleasing his Father and saving us. Ask God to help you serve your spouse out of joy in Christ's salvation.

March 16

We should rightly object to the binary choice that both traditional and contemporary marriage seem to give us. Is the purpose of marriage to deny your interests for the good of the family, or is it rather to assert your interests for the fulfillment of yourself? The Christian teaching does not offer a choice between fulfillment and sacrifice but rather mutual fulfillment through mutual sacrifice. (Hardcover, p. 47; paperback, p. 43)

WORKING FOR GOD. As we said yesterday, obedience can be a joy when we fix our hearts on how much we love our Savior and our spouse. And yet, in this world, obedience to the rules of service, repentance, and forgiveness is still hard, still costly. So when you make expensive sacrifices for each other, always remember that they are offerings primarily to God (Romans 12:1–2). If you are giving something up for your spouse when you don't really want to, look past the fallible human being before you and see God. Your spouse in him- or herself may not deserve what you are giving, but God always does.

Reflection: Make a list of recent changes you have made for the sake of your marriage and your spouse. Honestly assess whether or not you resent them. How can the concept in this devotional help you with that?

Thought for prayer: Meditate on Romans 12:1–2, about what it means to make your entire life a living sacrifice to God in honor of who he is and in gratitude for what he has done. Ask God to help you see sacrifices you've made for your family as sacrifices offered to him.

Subordinating ourselves to him, however, is radically safe, because he has already shown that he was willing to go to hell and back for us. This banishes fears that loving surrender means loss of oneself. (Hardcover, p. 47; paperback, p. 43)

IDENTITY AND MARRIAGE. Ephesians 5:21–22 famously speaks of wives submitting to their husbands and also to spouses submitting to each other. We will treat this later in this volume, but it is clear enough that marriage means the loss of freedom for the sake of love. Modern people regard this as diminishment, even the loss of one's identity. However, submission to God's plan did not injure Jesus, the Second Person of the Trinity, but rather led to him being exalted far above every other name. And Jesus called his disciples to "lose themselves" in order to find their true selves (Matthew 10:39)—and they did. So submission and service in marriage is the doorway into a deep, committed, truth-telling love relationship. And we always experience that as freedom.

Reflection: Men, have you experienced greater closeness to Jesus when your leadership calls for you to sacrifice? Women, have you experienced greater closeness to Jesus when, knowing your full equality, you lay it aside to serve?

Thought for prayer: Thank Jesus for how he laid aside his power and privilege in order to serve—all to save you. Admit your fears of submitting to him—or to anyone else—and ask him to help you follow his pattern of love.

On the one hand, the experience of marriage will unveil the beauty and depths of the gospel to you. It will drive you further into reliance on it. On the other hand, a greater understanding of the gospel will help you experience deeper and deeper union with each other as the years go on. (Hardcover, pp. 47–48; paperback, p. 44)

GOD'S SOVEREIGNTY. It is widely reported that younger adults in Western society are highly ambivalent about marriage and that they are opting out of marriage and childbearing more than any previous generation.[41] Singles should indeed approach the high calling of marriage with awe but also without fear. Jesus knows and rules your future, single or married, and nothing will happen to you that will not bring you closer to him if you offer him your trust. Married people can connect with him with identical comfort—Jesus rules your life, and even a less than perfect marriage, offered to him, will work toward the holiness in your life that God intends. He is working all things together for good (Romans 8:32). Your times are in his hand (Psalm 31:15).

Reflection: What areas of your life most need to be offered to God? You can discover them by finding where your fears live. Explore in prayer what you are afraid of, and offer it to God.

Thought for prayer: Ask God to remind your heart of three things: that you are *not* in control of your life—only he is; that he loves you far more than you love yourself; and that he is infinitely wiser than you are about what is best.

March 19

The reason that marriage is so painful and yet wonderful is because it is a reflection of the gospel, which is painful and wonderful at once. The gospel is this: We are more sinful and flawed in ourselves than we ever dared believe, yet at the very same time we are more loved and accepted in Jesus Christ than we ever dared hope. This is the only kind of relationship that will really transform us. (Hardcover, p. 48; paperback, p. 44)

RECONCILIATION. Our flawed and sinful nature leaves us alienated from God. No effort of ours would repair the damage, assuage the wrath, heal the brokenness, and release the chains of our self-chosen slavery. God did not choose between justice and love, but demonstrated his astonishing love for us by taking on *himself* the punishment due to us. Once we rest in this for ourselves by faith in Christ, it changes our relationships, especially marriage. The new security we have in him enables us to give each other an analogous love—speaking to each other about our flaws and sins and yet forgiving each other. Every incident of confrontation, repentance, and forgiveness is painful yet leads to deeper wisdom, love, and (eventually) joy in one another.

Reflection: When you are wronged in a relationship, how do you respond? Do you wait for the other party to make the first move? Or do you take whatever steps are necessary to repair the connection? How does the gospel of God's grace make that easier to do?

Thought for prayer: Ask God to give you a heart that can grant forgiveness and to teach you the skill of forgiveness.

Love without truth is sentimentality; it supports and affirms us but keeps us in denial about our flaws. Truth without love is harshness; it gives us information but in such a way that we cannot really hear it. God's saving love in Christ, however, is marked by both radical truthfulness about who we are and yet also radical, unconditional commitment to us. (Hardcover, p. 48; paperback, p. 44)

THE WOUNDS OF A FRIEND. Since God's relationship to us is meant to be our model for marriage, speaking the truth in love would be our goal even if we were not commanded to do it in Ephesians 4:15. Harsh denunciations, no matter how truthful, never change anyone. Sentimental—or, worse, fearful—approval of everything your spouse does is a form of stealth cruelty. It is not loving to see someone's faults, see how they hurt him or her and those around them, and yet say nothing. At the very least a marriage ought to be as good as a good friendship, where "iron sharpens iron" (Proverbs 27:17) and "wounds from a friend can be trusted; but an enemy multiplies kisses." (Proverbs 27:6)

Reflection: Couples, do you lovingly dare to help your beloved even if you know the truth will hurt? What measures do you take to make your communication as gentle as possible without compromising the truth?

Thought for prayer: Meditate on which side of Ephesians 4:15 is harder for you temperamentally—the truthfulness or the graciousness? Then ask God to strengthen you where you are weak.

The gospel can fill our hearts with God's love so that you can handle it when your spouse fails to love you as he or she ought. That frees us to see our spouse's sins and flaws to the bottom—and speak of them—and yet still love and accept our spouse fully. And when, by the power of the gospel, our spouse experiences that same kind of truthful yet committed love, it enables our spouses to show us that same kind of transforming when the time comes for it. (Hardcover, p. 48; paperback, p. 45)

GOD'S LOVE AND OURS. If your income increases dramatically your giving to charity can (and should) increase dramatically. In the same way each spouse must be full and overflowing with a love that comes from outside the marriage—God's love, poured into our lives through Christ's sacrifice (Romans 5:3–4). Only then can we deal appropriately with one another, speaking the truth in love, when our spouse hurts us or is hurting him- or herself with sinful behavior. We can love because we are supplied with an unending supply of divine love. As important as your spouse is to you, he or she is not the only or ultimate source of your love, significance, and security. This allows us not to panic when something "isn't right" in our marriage.

Reflection: Do you panic or get angry when your spouse is depressed, or hurting, or even sick? Is it because you expect the other person to be *your* rock and *your* redeemer, rather than Christ? What can you do to change this?

Thought for prayer: Meditate on Romans 5:3–4, about how patience and character growth result when we experience the love of God poured out into our hearts. Ask God to send his Spirit to effect this in your life.

"Submit to one another out of reverence for Christ." (Ephesians 5:21) . . . [Paul] is declaring that everything he is about to say about marriage assumes the parties are being filled with God's Spirit. Only if you have learned to serve by the power of the Holy Spirit will you have the power to face the challenges of marriage. (Hardcover, pp. 50–51; paperback, pp. 47–48)

LORD AND SERVANT. Marriage is not meant to be a transactional relationship, where I only give and stay involved if I am getting a good return on my investment. Rather, when each party in a marriage submits to the role to which he or she has been called, they do it out of reverence for Christ, not because of coercion by another human being. Husbands who accept their role of servant leadership when they would prefer to remain passive and wives who submit to their roles as suitable helpers when they might prefer to be more assertive should do it for the glory of Christ. And in the end each role is taken on out of a desire to emulate Jesus, who was both Lord and Servant of the covenant, as we love and build up our spouse.

Reflection: Men, are you passive in your role in the marriage and in the home? Does it frustrate your wife? Have you asked her? Women, are you frustrated in your role in the marriage and in the home? What about it frustrates you? Have you offered it to God as a way of glorifying him, or have you had your role imposed on you by cultural forces? Have you talked to your husband about what frustrates you?

Thought for prayer: Meditate on Philippians 2:7 and ask God to help you "take the very nature of a servant" for your spouse as Christ did for you.

[A]t the end of the day, Christ's love is the great foundation for build-ing a marriage that sings. Some who turn to Christ find that his love comes in like a wave that instantly floods the hard ground of their hearts. Others find that his love comes in gently and gradually, like soft rain or even a mist. But in any case, the heart becomes like ground watered by Christ's love, which enables all the forms of human love to grow. (Hardcover, p. 239; paperback, p. 276)

THE DYNAMIC THOUGHT. George Herbert, in his poem "Love (III)," depicts a weary man coming to an inn.[42] The inn-keeper is Love and the man feels that because of his "guilt and sin" he should depart in "shame." But Love says: "And know you not . . . who bore the blame?" "Love" is, of course, Jesus himself. And having silenced guilt by pointing to the cross, he invites him again. "'You must sit down,' says Love, 'and taste my meat.' So I did sit and eat." Philosopher Simone Weil was an agnostic, but when meditating on this poem, Jesus's love became so real that, she wrote, "Christ came down and took possession of me."[43] That is how it works. We meditate, pray, and read about the love of Christ until the Spirit makes some passage, text, or thought dynamically powerful. When we know his love, love for others can grow powerfully.

Reflection: It is one thing to read the Bible or devotional guides quickly. It is another thing to meditate long and thoughtfully over the many promises of the gospel in the Bible. How can you get more time to do this?

Thought for prayer: Meditate on Psalm 1, about the impor-tance of meditating "day and night." Ask God to move your knowledge and experience of him out of the shallows through the disciplines of the Word and prayer.

The Holy Spirit's task, then, is to unfold the meaning of Jesus's person and work to believers in such a way that the glory of it—its infinite importance and beauty—is brought home to the mind and heart. . . . The Holy Spirit's ministry is to take truths about Jesus and make them clear to our minds and real to our hearts—so real that they console and empower and change us at our very center. (Hardcover, p. 51; paperback, pp. 48–49)

THE BIBLE AND MARRIAGE. How does the Holy Spirit make Jesus real to us? Do we wait and listen for a voice? No. Extraordinary revelation ceased with the apostles; extraordinary guidance is rare. How can we know God's love experientially (Romans 5:3–4)? The Holy Spirit does this in a way that is very ordinary, even commonplace. He does it by illuminating the Scriptures as we pray and study them. (See Psalm 119.)[44] If we need the love of Jesus in our hearts in order to love our spouse well (see March 21 and March 26), and if we need the Scripture in order to know that love, then the Bible becomes central to a Christian marriage. Read it individually, jointly, regularly, attentively, and prayerfully.

Reflection: How can you make the Bible play a greater role in your life? In your marriage? Brainstorm some ways.

Thought for prayer: Meditate on Psalms 119:43–48 and 130–135 on the deep effects the Bible can have on one's life. Then ask the Lord to bring those things—freedom, courage, confidence, wisdom, discernment, and a sense of God's presence—into your life.

"Sing and make music in your heart to the Lord, always giving thanks to God the father for everything, in the name of our Lord Jesus Christ." [Ephesians 5:19–20] And because the object of this song is not favorable life circumstances (which can change) but the truth and grace of Jesus (which cannot), this heart song does not weaken in times of difficulty. (Hardcover, pp. 51–52; paperback, p. 49)

RADICAL GRATITUDE. In Ann Voskamp's book *One Thousand Gifts*, she tells of the transformation that occurred when she began keeping a record of each day's gifts and deliberately giving thanks for each one. This has the salutary effect of freeing us to focus on God's goodness rather than on our disappointing circumstances. My own (Kathy's) list, begun years ago, began very simply with "I am thankful for clean water to give to my children." This was something that many parents in the world do not have. The reason I did have it was largely due to where I was born and raised—all of these things being God's gifts. When I began to see things that I took for granted as things to be grateful for, it indeed injected a new music into my daily life.

Reflection: Do you keep a list of the things for which you are thankful about your spouse? If not, why not start today?

Thought for the day: Make your own list of very common, taken-for-granted things in your life for which you can be thankful to God. Then thank him directly for them.

March 26

> [T]he picture of marriage given here is not of two needy people, unsure of their own value and purpose, finding their significance and meaning in one another's arms. If you add two vacuums to each other, you only get a bigger and stronger vacuum, a giant sucking sound. Rather, Paul assumes that each spouse already has settled the big questions of life—why they were made by God and who they are in Christ. (Hardcover, p. 52; paperback, p. 49)

IDENTITY IN CHRIST. Everyone has to live for something—everyone bases his or her meaning and significance on something. If it is your career, you will give your spouse and family too little attention. But if it is your spouse, you may need them to always be perfectly affirming. If your meaning in life rests in another person's love, you will crush him or her. No human being can bear the full weight of the expectations of another person. Rather, with our identity found in Christ, we can give and receive love and support out of the fullness we have as God's children, the heirs of grace.

Reflection: Has your spouse become an idol in your life, someone you look to for all your happiness? Has this resulted in a happier marriage, or one in which you resent any problems your husband or wife may have, because it keeps him or her from focusing exclusively on you? How can you begin repenting for this?

Thought for prayer: To rest one's identity more in Christ and his love than anything else is a never-ending struggle. Ask God for the patience and wisdom necessary for continual progress.

No one lives a life of continual joy in God, of course. It is not auto-matic and constant. If that were the case, Paul would not have had to start [Ephesians] verse 18 with an imperative, exhorting them literally to "go on being filled with the Spirit!" We are often running on fumes, spiritually, but we must know where the fuel station is and, even more important, that it exists. (Hardcover, p. 52; paperback, pp. 49–50)

SPIRITUAL PROVOCATION. Just as it was not good for Adam to be alone, so it is impossible to grow spiritually by yourself. We need others to exhort, provoke, and stir us out of spiritual compla-cency (Hebrews 3:13, 10:24–25). Helping one another to find renewal in the Holy Spirit, therefore, may be the most important act of love we do for one another in marriage. This is rarely accom-plished by *nagging* (constant sermonizing) or *dragging* (forcing an unwilling spouse to accompany you to every church-sponsored event). We just received a letter this week from an eighty-seven-year-old woman who saw her husband become a Christian several years before he died—after quietly praying for him for decades. Other spouses have been helped into spiritual growth by more insistent (but still gracious) conversations. The only wrong thing to do is to be passive.

Reflection: Husbands and wives—when you see one another struggling, is your reaction one of compassion . . . or irritation? Do you pray for one another, or scold and harangue?

Thought for prayer: Meditate on 1 Samuel 12:23, in which it is said that failure to pray can be a sin. Ask your spouse for three things that they need and for which you could pray to God. Then do that at least once a week.

After trying all kinds of other things, Christians have learned that the worship of God with the whole heart in the assurance of his love through the work of Jesus Christ is the thing their soul was meant to "run on." That is what gets all the heart's cylinders to fire. If this is not understood, then we will not have the resources to be good spouses. If we look to our spouses to fill up our tanks in a way that only God can do, we are demanding impossibility. (Hardcover, p. 52; paperback, p. 50)

THE RIGHT AIM. Just because something is impossible doesn't stop us from wanting it. Expecting our spouse to supply all our needs for happiness (if we remain distant from God) is a futile impossibility. It is so easy to pay lip service to our faith in God, but functionally to rely on our spouse to make us happy. C. S. Lewis summarized a basic principle of the Christian life: "Aim at heaven and you'll get earth thrown in; aim at earth and you'll get neither." Happiness is an inevitable by-product of holiness, but pleasing God (not yourself) must be the primary aim. We can apply this to marriage. If we aim at God—at being faithful to him above all—we will be satisfied in our marriage; if we aim to find our happiness in our marriage alone, we will get neither.

Reflection: Functionally (meaning, *for real*), where do you look to fill your need for meaning, purpose, and happiness—in God or some human relationship (especially your spouse or a child)? What can you change to place more of your trust in God?

Thought for prayer: Meditate on Matthew 5:6, where Jesus says we experience blessedness if we hunger for righteousness rather than blessedness. Now ask God to help you do that.

In [Ephesians] verses 22–24, Paul says, controversially, that wives should submit to their husbands. Immediately, however, he tells husbands to love their wives as Christ loved the church and "gave himself up for her" (25), which is, if anything, a stronger appeal to abandon self-interest than was given to the woman. . . . [E]ach partner is called to sacrifice for the other in far-reaching ways. Whether we are husband or wife, we are not to live for ourselves but for the other. (Hardcover, p. 53; paperback, p. 50)

FORM YET FREEDOM. If we are to dance, the partners must have choreography that supports and honors the Other. If we are to sing, harmony is better than everyone singing only melody. If life-giving is the primary goal of marriage (whether in the creation of children, the growth of spouses toward holiness, and/or care for other image-bearers of God), then diversity of role is a creative necessity. Cultures and temperaments differ, and accordingly the Bible prescribes few details for what the husband and the wife in a marriage can or cannot do. It gives us plenty of freedom to work out what those roles are in a particular marriage, but nevertheless the roles exist.

Reflection: Husband, do you work to discover and encourage all the creative potential of your wife? Does she excel in ways you never expected? How have you helped her to develop her gifts? Wives, are you passive, doing little to stretch yourself and use the gifts and talents God gave you? Or are you trying to do everything at once, rather than focusing on the ways God wants you to contribute to your marriage, your church, and the world?

Thought for prayer: Ask God to, first, reveal to both of you your respective strengths and weaknesses, and second, how you can play to strengths and guard against weaknesses in the roles you adopt within your marriage.

Christians [are] to be *douloi* of one another (Galatians 5:13)—literally bond-servants . . . [b]ecause Christ humbled himself and became a servant and met our needs even at the cost of his own life. . . . [A] servant puts someone else's needs ahead of his or her own. That is how all believers should live with each other. And if all believers are to serve each other in this way, how much more intentionally and intensely should husbands and wives have this attitude toward one another? (Hardcover, pp. 53–54; paperback, p. 51)

DIFFERING GIFTS. Paul's explanatory treatise on the interlocking gifts of the Body (1 Corinthians 12:12–30) is crucial for married couples. A marriage is a small version of the Body of Christ. Paul argues first that every person is gifted differently— we are not interchangeable. He also argues that some gifts and abilities which "seem to be weaker are indispensible" (1 Corinthians 12:22). Therefore, within the Body of Christ those the world thinks "less honorable we treat with special honor" (verse 23). All this applies to marriage. Many chafe at the idea of a wife following her husband's leadership. But when we see that Christ himself was fully divine yet submitted to his Father, the terms "equality," "headship," and "submission" take on meaning beyond all our imagining.

Reflection: Married couples, do you honor the role to which your spouse has been called? Do you show your belief that you are equal in Christ (Galatians 3:28) even though you have been given different assignments in the Body?

Thought for prayer: Thank the Lord for his willingness to lose his glory and become a servant. Ask him to help you in your heart resist the world's teaching (Romans 12:2) that to give up power and to serve is always demeaning.

While Paul writes that the husband is "head" of his wife, it does not negate the fact he is also his wife's Christian brother and bond-servant according to Galatians 5:13. Husbands and wives must serve each other, must "give themselves up" for one another. That does not destroy the exercise of authority within every human relationship, but it does radically transform it. (Hardcover, p. 54; paperback, pp. 51–52)

THE TRANSFORMATION OF AUTHORITY. The early Christians astonished the world by welcoming in people of all races, social classes, gender, and ethnicities. In the book of Philemon, Paul told a Christian how he had to treat his servant as an equal brother in Christ, even though his time of service was not yet finished. This was a radical thing to say in that highly stratified, hierarchical culture. Historians have noted how this gospel principle undermined the powerful institution of slavery in the Western world. The New Testament does not eliminate authority within human institutions and relationships. For example, churches are still to have elders, but not domineering ones (1 Peter 5:3). Authority wielded for selfish purposes is the opposite of love. But loving authority transforms the curse put on relationships and marriage at the entrance of sin into the world.

Reflection: Men and women, married or single, how do you serve one another as brothers and sisters? If your service requires plain speaking of the truth in love, are you able to do that from a loving motivation?

Thought for prayer: Virtually all of us exercise some authority over others in various ways. Ask God to enable you only to do so with love and humility.

Can a man scoop fire into his lap and his clothes not get burned? Can a man walk on hot coals without his feet being scorched? So is he who sleeps with another man's wife; no one who touches her will go unpunished. (Proverbs 6:27–29)

DAMAGE. We have seen that adultery wrongs God, the spouse, and yourself. Here is why the damage is so extensive. Fire in the fireplace brought life through warmth and the cooking of food. But fire in the lap was death. Why? The fireplace is designed for fire, but the lap and clothes are not. So sex is designed for marriage—that is its fireplace—but outside of marriage it consumes and breaks things apart. God designed sex for marriage and outside of it you are going against the grain of the universe. Fire in the lap does not need to be punished—it is its own punishment. That's why the last sentence is literally true. Even adultery that is not caught by others will still catch you.[45]

Reflection: Think of other things that are its own punishment. Do you do any of these things in your marriage?

Prayer: Lord, remind me that, when I am tempted to wrongdoing, that there is no escaping the consequences, that no one ever gets away with anything. But I thank you for your grace. Amen.

Now Joseph was well built and handsome, and after a while his master's wife took notice of Joseph and said, "Come to bed with me!" . . . And though she spoke to Joseph day after day, he refused to go to bed with her or even be with her. One day he went into the house to attend to his duties, and none of the household servants was inside. She caught him by his cloak and said, "Come to bed with me!" But he left his cloak in her hand and ran out of the house. (Genesis 39:6–7, 10–12)

RESISTANCE TO TEMPTATION. The story of Joseph gives us insights into the Bible's teaching on how to resist adultery. His master's wife tries to wear him down, coming on to him "day after day" before she grabs him (verse 12). Temptation is ordinarily progressive. It seldom starts with someone just taking hold of us. It begins with attitudes of self-pity or resentment that speak to us, saying, "I deserve this; my life is full of stress." Sometimes your conscience becomes numbed through secret fantasies, or emotional affairs, or the use of pornography, so that eventually you can tolerate larger sins and dishonesties without being bothered. The Tempter can work on us for years, softening us up, before he actually grabs us.

Reflection: Are there any ways that you have been "softened up" for bigger sexual sin? How can you guard against the progressiveness of temptation?

Prayer: Lord, like Job, I want to make a "covenant with my eyes" (Job 31:1) so that I do not gaze longingly at anyone but my spouse—and you. Amen.

Now Joseph was well built and handsome, and after a while his master's wife took notice of Joseph and said, "Come to bed with me!" But he refused. "With me in charge," he told her, "my master does not concern himself with anything in the house; everything he owns he has entrusted to my care. No one is greater in this house than I am. My master has withheld nothing from me except you, because you are his wife. How then could I do such a wicked thing and sin against God?" (Genesis 39:6–9)

SELF-JUSTIFYING TALK. Joseph is a servant in the house of Potiphar and his master's wife wants to have sex with him. Joseph chooses a way to think about the woman's proposal that makes it easier to turn down. She calls it "come to bed" but he calls it a "wicked thing." Others might have seen their record of service and their freedom within the house as a warrant for indulgence, but he makes his success a ground for gratitude and self-control (verse 9). What tempts you, then, are not the circumstances themselves, but the things you say to yourself about the circumstances.

Reflection: How has your own experience confirmed this particular way that Joseph resists temptation? What can you personally learn from this way?

Prayer: Lord Jesus, you resisted temptation in the garden of Gethsemane, keeping your promise and being faithful to us. Now strengthen me to keep all my promises, and especially my promise to my spouse. Amen.

"How then could I do such a wicked thing and sin against God?" (Genesis 39:9)

GOD-CENTEREDNESS. Joseph finally says this sin would be "against God" (verse 9). He didn't think of sin as only breaking the law but also dishonoring God. Had he thought, "Well, if I do this, I might get caught," he would never have resisted. But instead he said, "This would be trampling on my Lord's glory and heart." That was a whole different way to think. Sin will always present itself to your mind under a false guise. You will have to unmask it for what it is. Joseph rooted his loyalty to his master down into his love and debt to God. That anchored it deep enough to survive this blast of temptation.

Reflection: How has your own experience confirmed this particular way that Joseph resists temptation? What can you personally learn from this way?

Prayer: Lord, sin does not want to admit that it is a stab at your very heart. Help me always see it for what it is when I'm tempted, so that I can resist it for your sake. Amen.

And though she spoke to Joseph day after day, he refused to go to bed with her or even be with her. One day he went into the house to attend to his duties, and none of the household servants was inside. She caught him by his cloak and said, "Come to bed with me!" But he left his cloak in her hand and ran out of the house. (Genesis 39:10–12)

CONTROL THE ENVIRONMENT. We have seen how Joseph controls his thoughts in order to overcome temptation. But when his master's wife tries to badger and wear him down, we are told, "he refused to . . . even be with her" (verse 10). Since she talked to him every day it meant he could not avoid her completely, but he tried to avoid being alone with her. So Joseph did not rely simply on his *inner* self-control. He avoided *outward* settings that he knew might be tempting. This is simply being humble and realistic. Working on changing one's outward environment is as necessary as working to unmask the sin and change one's inner thinking. We need to do both.

Reflection: How has your own experience confirmed this particular way that Joseph resists temptation? What can you personally learn from this way?

Prayer: Lord, how easy it is for me to take temptation lightly, to say, "I can handle this." But without you, I can do nothing. Help me to acknowledge my need and depend entirely on you. Amen.

One day he went into the house to attend to his duties, and none of the household servants was inside. She caught him by his cloak and said, "Come to bed with me!" But he left his cloak in her hand and ran out of the house. (Genesis 39:11–12)

FLEE TEMPTATION. Sometimes temptation comes upon us with a powerful frontal attack. When that happened to Joseph, he fled. (cf. 2 Timothy 2:22; 2 Peter 1:4). He doesn't remain and try to reason with temptation. He doesn't, like Eve, consider how nice the fruit looks (Genesis 3:6; cf. Joshua 7:21). Martin Luther supposedly said, "You can't stop birds from flying over your head, but you *can* stop them from making nests in your hair." In other words, you can't prevent a temptation from being proposed to you, but you can refuse to have any dialogue with it at all. Don't think: "Should I do this or not? What are the pros and cons?" No. In the iconic words of Doctor Who: *"Run!"*

Reflection: How has your own experience confirmed this particular way that Joseph resists temptation? What can you personally learn from this way?

Prayer: Lord, we are saved by grace and you love us despite our sin, but that does not mean that our sin does not grieve you deeply. Help me to have nothing to do with it. Amen.

April 7

Take care, brothers, lest there be in any of you an evil, unbelieving heart, leading you to fall away from the living God. But exhort one another every day, as long as it is called "today," that none of you may be hardened by the deceitfulness of sin. (Hebrews 3:12–13)[46]

FIND ACCOUNTABILITY. One of the main ways to guard against sexual temptation is through Christian community. There are three ways this can be done practically. First, deliberately cultivate a small number of one-on-one Christian relationships deep enough for speaking about personal matters. We need to keep each other accountable in our relationships, our use of money and time, our sexuality, and so on. Second, commit to being in a good small group that discusses and wrestles with the practical outworking of the Christian life. Third, regularly attend worship as a member of a congregation, even if the church is not perfectly to your taste. Each of these practices adds a level of accountability that the others do not.

Reflection: Do you already have these kinds of relationships? If so, be thankful! If you do not, do you have any candidates? What can you do to move forward?

Prayer: Lord, I ask you for encouragement and strengthening but so often you answer that prayer through other Christians. Help me to strengthen my relationships and friendships so that I can grow in grace and Christlikeness. Amen.

April 8

If two spouses are spending a day together, the question of who gets their pleasure and who gives in can present itself every few minutes. And when it does there are three possibilities: you can offer to serve the other with joy, you can make the offer with coldness or resentment, or you can selfishly insist on your own way. Only when both partners are most regularly responding to one another in the first way can the marriage thrive. But how hard that is! (Hardcover, p. 54; paperback, p. 52)

MY LIFE FOR YOU. As Luther said, we are "curved in upon ourselves"; we are self-absorbed, selfish, obsessed with our own needs and desires. Every day you face situations in which you can respond with the motivation of hell ("your life to serve mine") or of heaven ("my life to serve yours.") Each time you make your choice you form your soul, in a small but significant way, either outward or inward. Any step away from self-absorption entails a form of suffering, a putting to death of self in favor of the Other. Done habitually, it can transform a life, a marriage, a friendship, and a culture.

Reflection: Have you ever made an effort to step away from your own desires in order to give to another? Over time, does this balance out in your marriage, or does one (or both!) of you feel that you are always the one who makes the sacrifice? Discuss this honestly with your spouse.

Thought for prayer: Meditate on Philippians 2:5–11 and especially verse 5, "in your relationships with each other have the same mindset as Christ Jesus." Then ask God for it.

I didn't want to be served. I didn't want to be in a position where I had to ask for something and receive it as a gift. . . . I wanted to serve, yes, because that made me feel in control. Then I would always have the high moral ground. But that kind of "service" isn't service at all, only manipulation. But by not giving Kathy an opportunity to serve me, I had failed to serve her. And the reason underneath it all was my pride. (Hardcover, p. 55; paperback, p. 53)

PRIDE. Once while we were on vacation, Kathy encouraged me to go with our friend David to visit a theological bookstore, leaving her to handle our three energetic young boys alone for several hours. I knew it was a sacrifice for her, but I refused under the excuse that I didn't want her to be "put out." Later I realized I liked being in the position of having made the most sacrifices. My pride had prevented me from receiving the gift and also kept her from the joy of giving it. How can we untangle our selfish motives even for kindnesses? Repentance is the key to all of life, and nowhere more so than in marriage. Joyful repentance, even accompanied by "there I go again" laughter, is the mark of a mature and wise marriage.

Reflection: Consider ways in which selfish motives can be behind unselfish-looking behavior. Can you think of examples in your marriage?

Thought for prayer: Meditate on Psalm 139:23–24. Then ask God to help you know your own heart better, for his sake and your spouse's.

My reluctance to let Kathy serve me was, in the end, a refusal to live my life on the basis of grace. I wanted to earn everything. . . . I wanted to give undeserved gifts to others—so I could have satisfaction of thinking of myself as a magnanimous person—but I did not want to receive someone else's service. My heart still operated like this even though my head had accepted the basic gospel thesis that through faith in Christ we live by God's grace alone. (Hardcover, p. 56; paperback, p. 54)

SPIRITUAL SMELLING SALTS. Living a life based on the knowledge that we are justified by faith in Christ and not our own works takes constant effort. It said that the trouble with a living sacrifice (Romans 12:1–2) is that it keeps getting up off the altar! We must daily sacrifice our pride, our need to prove ourselves, our desire to find our identity in anything other than Christ. A marriage is a perfect vehicle to have your sins exposed, because your flaws cause friction between you and your spouse. That forces you to focus on them even though you would rather ignore them. Instead of silently complaining about the conflicts, give thanks for them because they can be like spiritual smelling salts. Repent and resolve to change as often as something comes to your attention.

Reflection: Married couples, you should each make a list of the top five ways in which your sinful heart works to defeat the grace shed abroad in your life by Christ. Ask your spouse for gentle, loving help in recognizing and eradicating these patterns. This will take courage and humility.

Thought for prayer: Meditate on friends "sharpening" each other in Proverbs 27:17. Then ask God to give you whatever it takes for clashes with your spouse to sharpen you spiritually rather than discouraging or embittering you.

That gospel message . . . teaches us that we are indeed self-centered sinners . . . [b]ut the gospel also fills us with more love and affirmation than we could ever imagine. It means we don't need to earn our self-worth through incessant service and work. It means also that we don't mind so much when we are deprived of some comfort, compliment, or reward. We aren't keeping records and accounts anymore. We can freely give and freely receive. (Hardcover, p. 56; paperback, p. 54)

PAST, PRESENT, FUTURE. Salvation by grace is instantaneous. We are justified and pardoned the moment we transfer our trust from our own works to Jesus for our standing before God. But living into the healing of that salvation is the work of a lifetime. We *have been saved* from the penalty of sin; we *are being saved* from the power of sin; and in heaven we *will be saved* from the presence of sin. Meanwhile, choose a spouse with whom you are willing to confront the continued power of sin in your life, postsalvation and preglorification. A pretty face or potential high earning power will be of no help at all in facing the indwelling sin in your own heart. Choose someone who can see who you are meant to become, and who loves you enough to be part of the process of getting you there.

Reflection: It is one thing to want your spouse to change to please you. It's another thing to help him or her change to please God. How do you help each other confront and overcome the sinful habits and temptations in your life?

Thought for prayer: Ask God to give you spiritual discernment and eyes to see what he wants your spouse to become. Then ask the Lord for the wisdom and grace to help him or her make progress.

The main barrier to the development of a servant heart in marriage is . . . the radical self-centeredness of the sinful human heart. Self-centeredness is the main problem in many marriages, and it is the ever-present enemy of *every* marriage. It is the cancer in the core of every marriage when it begins, and it has to be dealt with. (Hardcover, pp. 56–57; paperback, p. 55)

DEATH TO SELF. We said earlier that every step away from the self-absorption and self-centeredness in our marriages is a type of suffering; a death, if you will, to self. We are told that our old nature must be crucified (Galatians 5:24)—a slow and painful death. To live in Christ is to die to our own sinful desires. *Sacrifice* is not a word our culture prizes much, but it is the key to all growth, both personally and in a marriage. Sometimes it feels as if the longer you are married, the more abrasive you become with one another. That is merely the fragile shell of early infatuation wearing away and the irritations over long-standing issues surfacing. Finally, the real work can begin!

Reflection: What recurrent issues have surfaced in your marriage over the years, things that cause you to bicker and scratch with one another? How can those issues be addressed with the gospel?

Thought for prayer: Meditate on Philippians 4:5: "Let your gentleness be evident to all. The Lord is near." Then ask the Lord to make you significantly more gentle and gracious in your speech with your spouse, and especially when you disagree.

In Dana Adam Shapiro's interviews of divorced couples, it is clear that this was the heart of what led to marital disintegration. . . . [Each spouse] responded to the self-centeredness of their partner with their own self-centeredness. Why? Self-centeredness by its very character makes you blind to your own while being hypersensitive, offended, and angered by that of others The result is always a downward spiral into self-pity, anger, and despair, as the relationship gets eaten away to nothing. (Hardcover, p. 57; paperback, pp. 55–56)

NO CONDEMNATION! Romans 8:13 speaks about putting to death our lifelong hostility to God's lordship over our lives. Such a painful process must always be done against the background of the chapter's ringing first verse: *There is now no condemnation for those in Christ Jesus.* Knowing that our sins will not be met with condemnation, but with the help of the Holy Spirit, gives us the courage to confront the evils of our heart. In marriage Christian spouses must give each other something analogous. We must know that our sins and failures will be met with sympathy and forgiveness and help. This likewise gives us the freedom to be honest and the courage to tackle the changes we must make.

Reflection: How good are you at offering your spouse a critique against a background of "no condemnation"?

Thought for prayer: Meditate on Romans 8:1 and answer the question: "How would I be different if I believed this more deeply?" Then ask God to bring those things to reality in your life.

[T]he gospel, brought home to your heart by the Spirit, can make you happy enough to be humble, giving you an internal fullness that frees you to be generous with the other even when you are not getting the satisfaction you want out of the relationship. Without the help of the Spirit, without a continual refilling of your soul's tank with the glory and love of the Lord, such submission to the interests of the other is virtually impossible . . . without becoming resentful. (Hardcover, pp. 57–58; paperback, p. 56)

MAKING THE MARRIAGE FLOURISH. We should not think of marital differences as "zero sum," with one person always losing to the other. When writer Judith Viorst was asked for the secret of staying married for nearly sixty years, she replied: "The marriage is like a third thing. If we have a fight, if we make compromises, it's not to the other person, it's to the marriage. It's different from losing. This was a third thing that we treasured and took very good care of."[47] Many marry for the sake of their own personal flourishing, and if they find themselves sacrificing for the other's needs they are ready to leave. The goal of a Christian marriage is instead to see the marriage itself flourish, for a healthy marital bond honors God and serves you both.

Reflection: Discuss with each other how thinking of your marriage as a "third thing" can make sacrifices and compromises easier.

Thought for prayer: Ask God to help you avoid resentment over the compromises you have had to make in your marriage. Ask him to help you rejoice in the marriage itself and in the strengths of your spouse.

You can only afford to be generous if you actually have some money in the bank to give. . . . [So] if your only source of love and meaning is your spouse, then any time he or she fails you, it will not just be a grief, but a psychological cataclysm. If, however, you know something of the work of the Spirit in your life, you have enough love "in the bank" to be generous to your spouse even when you are not getting much affection or kindness at the moment. (Hardcover, p. 58; paperback, p. 56)

LOVE ECONOMICS. This thought was my (Kathy's) first introduction to the mind of Tim Keller. He wrote an article called "Love Economics" for a student Christian newspaper while still in college. Needless to say, I was impressed. Although he wasn't speaking specifically about marriage in the article, but relationships in general, nevertheless this principle has helped us understand each stage of our relationship (beginning as acquaintances, progressing to friendship, then marriage). It was the first, foundational plank on which all our days together have been built—God fills us first; then we give to the other, rather than looking for what only God can give in a poor, needy, sinful human. We can only give ourselves freely to the other if "our cup runneth over" (Psalm 23:5).

Reflection: How does this principle help you understand where your relationship is today?

Thought for prayer: Meditate on 1 John 4:19–20, on the relationship between receiving love from God and giving love to others. Spend some time repenting for not loving as he loved you.

April 16

> The deep happiness that marriage can bring, then, lies on the far side of sacrificial service in the power of the Spirit. That is, you only discover your own happiness after each of you have put the happiness of your spouse ahead of your own, in a sustained way, in response to what Jesus has done for you. (Hardcover, p. 58; paperback, p. 57)

ON THE FAR SIDE. Resurrection is promised, but it lies on the far side of crucifixion. In Psalm 34:19 and 20 it sounds as if God is giving a blanket promise that nothing bad will ever happen to one of his children: (19) "The righteous person may have many troubles, but the Lord delivers him from them all; (20) he protects all his bones, not one of them will be broken." The apostles rightly interpreted verse 20 as applying to Jesus, as his bones were not broken during the crucifixion. But notice that God's promised deliverance was on the far side of death and sacrifice, and not before. Every sacrifice of our self-absorption is a little crucifixion; life and restoration is promised as a result, not as a rescue from having to make the sacrifice.

Reflection: Husbands and wives, what was the last sacrifice you made for the other? Was he or she aware that you were making a sacrifice? Was it because you made a big deal out of it, or because you quietly put to death a selfish desire of your own?

Thought for prayer: Ask God for the patience to wait for the deeper love, freedom, and happiness that is only found on the far side of self-giving, self-control, and endurance.

Some will ask, "If I put the happiness of my spouse ahead of my own needs—then what do *I* get out of it?" The answer is—happiness. That is what you get, but . . . a happiness that won't be bad for you. It is the joy that comes from giving joy, from loving another person in a costly way. Today's culture of the "Me-Marriage" finds this very proposal— of putting the interests of your spouse ahead of your own—oppressive. (Hardcover, p. 58; paperback, p. 57)

HAPPINESS GROWS OUT OF SACRIFICE. In the years since we wrote *The Meaning of Marriage*, people have only become more averse to the idea of sacrificing one's interests and desires for the sake of anyone else. But therein lies the great paradox at the heart of our society. We want the happiness and liberation that comes from secure love relationships, but in order to get them one must surrender a great deal of one's individual autonomy. That, however, is what we absolutely will not do. We have created a culture in which, as it were, "food itself turns out to be the very thing you can't eat and home the very place you can't live. . . . Then indeed there is no rescue possible: the last card has been played."[48] The only alternative is to trust what the Bible says, namely, that you must lose yourself in service to God and others in order to find yourself (Matthew 10:39).

Reflection: Can your friends and neighbors see a difference in the way you treat one another? Or does your marriage resemble everyone else's "I'm for me" marriage?

Thought for prayer: Meditate on Romans 12:10 and Proverbs 11:25 about the "refreshment" of unselfish service. Then ask God to help both of you realize this freshness in your marriage.

April 18

Jesus . . . says, "Whoever wants to save his life shall lose it, but whoever loses his life *for my sake* will find it" (Matthew 16:25). He is saying, "If you seek happiness more than you seek me, you will have neither; if you seek to serve me more than serve happiness, you will have both." Paul applies this principle to marriage. (Hardcover, p. 59; paperback, p. 58)

SOLID JOYS AND LASTING TREASURE. The reason Christians are so out of step with the world is that we have a savior who lost his life for us, and called us to take up our cross—not a cranky mother-in-law, or overbearing father-in-law, but our own selfishness—and follow him into death and sacrifice. This is the *Good News* of the gospel. That we don't have to earn God's love and acceptance, but that Jesus, in this life and death, earned his reward and then bequeathed it to us! Following such a savior with joy and gratitude means that the insignificant victories, minor pleasures, and transient happiness of this world are shown up for the flimsy cobwebs they truly are.

Let the world deride or pity,
I will glory in thy Name:
Fading is the worldling's pleasure,
All his boasted pomp and show;
Solid joys and lasting treasure
None but Zion's children know.[49]

Reflection: Do you know the solid joys and lasting treasure of being a child of God? How does it reveal itself in your marriage?

Thought for prayer: Ask the Lord to help you remember that, in your marriage as well as in all you do, that "Only one life, 'twil soon be past; only what's done for Christ will last."[50]

April 19

Seek to serve one another rather than to be happy, and you will find a new and deeper happiness. Many couples have discovered this wonderful, unlooked-for reality. Why would this be true? It is because marriage is "instituted of God." It was established by the God for whom self-giving love is an essential attribute, and therefore it reflects his nature, particularly as it is revealed in the person and work of Jesus Christ. (Hardcover, p. 59; paperback, p. 58)

SERVE AND GIVE. Human beings were created in God's image. That means that we share some of the same characteristics that God himself displays—holiness, self-giving, generous creativity, compassion, justice, and forgiveness. To abandon those parts of our nature is to hate ourselves, to be out of joint with the universe, to be separated from all that is life-giving. To desire to be served rather than to serve separates us from our savior, who explicitly told his followers that "the Son of Man did not come to be served, but to serve, and to give his life as a ransom for many" (Matthew 20:28).

Reflection: Do you stand amazed and stunned by the generosity of God revealed in the person and work of Jesus? Does your spouse ever find herself or himself stunned by your generosity and sacrifice for her or his welfare and happiness?

Thought for prayer: Ask the Lord to prevent you from keeping accounts—of thinking what your spouse owes you, or even what you owe him or her. Ask him to give each of you his own spirit of generosity.

[T]o be part of . . . a greater unity, you have to surrender your independence. . . . Paul says that this ability to deny your own rights, to serve and put the good of the whole over your own is not instinctive; indeed, it's unnatural, but it is the very foundation of marriage. This sounds oppressive, but that's just the way relationships work. (Hardcover, p. 60; paperback, pp. 58–59)

INTERDEPENDENCE. The more our culture invests in online relationships, the harder it becomes for people to learn the skills necessary for maintaining actual face-to-face relationships. One can unfriend or ghost a person digitally without having to explain, apologize, or even acknowledge the issue that led to the dissolution of the relationship. This will make marriage all the more difficult, as the surrender of one's autonomy is almost the definition of marriage. The most basic of wedding vows is to love "for better, for worse, for richer, for poorer, in sickness and in health, to love and to cherish, till death do us part, according to God's holy ordinance; and thereto I pledge myself to you." With those words you exchange your independence for *interdependence*, which runs directly in opposition to our natural selfishness.

Reflection: Were there any relationships (roommates, siblings, parents, friends) that prepared you for the mutual surrender of independence that marriage requires? How well are you doing at consulting with one another before making decisions?

Thought for prayer: Meditate on Psalm 22:25, in which the suffering servant—Jesus—speaks of fulfilling his vows. Thank the Lord for being faithful to his vows to save us. Ask him to make you just as faithful to your wedding vows to love your spouse.

Fulfillment is on the far side of sustained unselfish service, not the near side. It is one of the universal principles of life. [As C. S. Lewis says:] Even in social life, you will never make a good impression on other people until you stop thinking about what sort of impression you are making. . . . The principle runs through all life from top to bottom. Give up yourself, and you will find your real self. Lose your life and you will save it. . . . Nothing that you have not given away will be really yours. (Hardcover, p. 60; paperback, p. 59)[51]

CULTURAL CONTRADICTION. This message is a direct contradiction to all the movies, television, self-help books, and messages of our culture. They tell us that the only path to fulfillment is to care about ME, and ignore the wishes and needs of everyone who might stand in our way. The end result of concentrating on ME is that all I end up with is myself—no love, no sustaining friendships, no viewpoints to challenge my own. The plunge in the fertility rate is directly tied to this attitude. Our culture tells us that no relationship should be a binding obligation, but of course parenting is—we can't divorce our children.[52] Children cannot be negotiated with. Their needs take priority no matter how busy or stressed we are. If you are unpracticed at sacrifice, children will come as a shock. So will marriage.

Reflection: Does "losing your life" sound like an invitation to abuse? When Jesus says "No one takes my life, I willingly lay it down" does that clarify things?

Thought for prayer: Thank the Lord that when he was dying on the cross and he saw us rejecting him, he stayed anyway and loved us. Ask him for the same faithfulness in all your relationships and especially marriage.

We are always, always the last to see our self-absorption. Our hurts and wounds can make our self-centeredness even more intractable. When you point out selfish behavior to a wounded person they say, "Well, maybe so, but you don't understand what it is like." The wounds justify the behavior. (Hardcover, pp. 61–62; paperback, pp. 60–61)

PAST HURTS AND PRESENT BEHAVIOR. Self-absorption derives from sinful selfishness, our desire to make the whole world revolve around us and our desires and needs. But it is not always right to simply tell self-absorbed people to "just stop it!" Those who have experienced physical, sexual, or extreme emotional abuse may not be able to change behavior with a mere exercise of the will. They may be trapped in bad relationships and behavior through a complex of fears, distorted beliefs, and false guilt. They will need patient gentleness and love as well as truth-speaking. Nevertheless, we must not use hurts inflicted on us in the past as excuses for irresponsible actions now. We must neither see abuse everywhere nor nowhere. How we need the Lord's wisdom (James 1:5) to help each other without hurting!

Reflection: A victim of extreme emotional abuse may not be able to confront his or her abuser without help. Have either of you experienced abuse? What effects of it are still with you? What can be done now?

Thought for prayer: Ask the Lord to show you if there are things done to you in the past that may still be controlling you through abiding anger, fear, or sorrow. Ask him to give you the tools of his grace to heal these wounds.

[I]t is argued it is only because they lack healthy self-esteem [that peo-ple are self-centered]. So . . . tell them to be good to themselves, live for themselves, not for others. . . . [But this] assumes that self-centeredness isn't natural, that it is only the product of some kind of mistreatment. No major religion in the world actually teaches that, yet this is the popular level view of many people. . . . But this view of things simply doesn't work. A marriage relationship unavoidably entails self-denial, even in the most mundane day-to-day living. (Hardcover, p. 62; paper-back, p. 61)

INFINITELY PRECIOUS. Arguing that self-centered people (which means all of us) need to become *more* self-centered as a cure for low self-esteem seems odd at best. Low self-esteem is still a way to concentrate on oneself, to obsess over one's own problems and deficiencies. If you are being mistreated, you must stop the perpetrator from doing so (see yesterday's devotional), but that alone is not the cure. Nor is having others tell you how good and talented you are at this or that. Only the unconditional loving arms of Jesus, who knows all our tears and sorrows better than we do ourselves, will be sufficient to fill us with what we need. He loved us enough to die for us; we are infinitely precious to him.

Reflection: In what ways do you convey the love of Christ to your spouse? When he or she is sad, lonely, hurting, or haunted by the past, how can your love, joined to that of Christ, aid in healing?

Thought for prayer: Ask God to give you such a strong sense of being *rich* in his love, his salvation, his blessings, his promises of future glory that you never feel impoverished or diminished by the ordinary daily sacrifices of marital love.

The Christian approach begins with a different analysis of the situation. We believe that, as badly wounded as persons may be, the resulting self-absorption of the human heart was not caused by the mistreatment, it was only magnified and shaped by it. . . . This is not to say that wounded people don't need great gentleness, tender treatment, affirmation, and patience. It is just that this is not the whole story. (Hardcover, pp. 62–63; paperback, pp. 61–62)

A MULTITUDE OF CAUSES. While we can be damaged by people sinning against us, nevertheless no one begins life in a pristine spiritual condition. Psalms 14:2–3 and 58:3 remind us that we are prone to sin, selfishness, and lying as soon as we are born. But just as a bodily infection can be exacerbated by poor nutrition, lack of sleep, and stress, so a sinful nature can be further inflamed by harsh treatment, isolation, ignorance, poverty, and other factors, both internal and external. Christians must address with compassion the social causes of spiritual ills without losing sight of the need for a new birth, a new heart, and the forgiveness offered in Christ. We cannot chalk up problems to *only* social forces (the default of liberal politics) or *only* personal irresponsibility (the default of conservative politics).

Reflection: What social ills may have injured those around you, including your spouse? As you hold out Christ to them as the lover of their souls, what are you *also* doing to alleviate the social conditions that make everything worse?

Thought for prayer: Ask God for wisdom and help in treating both your own flaws and sins and those of others with the balance that comes from knowing we both sin and are sinned against.

Both people crippled by inferiority complexes *and* those who are arrogant and have superiority complexes are centered on themselves, obsessed with how . . . they are being perceived and treated. It would be easy to help someone out of an inferiority complex into a superiority complex and have them no better furnished to live life well. . . . [A]ll people must be challenged to see that their self-centeredness hasn't been caused by the people who hurt them; it's only been aggravated. . . . And they must do something about it, or they're going to be miserable forever. (Hardcover, p. 63; paperback, pp. 62–63)

CHERISHED SIN. C. S. Lewis's novel *The Great Divorce* imagines a bus tour to heaven for people living in hell. They can stay if they repent, but all except one decides to return—most are too far gone in their self-centeredness to want anything to do with heaven. In one memorable scene, a woman "who began with a grumbling mood" has parlayed that into a life of grievance that has reduced her "to nothing but a grumble." If life goes on eternally (and it does), then a cherished sin or a posture of "your life to serve me" will indeed make you miserable forever. Acts of self-absorption—such as turning inward to nourish resentments, never forgiving others or letting go of grudges, and treating all relationships as transactional—consume the soul. What may have begun small, over the length of eternity, grows into a monstrosity.

Reflection: How do you challenge your own self-centeredness? Are you prepared to turn away from whatever idol you worship in order to give yourself wholly to God, and to his people?

Thought for prayer: Meditate on Psalm 73:16–17 and ask God to save you from the blurred vision, distorted thinking, and denial that increases our natural self-centeredness and tendency to self-justification. Ask him to help you see things clearly.

[T]hree things usually happen. First, you begin to find out how selfish this wonderful person is. Second, you discover that the wonderful person has been going through a similar experience and he or she begins to tell you how selfish *you* are. And third, though you acknowledge it in part, you conclude that your spouse's selfishness is more problematic than your own. This is especially true if you feel that you've had a hard life and have experienced a lot of hurt. (Hardcover, p. 64; paperback, p. 63)

FLAWED YET LOVED. This is the experience commonly referred to sardonically as "the honeymoon is over"—when the scales of ecstatic love fall from your eyes and you both notice that the person you married is a sinner. And as Jesus pointed out, the speck in that person's eye always appears greater to you than the beam in your own eye (Matthew 7:3–5). Surely if we have found our soul mate, if we have chosen our partner wisely, then this wouldn't be happening! Well, it always does, but we are more ill-prepared for it than past generations. There are two solutions. First, look at yourself and remember your spouse will find *you* hard to live with, and second, look at the Lord who loved you forever despite your flaws and sins.

Reflection: What "specks" do you focus on trying to make your spouse change? List the "beams" in your own life that need to be changed.

Thought for prayer: Ask God for the two things you will need in order to be able to regularly forgive and love your spouse despite their sins and failures: a view of your own sin, and a view of his infinite love for you.

[Y]ou could decide that your woundedness is more fundamental than your self-centeredness, and determine that unless your spouse sees the problems you have and takes care of you, it's not going to work out. Of course, your spouse will probably not do this—especially if he or she is thinking almost the exact same thing about you! And so what follows is the development of emotional distance. . . . No one changes for the other; there is only tit-for-tat bargaining. (Hardcover, p. 64; paperback, p. 64)

WHO HURTS MOST? When Tim and I were first married, one of us might say or do something intemperate. When the other spouse pointed it out, the response would be, "I've had a hard day." Rather than accepting this excuse the other would retort, "I've had a harder one." We eventually called this the "I'm more messed up than you" game. The "winner" wanted to be able to sulk, ignore responsibilities and relational necessities, while the "loser" had to put his or her own needs on hold to care for the other. We wasted a lot of time until we were able to name it as indeed a bitter "game" or contest. That helped us catch ourselves doing it in the early stages, mock ourselves, and move on. Usually.

Reflection: Are you familiar with "the game"? What if you both decided to be caregivers, in spite of your own pressing needs? Do you see any other such "games" in your relationship?

Thought for prayer: Ask God for the discernment and self-knowledge to identify "games" of self-justification in your marital relationship. Ask him also to help you to rest in your justification-in-Christ so that you can stop playing these games.

The alternative to this truce-marriage is to . . . treat [your selfishness] more seriously than you do your spouse's. Why? Only you have complete access to your own selfishness and . . . complete responsibility for it. So each spouse should . . . stop making excuses for selfishness, . . . to root it out as it's revealed to you, and to do so regardless of what your spouse is doing. If two spouses *each* say, "I'm going to treat my self-centeredness as the main problem in the marriage," you have the prospect of a truly great marriage. (Hardcover, pp. 64–65; paperback, p. 64)

THE ONLY PERSON. The truism "the only person you can change is yourself" is a hopeful thought for any married person, but particularly for those in difficult marriages. No amount of finger pointing, yelling, shaming, or arguing will change another person. But if *you*, with God's help, begin to change, at the very least life will become bearable; and at best your spouse may choose to begin making changes as well. Some people may need to change in the direction of speaking the truth in love; for others, it may mean giving your mouth a rest and loving with your actions.

Reflection: Do you tend to talk and nag people as a strategy for change? What would be a better place to start?

Thought for prayer: Meditate on Ecclesiastes 3:7 about "a time to tear and a time to mend; a time to be silent and a time to speak." Then ask God to help you know the difference, when it is time to do what.

April 29

It may be that [only] one of you decides to [work on your self-centeredness]. . . . Usually there is not much immediate response from the other side. But often, over time, your attitude and behavior will begin to soften your partner. . . . [I]t will be easier for your spouse to admit his or her faults because you are no longer always talking about them yourself. (Hardcover, p. 65; paperback, p. 65)

CHANGES. If you do decide to make sacrifices in your own habits and practices, try not to make an announcement with great fanfare. Just change! You aren't making changes for the applause of an audience (your spouse), but to please your savior, Jesus, who sees and knows and will help you to change.

Reflection: Without argument or debate, ask your spouse to help you make a list of things he or she would like to see you change.

Thought for prayer: Meditate on Galatians 1:10 and Romans 2:29. Ask God to help you want his approval and his applause so that you do not need it from human beings.

God asks that you deny yourself to find yourself, to lose yourself to find yourself. If you try to do this without the work of the Spirit, and without belief in all Christ has done for you, then simply giving up your rights and desires will be galling and hardening. But in Christ and with the Spirit, it will be liberating. (Hardcover, pp. 65–66; paperback, p. 65)

THE JESUS MOTIVATION. Unless Jesus is your motivation and your motive power, desire to change will soon give way to resentment—whether of your spouse not noticing (it takes a while to prove that you have really changed for good) or of he or she seeming not to care. Yet, ultimately, it is the love of Christ that compels you to respond in love to him. Your growth in Christ is assured if you belong to him. Otherwise, marriages fizzle out, worn out by too many fights and too little hope for any change. Instead, remember his promise that "he who began a good work in you will carry it on to completion until the day of Christ Jesus" (Philippians 1:6).

Reflection: Is your motive for change in order to please your savior? Or is it a way of seizing the moral high ground in your marriage in order to manipulate your spouse?

Thought for prayer: Meditate on Philippians 1:6 until you get a joyful hope for your future and the future of your marriage. Then thank him for it.

> That is why a man leaves his father and mother and is united to his wife, and they become one flesh. . . . Lamech married two women, one named Adah and the other Zillah. (Genesis 2:24, 4:19)

WHERE DID MARRIAGE COME FROM? Earlier in this book we explored the purposes of marriage. They include deep, joyful companionship, unity across difference, procreation, all through an exclusive covenant serving as a sign of Christ's salvation through sacrifice. Only against this backdrop can the Bible's various prohibitions—against polygamy and adultery, unwarranted divorce, homosexuality, or any sex outside of marriage—make sense. Many reading the Old Testament think it supports polygamy. But Genesis begins history with God giving Adam and Eve to each other alone. The two become one; there is no room for another. And the first person in the Bible to take two wives, Lamech, is a violent man (Genesis 4:23). Every place in Genesis we see polygamy, it results in misery. And Jesus himself says in Matthew 19:4–8 that God's intention in the beginning was for "two to become one flesh" (verses 5 and 6). The Bible's message is clear. Monogamy is not a Western idea—it is a biblical one.

Reflection: Consider the stories of Abraham and Jacob in Genesis, and of Hannah in 1 Samuel 1. How does polygamy violate the biblical purposes of marriage?

Prayer: Lord, keep me from giving my heart to other things in such a way that it could detract from my intimacy, friendship, and trust with my spouse. Amen.

You cover the LORD's altar with tears, with weeping and groaning because he no longer regards the offering or accepts it with favor from your hand. But you say, "Why does he not?" Because the LORD was witness between you and the wife of your youth, to whom you have been faithless, though she is your companion and your wife by covenant. (Malachi 2:13–14)[53]

THE LORD AS WITNESS. One way God's purposes for marriage can be thwarted is through unnecessary divorce. In the surrounding nations, marriage was a legal contract between the two partners witnessed by officials.[54] But the Israelites understood it to be a covenant with *the Lord as the witness.* Each partner first swore loyalty to the covenant God, and this "vertical" commitment made the horizontal commitment to each other all the more binding. This created a marital relationship unique in ancient times. "The word *companion . . .* used in the masculine of a close friend . . . is used only here of a wife."[55] The covenant with God made the marital bond more intimate, and the breaking of it more grievous.

Reflection: Why would more intimate friendship be enabled by deeper commitment and trust?

Prayer: Lord, as our friend you lay down your life for us (John 15:13). So help me to gladly surrender my selfish interests, comforts, and many of my goals as I seek to love my spouse as you loved me. Amen.

Has not the one God made you? You belong to him in body and spirit. And what does the one God seek? Godly offspring. So be on your guard, and do not be unfaithful to the wife of your youth. "The man who hates and divorces his wife," says the LORD, the God of Israel, "does violence to the one he should protect," says the LORD Almighty. (Malachi 2:15–16)

INJUSTICE. The first reason that divorce is so grievous is that it breaks a covenant with God. Here are two more reasons. One of the purposes of marriage is "godly offspring"—children who grow up to know, serve, and enjoy the Lord. Children of divorce have two to three times more negative psychological and socio-logical outcomes, in itself a reason to avoid divorce.[56] The third reason is that divorce commits injustice against your partner. The text literally says that divorce "covers your clothes with blood." Breaking a marriage promise is an act of violence against your spouse. Despite the exceptions (see the following days), marriage was meant to be for life.[57] We are to stay married for God's sake, the children's sake, and your spouse's sake.

Reflection: This seems to support "staying together for the children's sake." What kind of "staying together" would be good and what kind would be bad?

Prayer: Lord, I want to thank you for being patient with me and faithful to me, though I have been constantly a very imperfect spiritual spouse to you. Amen.

"Haven't you read," [Jesus] replied ... "'For this reason a man will leave his father and mother and be united to his wife, and the two will become one flesh'? So they are no longer two, but one flesh. Therefore what God has joined together, let no one separate." "Why then," they asked, "did Moses command that a man give his wife a certificate of divorce and send her away?" Jesus replied, "Moses permitted you to divorce your wives because your hearts were hard. But it was not this way from the beginning. I tell you that anyone who divorces his wife, except for sexual immorality, and marries another woman commits adultery." (Matthew 19:3–9)

THE FIRST GROUND FOR DIVORCE. The Bible allows grounds for divorce. Jesus says marriage was instituted by God as permanent, yet he recognized Moses' divorce laws because "the hardness of your hearts" brought about conditions in which it was warranted. The first condition is adultery. God designed sex as a covenantal act—as a way to signify and strengthen the giving of one's whole life to someone. So to have sex with someone else is to become "one flesh" with them (cf. 1 Corinthians 6:16). That breaks the "one-flesh" union with your spouse, freeing the party who has been wronged to divorce and marry again.[58] Such a solemn view of adultery seems quaint today, but divorce was even easier in Jesus's day, and so the teaching was as radical then as it is now.

Reflection: How would you respond to a married friend who said he had had a brief affair, "but it was just a lark—it meant nothing"?

Prayer: Lord, please help me guard my eyes and thoughts by remembering the solemn nature of sex and adultery. Amen.

May 5

If any brother has a wife who is not a believer and she is willing to live with him, he must not divorce her. And if a woman has a husband who is not a believer and he is willing to live with her, she must not divorce him. . . . But if the unbeliever leaves, let it be so. The brother or the sister is not bound in such circumstances; God has called us to live in peace. (1 Corinthians 7:12–15)

THE SECOND GROUND FOR DIVORCE. This is the second of the two grounds for divorce that the Bible permits. Paul says that if a Christian finds him- or herself married to a non-Christian, they should not divorce (verse 12–13). But he then asks: what if a spouse insists on leaving the marriage? Can the one who has been left divorce and remarry? The answer is yes; they are free and "not bound." Historically, "willful desertion" has been seen as a second ground for divorce.[59] Many have concluded that a spouse who engages in physical abuse can also be seen to be initiating a separation and so constitute grounds for divorce.[60] Anyone contemplating divorce should never do this in a vacuum, but should get good counsel from thoughtful believers for confirmation.

Reflection: This ground for divorce is not as easy to define as adultery. Think of the gray areas—behaviors that might or might not be considered "leaving" or "desertion." Do you see why it is important not to make this determination by yourself?

Prayer: Lord, divorce can never be considered or entered into without great wisdom and discernment. Make our churches places where the people considering or going through divorce get wisdom, love, and help—not indifference or rejection. Amen.

During the reign of King Josiah, the Lord said to me, "Have you seen what faithless Israel has done? She has gone up on every high hill and under every spreading tree and has committed adultery there. . . . I gave faithless Israel her certificate of divorce and sent her away because of all her adulteries." (Jeremiah 3:6, 8)

DIVORCE AND REDEMPTION. Marriage is meant to be permanent and so divorce is a very solemn decision. This might lead divorced people to feel they have been permanently disgraced. But in this text God has the audacity to call himself a divorced person. The self-righteous who want nothing to do with divorced persons will have to avoid God! But, you might ask, what if I was the one at fault in my divorce? Nothing in the Bible calls divorce the unforgivable sin. And never underestimate the redemptive power of God to work in an evil situation. Through David and Bathsheba's child, Solomon, God brings Jesus Christ into the world—out of a relationship that began as an illicit affair and led to murder. It's as if God is saying, "I love bringing good out of the hardest cases."

Reflection: Consider how different the Bible's attitude is toward divorce from Western cultures (where divorce is taken lightly) and traditional cultures (where it is a permanent disgrace). Why would the Bible be so balanced and different?

Prayer: Lord, I praise you that you are both holy and merciful, and therefore you both warn us strongly against divorce yet are gentle with those who have experienced it. Amen.

The Lord said to me, "Go, show your love to your wife again, though she is loved by another man and is an adulteress. Love her as the Lord loves the Israelites, though they turn to other gods and love the sacred raisin cakes." So I bought her for fifteen shekels of silver and about a homer and a lethek of barley. Then I told her, "You are to live with me many days; you must not be a prostitute or be intimate with any man, and I will behave the same way toward you." (Hosea 3:1–3)

A LAST RESORT. God calls the prophet Hosea to marry Gomer, a woman who is unfaithful to him (Hosea 1:2). Eventually she becomes a sexual slave of another man, but God directs Hosea not to give up on her and so he purchases her back from the man who owns her, and takes her home, seeking to restore the marriage. What does this show us? Even in the case of adultery God does not *command* divorce. It means that even a marriage seemingly broken beyond repair can sometimes be restored. Putting yesterday and today's devotionals together, the Bible could not be more nuanced. Seek with all your might to save your marriage, but if it cannot be saved, don't think of your life as permanently derailed.

Reflection: Work to save the situation with all your might but be at peace if you can't. What other areas of life can you apply this principle to?

Prayer: Lord, thank you that you love me continually, even though I constantly set my heart on other things and love them more than you. Help me to see this for what it is—spiritual adultery—and thank you for loving me despite it. Amen.

Spirit-generated selflessness . . . [is] taking your mind off yourself and realizing that in Christ your needs are going to be met . . . that you don't look at your spouse as your savior . . . [and] when [you] do that, [you] will discover sometimes an immediate sense of liberation, of waking up from a troubling dream. [You] see how small-minded [you] were being, how small the issue is in light of the grand scheme of things. Those who stop concentrating on how unhappy they are find that their happiness is growing. (Hardcover, pp. 66–67; paperback, pp. 66–67)

TWO CONCEPTS OF HAPPINESS. The Greek word *eudaimonia* (literally "good spirit") is usually translated as "happiness." But scholars tell us it would be better to translate it as "flourishing" because the ancients conceived of happiness in a different way than we do. Happiness was not seen as doing anything you wanted, but as conforming your life to the nature of reality, just as a trout is only "happy" when it is in water rather than in the air, or a robin is only "happy" when it is in the air and not underwater. The "happiness" of marriage only comes to us as we serve. In a review of the final Marvel movie, *Avengers: Endgame,* one of the screenwriters said that the ability to sacrifice for duty is the real heroism, not the superpowers.[61]

Reflection: What superpower would you most like to have? What sacrifices do you most need to make to be a hero in your marriage?

Thought for Prayer: Think of the ways that difficulties in your marriage have led to greater happiness. Then thank God for them.

What is it that most motivates and moves you? Is it the desire for success? The pursuit of some achievement? The need to prove yourself to your parents? The need for respect from your peers? Are you largely driven by anger against someone or some people who have wronged you? Paul says that if any of these things are greater controlling influences on you than the reality of God's love for you, you will not be in a position to serve others unselfishly. (Hardcover, p. 68; paperback, p. 68)

A NEW START. An adopted child leaves behind old ways of thinking and behavior to become a member of a new family. Having been adopted into God's family, we must leave our old baggage at the door of our new home in Christ. Our older preferences, hopes, dreams, fears, and hates must be left behind. We should walk in empty-handed, trusting that what God has for us is better than anything we had abandoned. C. S. Lewis famously said that we are like children playing in our familiar mud puddles when a holiday at the shore has been offered to us. We like what we know, and don't trust what we have never seen, but only God can offer us eternal, solid joy.

Reflection: What baggage have you dragged into your marriage that you thought would make you happy, but which is actually a source of unhappiness? Both of you think of an answer, and then discuss.

Thought for prayer: Meditate on 2 Corinthians 5:17—that in Christ we are a new creation, the old having passed away. Ask God to show you what older patterns of thinking, feeling, and behavior you may be clinging to, and the harm they may be doing to your marriage.

[I]t was wrong of her to seek to self-worth through male affection. . . . But now she was being asked to look to her career and personal independence as a way to feel good about herself. . . . And so she said, . . . "Would I not be as devastated then by career setbacks as I have been by romantic ones? No. I will rest in the righteousness of Christ. . . . Then I can look at males *or* career and say, 'What makes me beautiful to God is Jesus, not these things.'" (Hardover, pp. 69–70; paperback, p. 70)

SELF-TALK. One of the secrets of self-control is to realize that your emotions are not so much responses to events as they are created by what you *tell yourself* about the event. If someone you are dating drops you and you say to yourself, "I must be undesirable," your emotion is sadness; but if your self-talk is "They have no right to do that!" the same incident will produce anger instead. Teach yourself godly self-talk. The psalmist speaks to his own heart again and again: "Praise the Lord, my soul, and forget not his benefits" (Psalm 103:2).[62] If we don't talk to our hearts, telling them God's truth, our hearts will surely keep calling us like robo-scammers, telling us there's no hope. Learn to value what God values by learning to understand his Word and by deep communion with him in prayer.

Reflection: Do you pray together? Share insights with one another from your Bible study? Why or why not?

Thought for prayer: Meditate on Mark 1:35 and its context, in which Jesus, at the height of his ministry and intense demands on his time, rises early to spend time in prayer. Consider how the Son of God did not think he could get through a day without prayer. Now pray to God about your prayer life, whatever its condition.

But each of us comes to marriage with a disordered inner being. Many of us have sought to overcome self-doubts by giving ourselves to our careers. That will mean we will choose our work over our spouse and family to the detriment of our marriage. Others of us hope that unending affection and affirmation from a beautiful, brilliant romantic partner will finally make us feel good about ourselves. That turns the relationship into a form of salvation and no relationship can live up to that. (Hardcover, p. 72; paperback, p. 73)

EVERYONE WORSHIPS. Alexander Schmemann wrote that even the most atheistic people are nonetheless *homo adorans*—worshipping beings.[63] We must adore, center our lives, and base our meaning and worth on something. In David Foster Wallace's famous address, he makes the same point, saying "if you worship money and things . . . if they are where you tap real meaning in life, then you will never have enough." He includes sexual beauty, power, and artistic and intellectual achievement as other inadequate objectives of worship. Our culture says "live your own truth," but these replacement gods "will eat you alive." He ends: "The really important kind of freedom involves . . . being able truly to care about other people and to sacrifice for them over and over in myriad petty, unsexy ways every day. That is real freedom."[64] Right. Only worshipping the real God can give you that.

Reflection: We have been saying that we can't look to our marriage to give us what only God can give. But we won't have a good marriage if either spouse is looking to any other god-substitute either. Talk with each other about what things in this world can become god-substitutes for you.

Thought for prayer: Meditate on 1 John 5:21 and ask God to keep your heart from resting in idols.

> Only God can fill a God-sized hole. Until God has the proper place in my life, I will always be complaining that my spouse is not loving me well enough, not respecting me enough, not supporting me enough. (Hardcover, pp. 72–73; paperback, p. 73)

REORDERED LOVES. St. Augustine defined sin as "disordered love." The sin of cowardice is loving your own safety more than the good of someone else. Lying is loving your reputation or advantage over the good and right of others to the truth. If I love my career more than my family I will hurt or even lose my family. But the ultimate problem is that we love *anything* more than God. If I love my spouse more than God, then I look to him or her to provide the kind of steady, perfect, unconditional love only God can give. If I don't love God more than her, I don't love her for her sake. I'm using her to meet my needs and so it is mainly for my sake. There is only one solution. Do everything you can to provide "access to your hearts for the love of Him who is greater than the world."[65]

Reflection: Do some self-examination. Are any of your loves "out of order"? Think of the saying "The good is the enemy of the best." Are there any good things that you love too much in comparison to other things?

Thought for prayer: Consider the ways that the Lord is "greater than the world" and then ask him to convince your heart, not just your head, that this is so.

What . . . would the effect be if we were to go so deeply into Jesus's . . . promises and summonses, his counsels and encouragements, over time, that they just dominated our inner life, capturing our imagination? . . . When you received criticism, you would never be crushed, because Jesus's love and acceptance of you is so deeply "in there." When you give criticism, you are gentle and patient, because your whole inner world is saturated by a sense of Jesus's loving patience and gentleness with you. (Hardcover, p. 74; paperback, p. 75)

A KEY TO CHANGE. Christians are told if they knew God's grace and love sufficiently they would be liberated to forgive, love, change, and grow. But how do you do that? The answer is that Jesus must "capture our imaginations." Think of how that happens with a book, or music, or a movie that captivates us. We go back to it again and again to savor it. We think about it, or hum it, or relive it as we are walking about. We also get others in on it. To watch a beloved movie with someone who has never seen it is to discover it again. Now take the Gospels about Jesus and fall in love with him. The tools are private and corporate prayer, Bible reading, and praise.

Reflection: Get specific. How can Jesus capture your imagination so his love saturates your interior world? What can you do practically in the areas of prayer and reading that will help?

Thought for prayer: Ask: "Lord Jesus, make thyself to me a living bright reality."[66]

May 14

It is possible to feel you are "madly in love" with someone, when it is really just an attraction to someone who can meet your needs and address the insecurities and doubts you have about yourself. In that kind of relationship you will demand and control rather than serve and give. The only way to avoid constantly sacrificing your partner's joy and freedom on the altar of your need is to turn to the ultimate Lover of your soul . . . [who] voluntarily sacrificed himself on the cross. (Hardcover, pp. 75–76; paperback, p. 77)

DISORDERED LOVES. Of course both spouses are to meet one another's needs. But what are the signs that you are mainly using a person to affirm you and overcome your doubts about yourself rather than loving and serving the person's good? One bad sign is that you will not allow the person to have bad days or get down or discouraged. You need the person to be fine and pulled together so he or she can be attentive to you and not require too much unrequited affection from you. Another sign is that you either get too devastated by your spouse's criticism or else respond with such hostility that he or she takes it all back. Why? Because you need your spouse's constant praise and affirmation so much you can't bear their critique.

Reflection: Do you see these signs in your relationship to your spouse? If they are there, how strong are they?

Thought for prayer: Ask Christ to capture your imagination and heart (see yesterday's devotional) with his sacrificial love for you.

[When she said,] "Why do we need a piece of paper in order to love one another? I don't need a piece of paper to love you! It only complicates things." . . . She was assuming that love is, in its essence, a particular kind of feeling. She was saying, "I feel romantic passion for you, and the piece of paper doesn't enhance that at all, and it may hurt it." (Hardcover, p. 77; paperback, pp. 79–80)

FEELING AND ACTION. It is simplistic to say that love is an action and not a feeling at all. We shouldn't set those two things against each other. There must be deep affection and attraction in a marriage if it is to succeed. Nevertheless, parents know that love means meeting their children's needs even when they don't feel much affection at all for (what seem to be) the ungrateful little villains. So the essence or foundation of love is committed service to the good of someone, whether you feel like it or not. Arguably, it is a greater act of love to do things for someone when you *don't* particularly like them. And that is why the marriage vow is not to *feel* loving but to *be* loving, no matter what.

Reflection: Why have some said that the marriage license might hurt love rather than enhance it? What understanding of love does that reveal?

Thought for prayer: Thank the Lord that—when he was on the Cross and he saw us denying, betraying, mocking, and abandoning him—he stayed. Thank him for that kind of love.

May 16

[W]hen the Bible speaks of love, it primarily measures it not by how much you want to receive, but by how much you are willing to give of yourself to someone. How much are you willing to lose for the sake of this person? How much of your freedom are you willing to forsake? How much of your precious time, emotion, and resources are you willing to invest in this person? And for that, the marriage vow is not just helpful but it is even a test. (Hardcover, p. 78; paperback, p. 80)

TWO KINDS OF FREEDOM. The modern understanding of freedom goes something like this. "I should be free to live as I choose as long as I don't harm or restrict anyone else's freedom." In other words, the fewer restrictions on our independence, the freer we are. Let's call this "negative" freedom—freedom *from*. But that definition of freedom has a head-on collision with the requirements of any love relationship. The closer the relationship, the more you must make decisions and do things together, not independently. Yet the more you give up your negative freedom the more you can experience a positive freedom, an inner fullness of love and satisfaction that liberates you from fears, self-doubts, and sadness. You give up a lower freedom to gain a higher one.

Reflection: Do an inventory of yourself and your marriage by answering the three questions in the quote above.

Thought for prayer: Meditate on how much Christ was willing to lose in order to gain a relationship with us. Then ask for help in returning that kind of love to your spouse.

In so many cases, when one person says to another, "I love you, but let's not ruin it by getting married" that person really means, "I don't love you *enough* to close off all my options." . . . To say, "I don't need a piece of paper to love you" is basically to say, "My love for you has not reached the marriage level." (Hardcover, p. 78; paperback, p. 80)

JUST A PIECE OF PAPER? On a podcast a woman who had read *The Meaning of Marriage* argued that the last line in the quote above was unfair. She and her boyfriend were living together, had no intention of getting married, and wanted their love to be wholly voluntary, not forced by a piece of legal paper. Here again we see that modern people think of love in almost wholly subjective, emotional terms. I only am loving you if I am wanting you and feeling love for you at the present moment. But taking the vows is actually a way to say, "I love you enough to bind myself to you through the ups and downs of feelings and circumstances." To hear someone make such a promise is to feel grounded and secure in your spouse's love, and safe from the whims of changing feelings.

Reflection: Do you think the last line in the quote above is unfair? Why or why not?

Thought for prayer: Think of how Jesus "closed off his options" in order to save and love us (Philippians 2:4ff.). Thank him for it.

The biblical understanding of love does not preclude deep emotion. In fact, any marriage devoid of passion and emotional desire for one another isn't fulfilling the biblical vision. But neither does the Bible pit romantic love against the essence of love, which is sacrificial commitment to the good of the other. (Hardcover, p. 78; paperback, p. 81)

PLEASURE AND SERVICE. The ancients spoke of two kinds of love. There was the love of benevolence, which was a commitment to actively serve the good of someone regardless of how you felt about them at the moment. Then there was the love of "complacency," which was to take great joy and pleasure in someone. When we marry it is our pleasure-love that leads us to make a solemn promise of service-love.[67] But because our feelings wax and wane, it is our service-love that keeps us close and continually renews our pleasure-love. Since Jesus commands us to love our neighbor (and he can't mean we must always like our neighbor), the love of benevolence is perhaps more central to the biblical idea of love. But in marriage actions and feelings are mutually interdependent.

Reflection: Have you seen this dynamic between the two aspects of love play out in your own marriage?

Thought for prayer: Thank God that, in Christ, he not only loves us and gives us what we need, but he delights in us (Psalm 149:4). Let that sink in.

Modern people think of love in such subjective terms, that if there is *any* duty involved it is considered unhealthy. . . . If you won't make love unless you are in a romantic mood at the very same time as your spouse, then sex will not happen that often. This can dampen and quench your partner's interest in sex, which means there will be even fewer opportunities. If you never have sex unless there is great mutual passion, there will be fewer and fewer times *of* mutual passion. (Hardcover, p. 79; paperback, p. 81)

SEX AS A GIFT. Yesterday we spoke of two aspects of love—service-love and pleasure-love. In both parenting and in marriage it is impossible to sustain a long-term, healthy, loving relationship without both. They are mutually dependent. It is hard for younger adults to see that these two aspects of love are necessary for a long-term sexual relationship as well. It is thought to be almost hypocritical to be sexually intimate if you are not filled with desire, but why? Why can't you give yourself willingly to your spouse as a genuine gift even when, for myriad possible reasons, you are not emotionally or physically hungry for sex? Sometimes sex can be more of one aspect or the other, but they are both genuine acts of love.

Reflection: If your spouse said, "I don't particularly feel like sex, but I want to love *you*—so let's go to bed," would you be offended?

Thought for prayer: Ask God to give you a servant-heart in every aspect of your marriage.

Outside of marriage, sex is accompanied by a desire to impress or entice someone. It is something like the thrill of the hunt. When you are seeking to draw in someone you don't know, it injects risk, uncertainty, and pressure to the lovemaking that quickens the heartbeat and stirs the emotions. If "great sex" is defined in this way, then marriage . . . will indeed stifle that particular kind of thrill. But this defines sexual sizzle in terms that would be impossible to maintain in any case. (Hardcover, p. 79; paperback, p. 82)

MOTIVES FOR SEX. Sexual activity can often be a mask for other things, such as more fundamental idols. Some people make an idol out of human approval—they feel "if others like me, then I know I'm a worthwhile person." Being able to draw someone into a sexual liaison convinces such a person that they are approved. Others make an idol out of power—they feel "if I can get control over others then I know I'm a worthwhile person." For that person, being able to draw someone into sex gives a sense of conquest, of power. But notice how these are both ways of using the sex partner for your own emotional benefit. Here sex is about taking rather than giving.

Reflection: Using a sex partner for this outside of marriage is quite normal, perhaps even inevitable. But can this happen inside marriage?

Thought for prayer: Ask God to help you reflect his own self-giving love in your intimate sex life with your spouse.

[In sex the goals are] to be vulnerable to each other, to give each other the gift of barefaced rejoicing in one another, and to know the pleasure of giving one another pleasure. . . . Yes, it means often making love when sometimes . . . you are not "in the mood." But sex in a marriage, done to give joy rather than to impress, can change your mood on the spot. The best sex makes you want to weep tears of joy, not bask in the glow of a good performance. (Hardcover, p. 80; paperback, p. 83)

SEX AND PERFORMANCE. To convey love in any way takes skill. We have all tried to express our love in words and felt that we've come up short. Sexual love is no different. In sex we want to give the other person pleasure and that requires a knowledge of both their particular temperament and body. But in our culture sex has moved from being an intimate skill to a performance. Partners don't expect to start off being rather klutzy, laughing at themselves, but then to grow and learn together. Instead they want to know if they immediately have "sexual chemistry." Sex has to be great instantly, and that is enormous pressure. Outside of a marriage covenant, sex becomes an anxious encounter rather than a cradle of security in our moment of greatest vulnerability.

Reflection: How does the experience of sex before marriage teach habits that don't prepare you for the experience within the covenant of marriage?

Thought for prayer: Ask God to protect you from the culture's emphasis on sex as performance and to be instead grounded in the Bible's vision of sex as self-giving.

It is possible to see marriage as merely a social transaction, a way of doing your duty to family, tribe, and society. Traditional societies make the family the ultimate value in life, and so marriage becomes a transaction that helps your family's interests. . . . Contemporary Western societies make the individual's happiness the ultimate value, and so marriage becomes an experience of romantic fulfillment. (Hardcover, pp. 80–81; paperback, p. 83)

LEFT OR RIGHT? Liberals see your money as belonging largely to the state and poverty as due strictly to social structures. Conservatives see your money as belonging wholly to you, and if you are poor it's your fault and no one else's problem. The Bible says, instead, that all your money comes from God and belongs to him. This is not some halfway point between the world's options of left and right. Proverbs tells us that poverty can be caused both by injustice and oppression (13:23) as well as by laziness and irresponsibility (24:33–34). In the same way, traditional societies make an absolute of the family's interests over individual needs, and modern societies make individual choice the highest value. Both the needs of the family as well as those of the individual are considered significant by the Bible, but neither is ultimate.

Reflection: In what way does the biblical account address the concerns of both cultures, yet critique each culture as fundamentally wrong in its view of marriage?

Thought for prayer: Pray that Christians in your country would be more influenced by the Bible than by secular political options.

But the Bible sees *God* as the supreme good—not the individual or the family—and that gives us a view of marriage that intimately unites feeling *and* duty, passion *and* promise. That is because at the heart of the Biblical idea of marriage is the covenant. (Hardcover, p. 81; paperback, pp. 83–84)

WHO ARE YOU? Traditional societies see marriage as the fulfillment of a *duty* that you perform for your tribe and family. Romantic love is secondary and optional. Contemporary society sees marriage instead as a *choice* you make only if (and as long as) it is fulfilling to you as an individual. The idea of duty is negotiable, while romantic love is primary. Each approach is driven by the conviction that one's identity and worth is rooted in a particular thing. The traditional view is that you are who your community says you are, while modernity says you are who *you* say you are. But Christianity says that you are who God says you are, and your self-regard must be rooted in his love.

Reflection: How does the biblical view unite duty and desire?

Thought for prayer: Think of how in Jesus both duty and desire come together. He promises to save us out of love, and never flags in his duty. Ask him to unite those things in your own heart as you love those around you.

[T]here have always been consumer relationships. Such a relationship lasts only as long as the vendor meets your needs at a cost acceptable to you . . . [because your] individual needs are more important than the relationship. . . . There have also always been covenantal relationships . . . [in which] the good of the relationship takes precedence over the immediate needs of the individual. . . . Society still considers the parent-child relationship to be a covenantal one, not a [transactional] consumer relationship. (Hardcover, p. 81; paperback, p. 84)

PARENTING AS A MODEL. Because you sometimes can look at your child and find your heart bursting with love, you are able to give of yourself to him or her during the far more frequent times in which parenting is a drudge or a bore. For the present, at least, our culture still demands that we love our children like this even as it has redefined marriage to be conditional, to last only as long as it is personally fulfilling. Yet in our still-covenantal parenting we are given an inside look at how that kind of love works. When we "tie ourselves to the mast" (see February 13) to serve the needs of our children, it leads to deeper affection and love. Why can't we learn to give covenantal love to our spouses as well?

Reflection: Can you think of any other kind of relationship besides parenting that our culture has not turned into a transactional one?

Thought for prayer: Thank God for being a covenant God, who loved us faithfully even when we were not faithful to him.

[Today] the consumer model increasingly characterizes most relationships that historically were considered covenantal, including marriage. [W]e stay connected to people only as long as they meet particular needs at an acceptable cost to us. . . . [W]hen the relationship appears to require more love and affirmation from us than we are getting back—then we "cut our losses" and drop the relationship. . . . [In] "commodification" . . . social relationships are reduced to economic exchange relationships, and so the very idea of "covenant" is disappearing in our culture. (Hardcover, pp. 81–82; paperback, pp. 84–85)

COSTS AND BENEFITS. The heart of a transactional, consumer relationship is the calculus of cost and benefit. The relationship is completely disposable because it is based solely on profit. It is maintained only so long as the benefits outweigh the costs for each party. The Bible, however, presents marriage as a relationship like our relationship with God (Ephesians 5:22ff.) If God maintained his relationships on a cost-benefit basis, we'd all be lost. If you conduct marriage on a cost-benefit basis you will never succeed. And yet I would argue that taken over a lifetime the benefits of marriage outweigh the costs. Even a difficult marriage may drive you into God's arms, develop character, and impart other priceless spiritual goods to you.

Reflection: Make a list of the "priceless" goods that your marriage has led you to or has given you.

Thought for prayer: Thank God for the list above that you have made.

[The] marriage [covenant] has both strong horizontal *and* vertical aspects to it. In Malachi 2:14, a man is told that his spouse "is your partner, the wife of your marriage covenant" (cf. Ezekiel 16:8). Proverbs 2:17 describes a wayward wife who has "left the partner of her youth, and ignored the covenant she made before God." The covenant made between a husband and a wife is done "before God" and therefore . . . [t]o break faith with your spouse is to break faith with God at the same time. (Hardcover, p. 83; paperback, p. 86)

PRIMARY WITNESS. In traditional marriage the parents of the spouses, representing the society, are the primary witnesses. The bride is "given away" to the groom by her father. Modern marriage resists such symbolism and sees the two parties giving themselves to each other. But as we have seen (see May 2), it is the Lord who is both the primary witness (Malachi 2:14) as well as the one who gives the spouses to each other (Genesis 2:22). Christian marriage is therefore a deeper and more binding bond that does not let either your society or your spouse have the final word on how you are doing as a husband or a wife. You are accountable to God, and he is far more merciful than society or you yourself.

Reflection: How does it change things for you practically to think of God as the ultimate judge of your marriage?

Thought for prayer: Remember that, while God can see all your sins and flaws, he also loves you perfectly because you are "in Christ" (2 Corinthians 5:21). Thank him for those two truths.

Imagine a house with an A-frame structure. The two sides of the home meet at the top and hold one another up. But underneath, the foundation holds up both of the sides. So the covenant with and before God strengthens the partners to make a covenant with each other. Marriage is therefore the deepest of human covenants. (Hardcover, p. 84; paperback, p. 87)

TWO-WAY COVENANT. The physics of the A-frame structure serve as an instructional metaphor. No matter how sturdy and strong one side of the house may be, it cannot itself bear any weight if the concrete foundation slab under it does not bear *its* weight. If it is sinking into the ground, it cannot hold up the other side of the house at all. So in a Christian marriage the parties first make a covenant with God in the "I do" questions. That is the foundation. Then, having just heard the other person solemnly swear to God, each person is strengthened in their trust of the other. They can now turn to each other and literally put themselves in each other's arms. These two aspects of the covenant powerfully infuse and reinforce the marriage relationship.

Reflection: Do you think most people understand that the Christian marriage service has two covenants within it? How conscious are you of the twofold aspect of your marriage covenant?

Thought for prayer: Meditate on God as your "rock" and foundation (Psalm 18:2; Matthew 7:24). Thank God for being there to always support and strengthen you.

> What, then, is a covenant? It creates a particular kind of bond that is disappearing in our society. It is a relationship far more intimate and personal than a merely legal, business relationship. Yet at the same time it is far more durable, binding, and unconditional than one based on mere feeling and affection. A covenant relationship is a stunning blend of law and love. (Hardcover, p. 84; paperback, p. 88)

BLENDING LAW AND LOVE. We have been exploring various ways in which the Christian marriage covenant differs both from a traditional legal contract and from a modern transactional relationship. Here is another. Legal contracts require behavior but they can't create love. Cohabiting couples try to maintain loving feelings without any binding promises. But just as the original covenant between God and Israel both demanded behavior and offered intimate relationship ("You will be my people, and I will be your God," Exodus 6:7), so the Christian marriage covenant brings about a wonderful blend of love leading to vow, and then the commitment leading to greater love. Why can it do that? Because it is grounded not primarily in social approval or romantic love but in God's gracious, perfect love for you.

Reflection: Is your primary inspiration and motivation for fulfilling your marital vows: (a) the approval of your family and society, (b) your desire for your spouse's love and affirmation, or (c) responding to God's love for you? All these motives are good—but how can you increase the last one?

Thought for prayer: Meditate on the remarkable intimacy of God's offer that, in Christ, he can be not just God, but *"your* God."

[It is now seen as] common sense—namely, that love must be the response to spontaneous desire, never a response to a legal oath or promise. But the Biblical perspective is radically different. Love needs a framework of binding obligation to make it fully what it should be. A covenant relationship is not just intimate despite being legal. It is a relationship that is *more* intimate *because* it is legal. (Hardcover, pp. 84–85; paperback, p. 88)

LENGTHENING LOVE. In the Bible, covenants are literally everywhere. It is assumed that all love relationships need covenantal strengthening. Why? Covenants intensify both the length and the depth of love. Think about how covenants extend the length of love relationships. Our feelings will wax and wane for all sorts of physical and emotional reasons even if the loved one behaves perfectly. But of course they never do. Anyone we love is a sinner whose heart is prone to self-centeredness. Without the promises we would give up on the relationship. We would not get through the inevitable rough patches and conflicts. Without covenants our lives would be filled with broken relationships.

Reflection: Think of some times in which your marriage vow strengthened your resolve to work through problems you were having.

Thought for prayer: Meditate on Hebrews 13:5–6, on the infinite length of God's love for you in Christ. Then thank him for it.

Someone who says, "I love you, but we don't need to be married" may be saying, "I don't love you enough to curtail my freedom for you." The willingness to enter a binding covenant, far from stifling love, is a way of enhancing, even supercharging it. A wedding promise is proof that your love is actually at marriage level as well as a radical act of self-giving all by itself. (Hardcover, p. 85; paperback, p. 89)

DEEPENING LOVE. Covenants also intensify love by deepening it. They keep us in the marriage so we can make progress against several of the things that "clog" our ability to love each other well in this world.[68] The first is our inability to express our love properly. On the one hand, we often fail to give our spouse love in the form he or she most needs it. When our partner is upset, we may step in with a plan and a solution, making the mistake of "answering a feeling with a fact." On the other hand, we fail to express our love in ways that truly convey its magnitude. In heaven this problem will end and is part of the unimaginable joy of that place. Yet over the years we can grow in this ability in our marriages, if we stay together.

Reflection: Think of two or three times that this particular "clog" in your ability to love asserted itself in your relationship. How can you improve?

Thought for prayer: Thank God that he always loves us in exactly the way we need at the moment.

When dating or living together, you have to prove your value daily by impressing and enticing. . . . We are still basically in a consumer relationship and that means promotion and marketing. The legal bond of marriage, however, creates a space of security where we can open up and reveal our true selves. We can be vulnerable, no longer having to keep up facades. . . . We can lay the last layer of our defenses down and be completely naked, both physically and in every other way. (Hardcover, p. 85; paperback, p. 89)

MELTING AWAY FACADES. A second thing that "clogs" our love is that we tend to hide behind facades in order to guarantee that we will be loved. We fear we would not be loved if the truth were to be revealed. The close quarters of marriage show us our flaws as nothing else can. At the same time the security of the marriage vows enables us to be open about our true selves without the same fear of rejection we would have in other situations. If your spouse responds with love, it can be as healing an experience as is possible between two human beings. This dishonesty about ourselves is another way that the marriage covenant can help us deepen love.

Reflection: Think of two or three times that this particular "clog" in your ability to love asserted itself in your relationship. How can you improve?

Thought for prayer: Thank God for seeing us to the bottom, with all our sins, but loving us anyway.

Wisdom will save you from the adulterous woman . . . who has left the partner of her youth and ignored the covenant she made before God. (Proverbs 2:16–17)[69]

FRIENDSHIP ELEMENTS. The word for "partner" used in this verse means the closest of friends (cf. Proverbs 16:28). We speak often in this volume about the importance of friendship in a marriage. The book of Proverbs, however, details the elements that create a friendship. First, there is intentionality: we must "stick close" and deliberately spend face-to-face time together (Proverbs 18:24). Second, there is constancy: friends are there for you when the chips are down (Proverbs 17:17). Third, transparency: a willingness to be vulnerable and open to one another (Proverbs 27:5–6). Finally, there is sensitivity. A friend does not "sing songs to a heavy heart" (Proverbs 25:20). There is more to be said about how friendships develop, but these are the fundamentals.

Reflection: Look up the references in Proverbs to further understand each of the four elements. Which of these elements do you most need to work on in your marriage? In your other friendships?

Prayer: Lord, you called us friends (John 15:13–15) because you opened your heart and life to us and for us. Now help me to be a friend—to my spouse and to others—as you have been to me. Amen.

June 2

My son, keep your father's command and do not forsake your mother's teaching. (Proverbs 6:20)

LIFELONG LEARNERS. Old Testament scholar Bruce Waltke points out that in ancient times most women were not typically educated. Yet here we have a wife *teaching* her children, and in the book of Proverbs this would mean instruction in wisdom. Those trained in wisdom memorized a large number of sayings and poems. In other words, the wife was a colleague with her husband in intellectual pursuits. This biblical idea was revolutionary in its time. Today, however, even though men and women have equal access to education, that often doesn't carry over to spouses reading and learning together, sharpening each other's thinking on a variety of topics. In particular this is a call for spouses to study the ultimate source of wisdom together—the Bible itself.

Reflection: Do you have a systematic way to read the Bible together? Try this—read the same chapter of the Bible every day and note one thing that helped or impressed you most. That evening share it at bedtime and pray together.

Prayer: Lord, I pray that you would make us, as a married couple, interdependent students of your Word. Lord "teach us your way, that we may walk in your truth," and so "unite our hearts to fear your name" (Psalm 86:11).[70] Amen.

A loving doe, a graceful deer—may her breasts satisfy you always, may you ever be intoxicated with her love. . . . Charm is deceptive, and beauty is fleeting; but a woman who fears the Lord is to be praised. (Proverbs 5:19, 31:30)

TRUE LOVELINESS. A spouse is to not merely be a friend but also a lover and romantic partner. On the one hand you should be *intoxicated* and sexually attracted by features of your partner's body such as *her breasts*. But Proverbs 31:30 reminds us that physical beauty is *fleeting* and inexorably passes away with wear and tear and age. There is a deeper attraction, however, that comes from perceiving the beauty of character and also from years of sacrificing for each other and walking together through life's varied circumstances. The more we fix our gaze on the loveliness of our spouse's spirit, the more our physical attraction will grow, even as our physical attractiveness diminishes over the years.

Reflection: Have you embraced this understanding of "comprehensive attraction" or are you exclusively fixated on your partner's figure, weight, and physique for judging his or her desirability?

Prayer: Lord, help us both, not only in looking at the other but at ourselves, not to fix on outward beauty but on "the inner disposition of the heart," which is an "unfading beauty" (1 Peter 3:3–4). Amen.

June 4

She opens her arms to the poor and extends her hands to the needy. . . .
She speaks with wisdom, and faithful instruction is on her tongue.
(Proverbs 31:20, 26)

CHURCH IN MINIATURE. Husband and wife are to be ministry partners. The first verse implies that the family has a ministry to the poor. *Extending her hands* implies not just a general social concern but an invitation to the poor into one's home or delivering of concrete help. The second verse uses a Hebrew verb for "speaks" that means to speak publicly and expound on a subject at length.[71] The depiction is striking. Both husband and wife have turned their home into a ministry center, a church in miniature, where people are instructed in God's Word and wisdom, and where neighbors receive practical help for their needs, especially if they are poor or powerless.

Reflection: Are you and your spouse not only friends, lovers, and colleagues (see the rest of this week), but ministry partners?

Prayer: Lord, enable us to turn our home into a little church, where people find you, are built up in you, and get help for their needs. Give us a vision for this and the wisdom to know how to carry it out. Amen.

Her husband has full confidence in her and lacks nothing of value. (Proverbs 31:11)

CONFIDANTS. The Bible constantly condemns putting one's trust in anyone or anything other than the Lord (Psalm 118:8–9), so this verse is remarkable. Nowhere else do we see the Bible speak of, literally, entrusting one's heart to anyone beside God.[72] But in marriage spouses are to be confidants, to be intimate and vulnerable to one another, and to enjoy the highest level of spiritual trust. Such a relationship is hard won. No two flawed, sinful people can be married without letting each other down, so mistrust can easily grow. Only by keeping intimacy fresh through genuine mutual repentance and forgiveness can even the failures lead to deeper trust in one another. Only as we give our spouses the same grace that Jesus gave us will we be able to trust each other (Ephesians 4:32).

Reflection: Recall a time in which each of you let the other down. Did you use grace to repair and deepen trust?

Prayer: Lord, help us to forgive those times in which we have disappointed each other so that we don't lose confidence in one another. Give us grace so we can show one another grace, and let our trust in each other grow and grow. Amen.

She selects wool and flax and works with eager hands. She is like the merchant ships, bringing her food from afar. . . . She considers a field and buys it; out of her earnings she plants a vineyard. (Proverbs 31: 13–14, 16)

CO-EXECUTIVES. Again we notice how the Bible's assessment of a woman's calling contrasted remarkably with those of surrounding societies, most of which saw wives as mere possessions of their husband. The Bible calls the husband to be head of the home (Ephesians 5:22–26). Yet headship cannot mean that husbands are to make all management decisions, nor can it be defined as dictating that only the husband must have an income. Here wives are seen as breadwinners, and also as managing assets in the economy of the family. What each partner contributes to the economic prosperity of the household will depend on their gifts and skill sets, respectively. So spouses are friends, colleagues, lovers, ministry partners, confidants, and economic partners.

Reflection: Look at the list in the last sentence above. Which of these roles needs to be strengthened in your marriage?

Prayer: Father, you, the Son, and the Spirit have from all eternity been glorifying and lifting up one another, yet inhabiting different roles. Make us one in our marriage even as you are one (John 17:22–23). Amen.

If a man has recently married, he must not be sent to war or have any other duty laid on him. For one year he is to be free to stay at home and bring happiness to the wife he has married. (Deuteronomy 24:5)

DELIGHT. We are looking this week at all those things that spouses are to be to one another according to the Bible. This text made it law in Israel that when a man married he was exempt from military service or from any other kind of public service for one year. The most practical reason for this, of course, was that the man would not die before having a chance to have children and ensure the continuity of the family line.[73] But something much more is in view, because the last line says that he is to stay home for a year in order to "be a joy" to his wife. Are you, in the end, a source of joy to your spouse, or a drain on it? Do you bring each other joy?

Reflection: Among all the duties of spouses to each other, do you delight in each other?

Prayer: Lord, as you do not merely take care of us in general but actually take "great delight" in us and "rejoice over us with singing" (Zephaniah 3:17), so stir us up to do the same with each other.

Vows . . . give love a chance and create stability so the feelings of love, always very fitful and fragile in the early months and years, can grow strong and deep over time. They enable your passion to grow in breadth and depth, because they give us the security necessary to open our hearts and speak vulnerably and truthfully without being afraid that our partner will simply walk away. (Hardcover, p. 89; paperback, p. 94)

LOVE REFINEMENT. Another thing that impedes our love is how much we love others not for the sake of their happiness, but for our own. Jonathan Edwards says, "Most of the love which there is in this world . . . proceeds . . . from selfish motives." We love people because we think they can meet our needs, and if they do not we turn on them in anger. But marriage forces us to see how self-involved we are, and with God's help we can slowly learn to put our happiness *into* theirs—so that their joy becomes ours rather than the other way around. Then "the greater the [happiness] of the beloved is, the more the lover is pleased and delighted."[74] In heaven this kind of love is perfectly realized, but even tasted partially here on earth it is glorious.

Reflection: Think of two or three times that this particular "clog" in your ability to love asserted itself in your relationship. How can you improve?

Thought for prayer: Thank God for loving us selflessly in Jesus Christ, who gave up his glory for our joy and was satisfied to do so (Isaiah 53:11).

June 9

This blending of law and love fits our deepest instincts. . . . Lovers find themselves almost driven to make vow-like claims. "I will *always* love you," we say and we know that the other person, if he or she is in love with us, wants to hear those words. Real love, the Bible says, instinctively desires permanence. . . . So the "law" of vows and promises fits our deepest passions at the present. But it is also something the love of our heart needs. (Hardcover, pp. 85–86; paperback, pp. 89–90)

DESIRE FOR PERMANENCE. Look at the language of love songs. "I will always be with you; makes no difference where your road takes you to." "I'll be loving you eternally." "Longer than there've been stars up in the heaven, I've been in love with you." "I'll love you from now, till the end of time."[75] These lyrics are sentimental, but they exist because this is how romantic and sexual love makes you feel. Real love does not want independence, it wants permanence, and so, paradoxically, making vows "till death do us part" actually expresses our deepest passion and at the same time gives us the support we need to follow through on love's desire. And only in the Christian hope of eternity are the deepest desires of ordinary love fulfilled.

Reflection: How do these love songs make an argument for why the Bible's prohibition of sex outside of marriage is right?

Thought for prayer: Thank God that, in Christ, his love for you and yours for him will literally last forever.

Wedding vows are not [primarily] a declaration of present love but a mutually binding promise of future love. A wedding should not be primarily a celebration of how loving you feel now—that can safely be assumed. Rather, in a wedding you stand up before God, your family, and all the main institutions of society, and you promise to *be* loving, faithful, and true to the other person in the future, regardless of undulating internal feelings or external circumstances. (Hardcover, p. 87; paperback, p. 91)

KEEPING LOVE KINDLED: 1. When we promise future love at our wedding, what does that mean? Of course it means behavior. We are to be sexually faithful, we are to serve and protect, and we are to be kind, gracious, and patient while we are doing so. But is the promise to love confined to actions? How can we promise feelings? Of course we cannot promise to always have particular levels of joy and attraction to another person. Emotions, in some sense, are not ours to command. But there are four things that we can promise to do that are directly tied to our feelings for our spouse. The first one is this. We can promise to engage sexually (1 Corinthians 7:2–5). Sex can be done as a kind of "covenant renewal ceremony" in which both spouses remember the other person's strengths and give themselves to one another afresh. This can continually rekindle romantic love.

Reflection: Reflect on how thoughtfully you engage sexually in your marriage in this way.

Thought for prayer: Ask God to help you, when you have sex, to fill your mind and heart with all your spouse has done for you and means to you as you give yourself to him or her anew.

[T]wo-thirds of unhappy marriages will become happy within five years if people stay married and do not get divorced. . . . What can keep marriages together during the rough patches? The vows. . . . [That] keeps you in the relationship when your feelings flag, and flag they will. By contrast, consumer relationships cannot possibly endure these inevitable tests of life. (Hardcover, p. 87; paperback, pp. 91–92)

KEEPING LOVE KINDLED: 2. There are three other things that you can promise to do that lead directly to the maintenance and growth of loving feelings in marriage. First, we can promise forgiveness, which is granted before it is felt. Without continual forgiveness resentment grows, and it is one of the main things that eats away at affection. Second, we can also promise to promptly and ungrudgingly admit when we do wrong. Without constant humble repentance a kind of self-pity and superiority grows that eats away at affection. Finally, we can promise to take time to praise one another. Christians in general are told to praise the accomplishments of one another and to affirm gifts and abilities (Romans 12:3–6, 10). How much more should spouses do this regularly! As you will discover, what you praise more, you enjoy more.

Reflection: Reflect on how well you practice these three behaviors that lead to sustained affection and feelings of love.

Thought for prayer: Ask God to especially help you to admit to your spouse when you've done wrong "promptly and ungrudgingly." Ask the Lord to help you avoid defensiveness and blame shifting, and repent without excuses.

[In Matthew 19] Jesus denies that you can divorce for any reason. . . . [H]e confirms that marriage is a covenant . . . [that] creates a strong new unity that must only be broken under very serious conditions. But he goes on to say that these serious conditions do exist, because of "the hardness of your hearts." That means that sometimes human hearts become so hard because of sin that it leads . . . to a severe violation of the covenant, without prospects of repentance and healing, and in such cases divorce is permitted. (Hardcover, p. 88; paperback, p. 93)

DIVORCE: THE REALISM. 1 John 5:3 says that God's commandments are "not burdensome." Knowing we are sinners saved by sheer grace changes our motivation toward obedience from the merely dutiful "I have to" to the grateful joy of "I want to." Further, God knows we will sometimes break our covenant with him and with each other, and he provides means for reconciliation that may or may not be successful (see Matthew 5: 23–24; 18:15–17). In the same way, God knows that some will break their marriage covenants with one another and in his wisdom and mercy he provided for divorce. A marriage can be so violated that even when forgiveness is given, the trust basis of the covenant is damaged beyond repair in this world. How realistic and understanding is this holy God.

Reflection: Think of other ways in which God's commands—though no one can keep them perfectly—are not burdensome.

Thought for prayer: Ask God to help you know your own heart and to deal with problems and conflicts rather than letting them fester, so that you can avoid the pain of divorce.

The only such violation that Jesus names in [Matthew 19] is adultery. In 1 Corinthians 7, Paul adds another ground [for divorce]—namely, willful desertion. These actions essentially break the covenant vow so thoroughly, that, as Paul says in 1 Corinthians 7:15, the wronged spouse "is not bound." . . . Divorce should not be easy; it should not be our first, second, third, or fourth resort. (Hardcover, p. 89; paperback, p. 93)

DIVORCE: THE BALANCE. Our God is both perfectly holy and yet infinitely merciful. This must be borne in mind when we approach the subject of divorce. If we forget God's awesome holiness we will remember how solemn it is to take a marriage vow before him as primary witness. God says that he hates divorce (Malachi 2:16) and we should as well. It must never be entered into lightly and it must be a very last resort. But if we forget God's infinite mercy, and Jesus's direct teaching that he provided for divorce because human sinfulness would sometimes warrant it, then we also fail to do justice to God's character and the biblical teaching on marriage.

Reflection: Do you personally have an equally good grasp on these two aspects of God's character? Or do you have more of a grasp on one rather than the other?

Thought for prayer: Ask the Lord to help you avoid the legalism of a "God is mainly holy" mindset or the relativism of a "God is only love" mindset, and to avoid the particular sins to which each habit of mind can lead.

Jesus knows the depths of human sin and holds out hope for those who find themselves married to someone with an intractably hard heart who has broken his or her vow in these ways. Divorce is terribly difficult, and it should be, but the wronged party should not live in shame. Surprisingly, even God claims to have gone through a divorce (Jeremiah 3:8). He knows what it is like. (Hardcover, p. 89; paperback, p. 93)

SUPPORT FOR THE DIVORCED. In a culture that has lost its grip on the holiness of God (such as ours), divorce is too common and no big deal, despite the awful statistics about its effects. But in churches that have lost their grip on the mercy of God, divorced persons often must live with stigma and shame. No one enters the world as a divorced person with ease. They need comprehensive support, and many churches fail in this. It is remarkable that God is willing to call himself a divorced person (Jeremiah 3:8), having lost his relationship with his people Israel. If you have been divorced, you can go in prayer to a God who has been through it himself. There's no other religion that offers that.

Reflection: Think of the churches that you have been part of—how do they handle the subject of divorce? How do they treat divorced people?

Thought for prayer: Thank him for being a God we can turn to in our troubles, a God who knows what it is like to be rejected, even to the death on a cross.

June 15

W. H. Auden . . . wrote: "Like everything which is not the involuntary result of fleeting emotion but the creation of time and will, any marriage, happy or unhappy, is infinitely more interesting than any romance, however passionate." (Hardcover, pp. 89–90; paperback, p. 94)

MORE INTERESTING. The quote above, from the prominent twentieth-century poet and author W. H. Auden, is meant to be startling. But we believe that the statement holds up to scrutiny. Some argue that living together as long as there is sexual attraction is a more voluntary kind of love than legal marriage. But Auden depicts romantic relationships outside of marriage as *less* voluntary. They almost "happen to us" as we sense the sexual chemistry and are drawn in. They are also, therefore, not lasting. Marriage, however, is an act of the will—a vow and commitment— that is sustained over time. They involve every part of your life— not just the weekends or getaways. They are then infinitely more "interesting" because marriage will tell you far more about yourself, human nature, and life itself.

Reflection: Do you agree with the statement? Think of other ways that marriages, even difficult ones, are "infinitely more interesting."

Thought for prayer: Meditate on Jesus's endurance to the end in order to love and save us (Hebrews 12:1–3). Ask God for spiritual endurance over the long run, not just to be faithful to your spouse but faithful to him as well.

[I]t is our promises that give us a stable identity, and without a stable identity, it is impossible to have stable relationships. Hannah Arendt wrote: "Without being bound to the fulfillment of our promises, we would never be able to keep our identities; we would be condemned to wander helplessly and without direction in the darkness of each person's lonely heart, caught in its contradictions and equivocalities." (Hardcover, p. 91; paperback, p. 96)

IDENTITIES ARE FORGED. The word "identity" literally means "sameness." If there is nothing about you that is the same—if you are completely different in every situation and relationship—you have no identity. An identity is a core *you* that is continuously there. Our culture tells us to look into our heart and discover who we are, but every person's heart is filled with contradictory desires and impulses. How can I know who the real *me* is? Identity is not discovered, it is forged, and it is forged through discovering truth outside of ourselves and bringing ourselves into alignment with it. That is, through faith and promise. Marriage is one key way to do this. To make a promise is to say, "In spite of changing feelings and circumstances, this is who I am, this is what I will always do and be."

Reflection: Think of some examples besides the marriage vow where promises help to forge identity.

Thought for prayer: Meditate on John 1:12–13. Then ask God to show you the truth, to help you be true to the truth, and thereby become his child, the one identity that is safe and forever true.

[Lewis Smedes wrote:] "My wife has lived with at least five different men since we were wed—and each of the five has been me. The connecting link with my old self has always been the memory of the name I took on back there: 'I am he who will be there with you.' When we slough off *that* name, lose *that* identity, we can hardly find ourselves again." (Hardcover, p. 92; paperback, p. 97)

IDENTITIES IN FLUX. This quote by Lewis Smedes observes that identities are inevitably in flux over time. An older man who cannot admit his age, who wants to appear and be treated as much younger, is refusing to accept this process. When you change careers, or you move to a different country, or retire, or have grandchildren, you become a slightly different person than you were. When you suffer—if you go through the death of loved ones, or a debilitating illness—that makes you a different person, too. But the change must not be total. There needs to be a core identity that doesn't change and that stabilizes and anchors you through life changes. The wedding vow is one of them. It becomes the thread keeping your different "selves" united in love to one another.

Reflection: If you have been married for a number of years, what personal changes in you has your marriage had to weather? If you are newly married, think of the changes that are coming.

Thought for prayer: Meditate on Psalm 116:17–18. Ask God to help you fulfill the vows made at your baptism and at your wedding. Ask him to make you the same kind of promise-keeper that he is.

[Many argue] that striving for permanence through traditional marriage stifles freedom. . . . But Smedes argues eloquently that promising is the *means* to freedom. In promising, you limit options now, in order to . . . be free to be there in the future for people who trust you. When you make a promise to someone, both of you know that you are going to be there with and for them. "You have created a small sanctuary of trust within the jungle of unpredictability." (Hardcover, p. 93; paperback, p. 98)

MONOTONY. We want the freedom we feel when we are in a great love relationship. But learning to give love in the particular ways that your spouse wants and needs, to give love that grows rather than diminishes through conflict, is learned through the discipline of sticking with each other at times when the marriage is, frankly, somewhat monotonous. A famous trumpet instructor said: "There are no shortcuts to learning how to play the trumpet. It takes practice and patience. I know that it is monotonous. But finally comes a time when you [are free to] express your emotions through music. And this brings such a pleasure that all the dull hours are forgotten. All you have to do is practice scales . . . scales . . . and more scales."[76] A good marriage grows in the same way.

Reflection: To extend the metaphor—what are the somewhat boring "scales" to be practiced in marriage that can lead to a relationship of the greatest delight?

Thought for prayer: Meditate on Romans 15:5. Then ask God to give you his endurance and encouragement so you can patiently but gladly love your spouse and others even when there is little reward for doing it.

[Smedes writes:] "When I make a promise, I bear witness that my future with you is not locked into . . . the hand I was dealt out of my . . . genetic deck . . . [or] the psychic conditioning visited on me by my . . . parents. . . . No home computer ever promised to be a loyal help. . . . Only a person can make a promise. And when he does, he is most free. (Hardcover, p. 94; paperback, pp. 98–99)

THE FREEDOM OF PROMISING. Lewis Smedes's point is that computers are incapable of rising above their "programming." They cannot change beliefs or make choices that go against their programming. Even if Artificial Intelligence computers become capable of developing consciousness, they will not get a "heart"—a set of deep, chosen commitments and beliefs about reality that animate feelings and behavior. When I promise something like a wedding vow, I am not really giving away my freedom. I'm proving I actually have it. If I can't make promises, I'm a bit more like nonhuman things.

Reflection: Think of other promises that you can make that move you from being creatures of instinct and impulse or make you pawns of your own past.

Thought for prayer: Meditate on Psalm 119:45, on how the more you obey God's commands the more free you are. Now ask God to help you know the kind of freedom that comes from keeping vows and obeying the Lord.

When you first fall in love, you think you love the person but you don't really. You can't know who the person is right away. That takes years. You actually love your idea of the person—and that is always one-dimensional and somewhat mistaken. . . . [R]omantic flings are so intoxicating largely because the person is actually in love with a fantasy rather than a real human being. (Hardcover, pp. 94–95; paperback, pp. 99–100)

THE HIDDEN SPOUSE. Every person is created in the image of God, "made a little lower than the angels" and "crowned with glory and honor" (Psalm 8:5). Yet Jesus can say casually, "you are evil . . ." (Luke 11:13). He is addressing his apostles! Jesus is saying that every human being is evil and capable of terrible things. In short, human beings are infinitely complex, contradictory beings. The more sinful aspects are usually not the first things we see in a person. So when you begin your marriage you have only a superficial grasp on both how good and how flawed your partner is. No wonder we need a marriage vow to help us learn to love the real person we married.

Reflection: Set aside some time to be alone and to talk to each other, in great charity and grace, about the strengths and weaknesses you have discovered in each other.

Thought for prayer: Ask the Lord that your knowledge of your own evil heart and of your spouse's would increase at the same pace, so that together you can offer each other accountability yet humble grace.

[N]ot only do you not know the other person, but the other person does not really know you. You have put on your best face (often quite literally). There are things about yourself that you are ashamed of or afraid of, but you don't let the other person see your flaws. And, of course, you cannot show your partner those parts of your character that you cannot see yourself and which will only be revealed to you in the course of the marriage. (Hardcover, p. 95; paperback, p. 100)

THE HIDDEN SELF. We looked yesterday at how infinitely complex and contradictory human nature is, so it takes years to come to know the person we marry. But while you know yourself far better than your spouse, you are largely blind to who you are as well. The mark of a fool is that he looks wiser to himself than he really is (Proverbs 12:15) and all of us are born sinful and therefore foolish (Proverbs 22:15). In every marital conflict, then, the great temptation will be to be blind to our own flaws and our contribution to the problem. No wonder we need a marriage vow, not only to help us learn to love the real person we married, but also to help our spouse love us.

Reflection: Again, set aside some time to be alone and to talk to each other, in great charity and grace, about the strengths and weaknesses you have discovered in each other.

Thought for prayer: "Search me, God, and know my heart; test me and know my anxious thoughts. See if there is any offensive way in me, and lead me in the way everlasting" (Psalm 139: 23–24).

There is an emotional "high" that comes to us when someone thinks we are so wonderful and beautiful, and that is part of what fuels the early passion and electricity of falling in love. But the problem is . . . the person doesn't really know you and therefore doesn't really love you [nor you him or her], not yet at least. [The "high" is] in large part a gust of ego gratification, but it's nothing like the profound satisfaction of being known *and* loved. (Hardcover, p. 95; paperback, p. 100)

NOT FULLY KNOWN. In the Garden of Eden, Adam and Eve were originally "naked and unashamed." They were *naked*, meaning they could see each other wholly, all the way to the core. Also, they were *unashamed*, meaning that they were not rejected but completely loved and accepted. So the Bible depicts the situation we were designed for—to be fully known *and* fully loved. There are two situations that fall short of this. The first is to be loved but not known for who you are. That is fleetingly pleasant, but it creates anxiety and leads to hiding and shame as well. If we are sure we would be rejected if we are known, we won't be able to enjoy and rest in the love we are getting at the present.

Reflection: What are the disadvantages of being loved but not to have your sins and flaws fully known by the lover?

Thought for prayer: Meditate on 1 John 3:19–20, that when our hearts condemn us, God is greater than our hearts; he knows everything, but accepts us. Ask him to give you that assurance, so you can have the courage to be honest with your spouse.

June 23

To be loved but not known is comforting but superficial. To be known and not loved is our greatest fear. But to be fully known and truly loved is, well, a lot like being loved by God. It is what we need more than anything. It liberates us from pretense, humbles us out of our self-righteousness, and fortifies us for any difficulty life can throw at us. (Hardcover, p. 95; paperback, p. 101)

NOT FULLY LOVED. We saw yesterday that we want to be fully known and fully loved at the same time. One way to fall short of that in marriage is "love without truth"—loving someone but not knowing about their flaws. The second way is when a person who loves us makes a deeper discovery of our selfishness, foolishness, and flaws—and responds with disillusionment, anger, and recriminations. This is "truth without love," and unfortunately it is a natural response. Only the gospel can make each spouse capable of seeing each other to the bottom and still forgiving and loving. It starts with remembering that Jesus saw *us* wholly and yet loved us fully, forgiving us eternally.

Reflection: How, specifically, can you use the knowledge of Jesus's saving love for you to help you love a flawed spouse?

Thought for prayer: Meditate on Hebrews 4:13, which says nothing is hidden from God, but also John 17:23, which says the Father loves you *even as* he loves Jesus. Thank God for knowing you fully and yet loving you completely.

June 24

The kind of love-life I am talking about is not devoid of passion, but it's not the same kind of passion. . . . When Kathy first held my hand, it was an almost electrical thrill . . . [b]ut as I look back on that initial sensation, I realize that it came not so much from the magnitude of my love for her, but rather from the flattery of her choice of me. . . . There is no comparison with what it means to hold my wife's hand now, after all we've been through. (Hardcover, pp. 95–96; paperback, p. 101)

THE PROCESS—RECONCILIATION. Over the years in a healthy marriage there will be a process of discovering more and more sin in one another and doing mutual repentance and forgiveness. The repentance offered humbles you away from the superiority and self-pity that makes forgiveness hard. But forgiveness offered builds you up so you can more readily admit your flaws. After every cycle of mutual repentance and forgiveness, you are slightly better known and slightly better loved. As time goes on, this leads to a deep love and passion for each other, but it may feel different from the "sexual chemistry" that occurs between two people who mainly love each other's admiration.

Reflection: Think of ways that the two kinds of love and passion—that of new lovers and that of spouses in healthy marriages after decades—would differ.

Thought for prayer: Think of the line of the hymn: "'Twas grace that brought us safe thus far; And grace shall lead us home." Simply thank God for this fact and promise.

[After thirty-five years] we know each other thoroughly now, we have shared innumerable burdens, we have repented, forgiven, and been reconciled to each other over and over. There is certainly passion. But the passion we share now differs from the thrill we had then like a noisy but shallow brook differs from a quieter but much deeper river. Passion may lead you to make a wedding promise, but then that promise over the years makes that passion richer and deeper. (Hardcover, p. 96; paperback, p. 101)

THE PROCESS—TRIALS AND TRIBULATIONS. Another way that love deepens over time is through suffering. Suffering is inevitable. No amount of success or planning can make you impervious to troubles like the loss of a loved one, debilitating illness, relational betrayal, financial and career reversals. When these things happen, your spouse needs to be the most primary of your comforts. Your marriage should be a shock absorber. Usually it takes time and many painful conversations to discover how to best support your spouse in such times. But if you push on together through these times, you will be amazed at how they weld you together at a level impossible to reach any other way.

Reflection: Think of ways that trials and troubles have brought you together with your spouse.

Thought for prayer: Meditate on Hebrews 12:11, on how suffering is like sowing seeds—at first it is laborious and you see nothing good, but later it yields fruit. Ask God to help you take that perspective on the difficulties you are experiencing now.

Isn't romantic love something that must be completely free and unco-erced? And isn't it inevitable that intense desire for someone else sim-ply can't be sustained and, therefore, it is inevitable that we must be free to seek another person who can reawaken the joy of love in us? Therefore, isn't it true that fully monogamous, lifelong marriage is the enemy of romantic affection? (Hardcover, p. 96; paperback, p. 102)

THE PROCESS—LIFELONG. To answer those questions above, let's summarize what we have been learning. The roman-tic love we know in the beginning of our relationship is based on the initial pleasure of ego affirmation, and on an image of the other person that is in part illusion. A deeper, less self-involved, and more sustained passion comes from repeated cycles of repentance and forgiveness and of bearing each other's burdens in times of trial, until you slowly experience what it means to be both known and loved at the same time. That known-and-yet-loved experience, the greatest of all, is not possible without all of this. Lifelong monogamy, therefore, is not the enemy of romance, it is one of its conditions.

Reflection: Answer the questions (in the quote above) in your own words, drawing on your own experience.

Thought for prayer: Meditate on Malachi 1:2 and 3:6, which say that because God's love is absolutely unchangeable, we are not destroyed. Ask God to give you both something of his unchangeable love for one another.

June 27

> [Kierkegaard describes "the aesthete" who] claims to be a free indi-
> vidual. Life should be thrilling, full of "beauty and sparkle," he says. . . .
> But Kierkegaard says . . . [he] is not master of himself at all . . . If [your]
> wife loses her beautiful skin and countenance or [your] husband puts
> on the pounds, the aesthete begins to look around for someone more
> beautiful. If [your] spouse develops a debilitating illness, the aesthete
> begins to feel that life is pointless. But, says Kierkegaard, such a person
> is being completely controlled by external circumstances. (Hardcover,
> p. 97; paperback, pp. 102–3)

BLOWN ABOUT. Here we have Kierkegaard using his own
terms and images to argue for the Christian understanding of
romance and marriage. He uses the term "aesthete" to describe a
man or woman whose attraction to a spouse is highly superficial. The moment the spouse begins to lose his or her looks or
become high maintenance, the aesthete finds "the love going out
of the marriage." The glow and electricity of the romance for the
aesthete comes from the thought that *this* beautiful, cool, sophisticated, pulled-together person loves *me*. But when the person
starts to look less beautiful, the aesthete's ability to affirm diminishes. Kierkegaard adds that the aesthete is like a weather vane
totally blown about by the winds of life. The love that comes
from vows is different.

Reflection: "The aesthete" is a negative image but it is somewhat
true of most of us. To what extent have the attitudes Kierkegaard
mentions been true of you?

Thought for prayer: Meditate on Romans 5:8, how Christ
loved us and gave himself for us "while we were yet sinners." Ask
for help to love your spouse and others in the same, sustained,
unconditional way.

Only if you commit yourself to loving in action, day in and day out, even when feelings and circumstances are in flux, can you truly be a free individual and not a pawn of outside forces. Also, only if you maintain your love for someone when it is not thrilling can you be said to be actually loving a *person* . . . [and not merely] the feelings, thrills, ego rush, and experiences that the other person brings. (Hardcover, p. 97; paperback, p. 103)

LOVE THEM FOR THEIR SAKE. When we begin with the Lord, we are concerned more about what God can give us than with God himself. We come seeking meaning, or forgiveness, or strength, or happiness, or direction, or hope. These are all things we can't live without, and it is right to seek them in God. Yet if we grow in our relationship with the Lord, we will come to see we at first were loving the things we got from God, rather than God himself. We did not get our highest delight in delighting him—which is the essence of real, self-giving love. Well, that's how we start in marriage, and that's the goal of marriage—to love your spouse for who they are, not what they bring you.

Reflection: If you are meant to grow toward loving God and loving your spouse for themselves alone, how are you doing in both relationships?

Thought for prayer: Meditate on Psalms 62:1–2 and 27:4. Then admit to God you are helpless to love him for himself alone unless he intervenes and shows you more of his beauty and excellence.

[I]t is the covenantal commitment that enables married people to *become* people who love each other. Only with time do we really learn who the other person is and come to love the person for him- or herself, and not just for the feelings and experiences they give us. . . . Eventually all this leads to wells of memory and depths of feeling and enjoyment of the other person that frames and enhances the still crucial episodes of romantic, sexual passion in your married life. (Hardcover, p. 98; paperback, p. 104)

THE ATTRACTION OF HISTORY. Most young couples fear the loss of sexual energy as the years go by and their bodies age and become less attractive. However, the visual stimulation of a beautiful physique is not the only factor in attraction. Others are character and history. The more you have seen a person act admirably and courageously, act lovingly and graciously, act selflessly and sacrificially, the more your attraction grows even as the body ages. We have said that sex is a "covenant renewal ceremony," a time in which your life together can flash before your eyes and you remember all you've been through and all you mean to each other. That creates passion and intimacy as well. Physical beauty becomes more like icing on the cake.

Reflection: Do you have sex the first and early way, or have you begun to transition to the long-term way?

Thought for prayer: Make a simple list of a half dozen things about your spouse that you have witnessed over the years for which you are thankful. Then, in the presence of one another, thank God for them.

Our emotions are not under our control, but our actions are. Most of our likes and dislikes are neither sins nor virtues—no more than our tastes in food or music. What matters is what we do with them. If, as our culture encourages us, we go so far as to define love *as* "liking"—if we only feel that actions of love are "authentic" if there are strong feelings of love present—we will inevitably be bad friends and even more terrible . . . spouses. (Hardcover, p. 99; paperback, p. 105)

SELF-COMMUNION. It helps to think of yourself as the Scripture does—having more than one self—an old self still operating on the principles of fear and pride and a new self grounding itself in God. Dr. D. M. Lloyd-Jones sees Psalm 42 as an example, and asks: "Take those thoughts that come to you the moment you wake up in the morning . . . they bring back the problem of yesterday, etc. . . . Who is talking to you? Your self is talking to you." Instead the psalmist says: "'Why art thou cast down, O my soul?' . . . His soul had been repressing him, crushing him. So he stands up and says: 'Self, listen for a moment, I will speak to you.'"[77] Don't identify the fearful, angry self as your truest self. "Put off the old self . . . be made new in the attitude of your minds" (Ephesians 4:22–23).

Reflection: Choose one problem or issue in your life and think of how this approach could be used on it.

Thought for prayer: Meditate on Psalm 42–43. See how the psalmist deals with himself. Ask God for help in doing the same thing with a fear you are experiencing now.

> Be devoted to one another in love. Honor one another above your-selves. (Romans 12:10)

ONE ANOTHER. The New Testament calls Christians to a mutual ministry to "one another." We will look at some of them this week. If all believers are required to do these things, how much more effort should Christian spouses make to intention-ally weave these practices and attitudes into their relationship? Here's the first one. To "honor" means both to show respect in general and to give credit for accomplishments and sacrifices. "Above yourselves" means to be more concerned to give praise than to seek it. Remember Jesus, seeing his disciples fall asleep on him in his moment of greatest need, said, "The spirit is willing but the flesh is weak" (Matthew 26:41). That is like saying, "I know you meant well." Amazing that he found something to affirm in them even when they were letting him down.

Reflection: Do you regularly acknowledge and sometimes cele-brate what your spouse has done? How good are you at this?

Prayer: Lord, the very wonder and glory of our salvation is that you love and accept us, and even praise us (Romans 2:29) despite our sin. Make us people who love to affirm and give praise to others.

Don't grumble against one another, brothers and sisters, or you will be judged. The Judge is standing at the door! (James 5:9)

DON'T GRUMBLE. The word "grumble" (*stenazdo*) means to groan or sigh, to express frustration and disdain, especially non-verbally. It means to talk to your spouse with a dismissive tone of voice, or with the rolling of your eyes that belittles or makes the other person feel small. It can also mean speaking with a complaining tone that makes your spouse feel browbeaten. This is not merely a failure to give honor (see yesterday). It takes away honor by chipping away at his or her self-respect rather than building it up. There is a sting in the tail of this exhortation. Christians know Jesus came to bear our judgment so that on the Last Day we will not be condemned. How inappropriate to be judgmental to our spouse even in little things!

Reflection: Assess together how good (or bad) each of you are at this in your marriage.

Prayer: Lord, even though you have showered us with both supernatural and natural gifts and blessings, we are quick to grumble against you and each other. Help us come to our senses, get perspective, and always have a spirit of gratitude and joy in you. Amen.

In Christ we, though many, form one body, and each member belongs to all the others. We have different gifts. . . . [I]f it is serving, then serve; if it is teaching, then teach; if it is to encourage, then give encouragement. . . . Do not be proud. Do not be conceited. (Romans 12:5–8, 15)

AFFIRMATIVE DISCERNMENT. The church must help its members discern and use the spiritual talents and gifts that they have been given by God. Spouses should do this, too. Don't just be affirmative in general. Say: "You are very good at this. How can you do more of it?" Discern the specific gift and support them in using it. Paul adds, a few verses later, that we cannot do a good job of such affirmative discernment if we are self-absorbed. It takes sustained, patient observation and listening. Both the arrogant and those filled with self-pity have their eyes too fixed on themselves to notice the perhaps only embryonic gifts and abilities in their spouse.

Reflection: In general, how good are you at "affirmative discernment" with one another? Make a short list of two talents or gifts the other spouse has and share it with them.

Prayer: Lord, you don't just love us in general, you have given each of your children gifts and distinct ways to serve people and meet needs. Help us to help each other better know the unique mission in life you have given us to do. Amen.

All the brothers and sisters here send you greetings. Greet one another with a holy kiss. (1 Corinthians 16:20)

AFFECTION. Christians are often told to "greet one another with a holy kiss" (Romans 16:16; 1 Corinthians 16:20; 2 Corinthians 13:12) or "with a kiss of love" (1 Peter 5:14). It was a way to testify that in Christ they were truly a reconciled family.[78] The point was that Christians were to communicate love and affection in a visible way. How much more should spouses not be cold, clipped, abrupt, indifferent, and harsh with one another. More than that, we must be willing to actually talk about how much we love each other. This does not come easy to some of us who (we would say) are not naturally "gushy" and sentimental. But regardless of temperament, we must concretely communicate love through word and gesture daily, even hourly.

Reflection: Talk frankly to each other about how well each of you does in showing visible affection to each other. Tell each other two or three ways you enjoy receiving affection from the other.

Prayer: Lord, you don't just tell us you love us in the abstract, but you pour out your love in our hearts so we can feel it (Romans 5:5). Show us how to not just claim to love but to pour it out on each other so it affects our hearts. Amen.

July 5

Bear one another's burdens and so fulfill the law of Christ. (Galatians 6:2)[79]

HELPING. This famous text tells us both what we should do with our spouse and why we should do it. A "burden" can range from a practical problem (like caring for a child on a given day) to major illnesses and deep sorrows. And Paul does not merely say "help" but "bear" the burdens. The image entails coming very close to the burdened person, virtually standing in their shoes, and then allowing some of the weight of things to fall on you, thus lightening the load for the other. This implies both listening and understanding with deep sympathy (that is, letting the weight come upon you emotionally), as well as practically investing time and effort so that much of the inconvenience, cost, and trouble falls on you.

Reflection: There are two aspects of burden bearing: real sympathy and practical help. Assess together how good each of you are at this in your marriage.

Prayer: Lord, you told us to "cast our burdens on you" (Psalm 55:22), but it wasn't until you came to earth that we realized what it would cost you to take on our ultimate burdens—of sin and death. In light of that, let me gladly bear burdens for others and my spouse. Amen.

July 6

Bear one another's burdens and so fulfill the law of Christ. (Galatians 6:2)[80]

BEING HELPED. There is a hidden reciprocity in this text that should not be overlooked. Notice it does not only say "bear others' burdens" but "bear *one another's* burdens." It is possible for spouses to get into a pattern in which one person is always in difficulty and the other is always rescuing. It is not enough to help others—you must be willing to be helped. The gospel removes the proud self-centeredness that despises people who are in weakness. But it also removes the proud self-centeredness that despises and hates to admit any of your own weakness and need. Anyone who is afraid to admit weakness and accept help hasn't really grasped fully the gospel of grace.

Reflection: It can feed your pride to help others—but it takes real humility to allow yourself to be helped. In your marriage, is one of you more reluctant to be helped? What can you do to change?

Prayer: Lord God, the gospel offers free grace and mercy through Christ, and only those who are too proud to be helped by it are lost. Hatred of being helped is eternally fatal. Don't let it characterize my life—help me remove it. Amen.

Brothers and sisters, if someone is caught in a sin, you who live by the Spirit should restore that person gently. But watch yourselves, or you also may be tempted. (Galatians 6:1)

GENTLE CORRECTION. We are told to correct one another (Hebrews 3:13; Luke 17:3–4), but when? Every time we see someone do wrong? No. 1 Peter 4:8—"love covers a multitude of sins"— means that we should cover many or most sins with a forgiving, generous spirit rather than rebuking people constantly. We should correct when the person is "caught" or trapped in the behavior, that is, when we see them doing wrong in a habitual pattern that is harming them and others. But also, we should correct them with the utmost gentleness, in full awareness that we are flawed people as well with our own blind spots. Finally, we do it to *restore* them, never to just tell them off and make them feel bad.

Reflection. Analyze the way each of you gives the other criticism in light of these three criteria. Where do you need to improve?

Prayer: Lord Jesus, you fearlessly denounced sin yet you were "gentle and humble in heart" (Matthew 11:29). Help us to combine those qualities as we speak to one another. Amen.

July 8

It is a mistake to think that you must feel love to give it. If, for example, I have a child, and I give up my day off to take him to a ballgame to his great joy, at a time when I don't particularly like him, I am in some ways being more loving to him than if my heart were filled with affection. (Hardcover, p. 99; paperback, p. 105)

EMOTIONS AND BELIEFS. Emotions are not something we can just turn on or off, but our beliefs *about* our emotions are under our control. If we begin to resent someone, do we give in to that, or do we say, "That is not the person Christ is creating in me, the one who believes that I live only by God's mercy and grace"? This changes our attitude. We can resist thoughts of superiority and resentment, and encourage thoughts of humility and forgiveness. So beliefs lead to attitudes, and attitudes lead to behavior and that can have an impact on the original emotion. We are not helpless in the hands of our emotions.

Reflection: Think of a strong, negative emotion. How can you, through belief and behavior, change the hold that emotion has over you?

Thought for prayer: Meditate on Psalm 77:12, where the distressed psalmist says to God: "I *will* . . . meditate on all your deeds." Ask God for the same steely resolve to center your thoughts on his Word, especially when your emotions are high.

July 9

[C. S. Lewis wrote:] "Do not waste time bothering whether you 'love' your neighbor; act as if you did. . . . If you injure someone you dislike, you will find yourself disliking him more. If you do him a good turn, you will find yourself disliking him less. . . . The worldly man treats certain people kindly because he 'likes' them: the Christian, trying to treat everyone kindly, finds himself liking more and more people as he goes on—including people he could not even have imagined himself liking at the beginning. (Hardcover, pp. 100–101; paperback, p. 107)

EMOTIONS AND BEHAVIOR: 1. C. S. Lewis argues that "The Germans, perhaps, at first ill-treated the Jews because they hated them; afterwards they hated them much more because they had ill-treated them."[81] Here Lewis is drawing on his reading of Aristotle, who taught that we become good not by feeling good but by practicing goodness. For example, a courageous man is not one who feels brave but who acts brave despite fears. If he wasn't afraid, his action wouldn't be courageous. So a loving person is not necessarily one who feels love for someone at the moment. Love is doing someone good, even if it means a sacrifice of your own interests. If you are filled with affection, there wouldn't be much sacrifice in it. Feelings tend to follow actions.

Reflection: Is Lewis saying we should pretend we feel loving and brave even though we aren't? Have you ever seen what Lewis says work?

Thought for prayer: Meditate on Hebrews 12:12–13, which say that just as we should exercise an injured limb though it hurts in order to heal it, so we should obey God and love and serve others whether we feel like it or not. Ask God to help you remember that and practice it.

Our culture says that feelings of love are the basis for actions of love.... But it is truer to say that actions of love can lead consistently to feelings of love.... Married love is a symbiotic, complex mixture of both [emotion and action]. Having said this, it is important to observe that of the two ... it is the latter that we have the most control over. It is the action of love that we can promise to maintain every day. (Hardcover, p. 103; paperback, pp. 109–10)

EMOTIONS AND BEHAVIOR: 2. Another example of how actions lead to feeling is found in Edmund Morgan's classic historical study *American Slavery, American Freedom.* He shows how white colonial Virginians had shown little or no animus toward blacks until they began to enslave them. This was done originally for economic purposes, but once they had done so they began to feel and express increasing racial contempt for them.[82] They did not, at first, enslave Africans because they despised them, but they came to despise them because they enslaved them. If you treat your spouse with respect, serve them in love, and act loving, in the long run, it is the most fruitful way to experience love.

Reflection: Think of several ways that you have seen negative emotions (like disdain or animosity) grow from negative behavior (like mistreating or shunning).

Thought for prayer: Ask God to save you from the vicious cycle of avoiding leading to despising leading to more avoiding, making the relationship worse and worse. Ask for the discernment and self-control it takes to avoid that human and sinful spiral.

I am not proposing that you deliberately marry a person you don't like. But I can guarantee that, whoever you marry, you *will* fall "out of like" with them. . . . [O]ur emotions are tied to so many things within our physiology, psychology, and environment. Your feelings will ebb and flow and, if you follow our culture's definition of "love," you may conclude that . . . "[i]f this was the person for me to marry, my feelings wouldn't be so up and down." (Hardcover, pp. 103–4; paperback, pp. 110–11)

EMOTIONS AND COMMITMENTS. Robert Bellah wrote that we now have a culture of what he called "expressive individualism." We are taught that "each person has a unique core of feeling . . . that should unfold or be expressed if [identity] is to be realized."[83] Supposedly, our deepest authentic identity is in what we *feel*. But this makes a long-term marriage impossible. It means efforts to rekindle love are "inauthentic." The fact is that our changing and contradictory emotions cannot be the deepest foundation of who we are. Our deepest identity is rooted in our commitments—our promises, trusts, and vows. Your wedding promise is a bigger part of who you are than your fluctuating feelings.

Reflection: What are your most foundational commitments? How do they constitute a more stable identity than do your emotions?

Thought for prayer: Ask God to help you look to your identity as a child of God, adopted by grace (John 1:12–13), rather than to your feelings when you are having trouble loving your spouse.

You must stick to your commitment to act and serve in love even when—no, *especially* when—you don't feel much delight and attraction to your spouse. And the more you do that, slowly but surely, you will find your more ego-heavy attraction being transformed into a love that is more characterized by a humble, amazed reception and appreciation of the other person. The love you will grow into will be wiser, richer, deeper, less variable. (Hardcover, p. 105; paperback, p. 112)

EMOTIONS AND HABIT. Anything we do once becomes easier to do again, since we are creatures of habit. It makes sense that you become brave by acting brave, not waiting until you feel brave.[84] But is that also true for love? Yes, it is. If you serve someone to whom you are strongly attracted at the moment, your deeds are partially for yourself. You are inviting and stirring the other person's affection, which is something you desire greatly. However, when you love and serve someone who at the moment you don't even like, then you are doing it for their sake, not yours. In some ways loving someone you don't like is more truly love and a way to become a more loving person.

Reflection: Think of some ways in which this principle worked for you in a relationship outside of marriage. Think of some ways in which this principle worked for you inside your marriage.

Thought for prayer: Be thankful to God for the situations in which you can serve your spouse when you don't feel like it. Ask God to help you see these situations as opportunities for deepening your character, relationship, and love.

It is not surprising, then, that after the children leave home, many marriages fall apart. Why? Because while they treated their relationship with their children as a covenant relationship—performing the actions of love until their feelings strengthened—they treated their marriages as a consumer relationship and withdrew their actions of love when they weren't having the feelings. As a result, after two decades, their marriages were empty while their love for their children remained strong. (Hardcover, p. 108; paperback, p. 116)

THE PARENTING TEST CASE. When children fail to be grateful or to reciprocate friendship and service, we remain faithful parents because of their dependent condition. And as the years go by our love for them gets stronger. But if your spouse fails to be grateful or to reciprocate actions of love, it feels fair to draw back from your spouse and to think, "If you aren't being the spouse you should be, don't complain if I am not being the spouse I should be." It has the appearance of justice, but that attitude has deadly consequences. While your love for your children grows because you love them unconditionally, your marriage is dying the death of a thousand cuts. Parenting is a "test case" that proves that the feelings of love follow the actions of love.

Reflection: Think of various ways that a marriage can die through "a thousand cuts"—small, barely perceptible ways of compromise or withdrawal.

Thought for prayer: Thank God for being the perfect Father—just yet merciful; and thank Jesus for being the perfect spouse—infinitely loving yet insisting we change for the better. Ask the Lord to renew you in his image.

July 14

[W]e must say to ourselves something like this: "When Jesus looked down from the Cross . . . [and saw us] denying him, abandoning him, and betraying him . . . in the greatest act of love in history, he *stayed.* . . . He loved us, not because we were lovely to him, but to make us lovely. That is why I am going to love my spouse." Speak to your heart like that, and then fulfill the promises you made on your wedding day. (Hardcover, p. 109; paperback, pp. 116–17)

EMOTIONS AND MEDITATION. What do you do when you find your feelings for your spouse flagging? Look at the various "languages" of love that will be covered later in this devotional and in *The Meaning of Marriage.* Be sure to use them all, and to especially use the one(s) most valuable to your spouse. But as important as the behaviors are, work on the heart itself. Here is a simple, practical proposal. Meditate on Christ's love for his disciples when they were abandoning him. Meditate on his love for you over the years when you ignored him or at least did not love him back as you should have. Think of his unflagging love for you despite all that, and what it cost him. Let that stir you to love your spouse.

Reflection: What things do you do that makes it harder for your spouse to love you? Share them with each other.

Thought for prayer: Meditate on Psalm 1:1–6, which is a meditation on meditation. Then ask God to show you how not to simply pray but to meditate to the point of delight (Psalm 1:2).[85]

It is striking, then, that after God creates the first man, he said, "It is *not* good that the man should be alone." (Genesis 2:18) . . . The Genesis narrative is implying that our intense relational capacity, created and given to us by God, was not fulfilled completely by our "vertical" relationship with him. God designed us to need "horizontal" relationships with other human beings. That is why even in paradise, loneliness was such a terrible thing. (Hardcover, pp. 110–11; paperback, p. 120)

FRIENDSHIP OR PERISH. Our individualistic culture promotes the illusion that what we are and will be is mainly the result of our personal decisions. When we come to faith, we likewise assume that our new connection with God and his power will give us all the resources we will need to be happy and reach our goals. In reality, we are irreducibly relational beings. We are perhaps more the product of our family and social relationships than of our own conscious choices. And so, after getting a new relationship with God through Christ, it is only through a whole community of believers that God changes us, "for we are members of one another" (1 Corinthians 12:12–27). We were built to have friends or perish.

Reflection: Do you have three kinds of friends: Among neighbors whom you live and work with? Among Christian brothers and sisters? Is your spouse your friend?

Thought for prayer: Spend some time thinking of two or three people who have had an enormous impact on you—who were almost literally (or literally) lifesavers for you. Thank God for them heartily, and then ask him to provide more of the same in your life.

While erotic love can be depicted as two people looking at one another, friendship can be depicted as two people standing side by side looking at the same object and being stirred and entranced by it together. . . . The paradox is that friendship cannot be merely about itself. It must be about something else, something that both friends are committed to and passionate about besides one another. (Hardcover, p. 113; paperback, pp. 122–23)

FRIENDSHIP AND PRAISE. After you've watched a movie you really loved you will find that your pleasure is exponentially enhanced if you can watch it again with someone who hasn't seen it yet. Your joy in the story is deepened by the wonder and praise of the other person. This is true of everything. You remember, understand, and appreciate things better when you do them with someone else. Not only that, but their enjoyment enhances your own. The experience deepens the relationship and the relationship deepens the experience. That's one of the ways friendship enriches our lives. At the root of friendship is our need to complete our enjoyment of things through others.

Reflection: What activities that bring real joy to you can you do with your spouse? How can you increase the amount of time you spend in such activities?

Thought for prayer: Praise God that praising him creates joy (Psalm 84:1–2). Praise God that we, made in his image, get joy through praising. Ask him to give us a spirit of praise rather than one of crankiness and faultfinding.

July 17

C. S. Lewis wrote: "The very condition of having friends is that we should want something else besides friends. Where the truthful answer to the question *'Do you see the same truth?'* would be *'I don't care about the truth—I only want [you to be my] friend,'* no friendship can arise. Friendship must be *about* something. . . . Those who have nothing can share nothing; those who are going nowhere can have no fellow-travelers." (Hardcover, pp. 113–14; paperback, p. 123)

FRIENDSHIP WORTH A FIGHT. It is well known that over the years you have to work to keep the romance in a marriage. But it can be just as much of a fight to keep the friendship in it. As careers get more demanding and children become higher maintenance, it is easy to become mere roommates or parental managing partners. You must find time not just for romantic evenings, but also for delighting in and discussing the same books, for giving each other counsel, for exploring the same landscapes, for affirming one another's gifts, for prayer and worship together—for becoming better and better friends. Friendship is always worth the fight.

Reflection: Friendships must be *about* something besides the friendship. There are an infinite number of such things. In your marriage, what things can your friendship be about?

Thought for prayer: Pray about your devotions for July 15–23 on friendship. Ask him for deeper insight and for at least one very concrete, practical idea for how you as a couple can strengthen your friendship.

For believers in Christ, despite enormous differences in class, temperament, culture, race, sensibility, and personal history, there is an underlying commonality that is more powerful than them all. . . . Christians have all experienced the grace of God in the gospel of Jesus. We have all had our identity changed at the root, so now God's calling and love are more foundational to who we are than any other thing. (Hardcover, p. 114; paperback, p. 124)

FRIENDS SHARE A PAST. The usual plot of "buddy movies" requires individuals who dislike each other to have a common experience of danger and loss that forges them into a cohesive, interdependent "band of brothers." Christians share a deep common experience that is unique, a conviction they are sinners who can't save themselves, and a recognition of an unmerited full salvation that saves by grace. That both humbles us—so we can't look down on anyone else—but it also grounds us in a certainty about our worth that other identities cannot provide. When any Christian meets another Christian whose identity has been transformed by grace, they recognize the joy in one another. There is an instant bond and basis for a deep friendship.

Reflection: Recount with one another how you were led through the stages to see that you were trying to save yourself, how it was impossible, and that Christ's salvation was unmerited and available.

Thought for prayer: After reminding each other of your respective "stories of grace," pray for one another together, thanking God for his work in your spouse's life.

And [all believers] also long for the same future, journey to the same horizon, what the Bible calls the "new creation." . . . We will become our true selves, the persons we were created to be, freed from all flaws, imperfections, and weaknesses. [Paul] speaks of "the glory that will be revealed in us" (Romans 8:18, 20). . . . We "hope" and "wait eagerly" for this final and full redemption (Romans 8:23). (Hardcover, p. 114; paperback, p. 124)

FRIENDS SHARE A VISION. Paul speaks of a process of change into Christlike character (2 Corinthians 3:18) that begins now and comes to perfect completion in the future (Philippians 1:6). This means that even now there is a process going on in which we are each being spiritually formed into someone unique and beautiful, as the sinful accretions are being loosened and removed while the virtues of faith, hope, and love are growing and strengthening. Here is a second thing that Christian friendships are about. We get a vision for the "best self" that God is creating in our friend. Christian friends partner with Christ to help one another toward this great future. We do it through affirming, critiquing, exhorting, loving, weeping, and rejoicing with one another.

Reflection: Make a list of three great things you see Christ creating in your spouse.

Thought for prayer: Yesterday you prayed in each other's presence, thanking God for his work of grace in your spouse's life. Today pray again, this time asking him to continue it, and to make you a partner with God in it.

July 20

> [A]ny two Christians, with nothing else but a common faith in Christ, can have a robust friendship. . . . Friendship is a deep oneness that develops as two people, speaking the truth in love to each other, journey together to the same horizon. (Hardcover, pp. 114–17; paperback, pp. 124–27)

FRIENDS AND FORMATIVE PRACTICES. For centuries believers were formed as Christians by a set of communal practices. These are tools that Christian spouses can use for intensifying their own friendships with each other. You can study the Bible and theology together (Acts 2:42). You can hold each other accountable for spiritual growth goals (Hebrews 3:13). You can help each other identify your particular gifts for ministry and then support each other in their use (Romans 12:4–8). You can open your home to others in the name of Christ, providing hospitality (Romans 12:13). You can think of ways to nurture your children's faith together (Ephesians 6:1–4). All of these ordinary Christian practices, when done intentionally together as spouses, become the basis for a spiritually rich friendship.

Reflection: Which of the practices listed above do you currently do as a couple? Which ones could you add?

Thought for prayer: Going through the list in the devotional above, thank God for each particular means of grace and ask him for the wisdom and self-discipline to make better uses of them both in your marriage and in the church.

Proverbs 2:17 speaks of one's spouse as your '*allup* . . . —"best friend."
In an age where women were often seen as the husband's property . . .
[this] was startling. . . . But [today] . . . it is just as radical. . . . In tribal
societies, romance doesn't matter as much as social status, and in
individualistic Western societies, romance and great sex matter [the
most]. The Bible, however, without ignoring responsibility to the community or the importance of romance, puts great emphasis on marriage as companionship. (Hardcover, p. 117; paperback, pp. 127–28)

FRIENDS TO THE END. In ancient times, the chief purpose of
marriage was to secure social stability and status through the
bearing of children. Romantic happiness was optional and friendship not even imagined. Today the main concern is for sexual and
personal fulfillment. Children are optional and, again, friendship
is not the focus. However, we should bear in mind that in Genesis, the text doesn't say that Eve was brought to Adam because he
needed sex or children, but because "it was not good that he be
alone." And if you live into an advanced age together, neither
child-rearing nor sex will be the glue for your relationship. But
friendship lasts until the end.

Reflection: The Bible puts emphasis on all these various aspects
of marriage. List them. Are some of them dominating and others
taking a backseat right now? What can you do about that?

Thought for prayer: Today, simply thank God for the unequalled, multidimensional richness of the institution of marriage, and ask him not to allow any of those wonderful aspects to
atrophy in your relationship, especially not friendship.

This principle—that your spouse should be capable of becoming your best friend—is a game changer when you address the question of compatibility in a prospective spouse. If you think of marriage largely in terms of erotic love, then compatibility means sexual chemistry and appeal. If you think of marriage largely as a way to move into the kind of social life and status you desire, then compatibility means . . . common tastes and aspirations for lifestyle. (Hardcover, pp. 119–20; paperback, p. 130)

FRIENDS: AN OVERVIEW. What, then, are the marks of a person who can be not just your spouse but also your best friend? Two pairings.[86] First candor and counsel. They need to be willing to speak the truth, to say painful things that you need to hear, and to not merely rebuke but give wise advice for a way forward. Then, constancy and carefulness. The truthfulness must be embedded in unconditional love, in tactfulness and graciousness. A friend knows how to speak the truth in the way and at the moment when it can be best received. What are the marks that should be in *you* if you are to be a friend to your spouse? The same list.

Reflection: Look at these four marks of friendship with your spouse. Which ones are you each strongest at? Weakest at?

Thought for prayer: After concluding your self-examination in the Reflection above, ask God for help in the area you have identified as the weakest. Ask him for practical insight as to how to improve.

Physical attractiveness will wane, no matter how hard you work to delay its departure. And socio-economic status unfortunately can change almost overnight. . . . [And] sexual attraction and social class "relatability" does not give you any common vision. . . . But such goals do not create the deep oneness. . . . If you marry mainly a sexual partner, or mainly a financial partner, you are going nowhere together, really. And those who are going nowhere can have no fellow-travelers. (Hardcover, p. 120; paperback, pp. 130–31)

FRIENDS IN MISSION. As we have seen, friendships must be *about* something, including shared goals. Many couples share good goals such as owning a home or attaining some level of financial sufficiency. A much more substantial and long-term goal is the rearing and nurturing of children. But we all know that such goals do not necessarily bind hearts together in love. Many people who are divorced and alienated can work together on financial and parenting matters without drawing closer. The greatest, deepest, most heart-bonding goals to share include a desire to see God's kingdom grow in the world, in your community, and in your spouse, through Spirit-changed lives.

Reflection: What goals regarding God's kingdom in the world and in your community can you set as a couple?

Thought for prayer: Meditate on Psalm 48:1–2. Pray together that God's kingdom—his saving grace and the resulting human community based on peace, justice, and love—would become "the joy of the whole earth."

Paul [writes in Ephesians 5 that] the primary goal of marriage is not social status and stability . . . nor is it primarily romantic and emotional happiness. . . . [T]he goal . . . is "to sanctify her" (verse 26) to "present her to himself" in radiant beauty and splendor (verse 27a), to bring her to be perfectly "holy and blameless" (verse 27c) . . . to remove all spiritual stains, flaws, sins, and blemishes, to make us "holy," "glorious," and "blameless." (Hardcover, p. 118; paperback, p. 128)

GROW IN GRACE. Yes, we are to love our spouse by seeking his or her good, and yes, your spouse should be seeking to love and please you. But there is nothing better your spouse can do for you—and nothing better you can do for him or her—than to grow in grace and in the knowledge of Jesus Christ (2 Peter 3:18). We should not, however, pit this goal of marriage against the others. There is no better way to enhance your romantic attractiveness to your spouse than to listen to his or her spiritual counsel and become more the person Christ is calling you to be.

Reflection: In gentleness and with all the graciousness you can muster, make a list of one another's character "blemishes." Now each of you choose one to work on. Get your spouse's counsel as to how to go about it.

Thought for prayer: Read 2 Peter 3:18 aloud and pray it for one another, in each other's presence.

Husband and wife are to be both lovers and friends to one another as Jesus is to us. Jesus has a vision of our future glory (Colossians 1:27; 1 John 3:2–3) and everything he does in our lives moves us toward that goal. Ephesians 5:28 directly links the purpose of every human marriage to the purpose of the Ultimate Marriage.... If any two unrelated Christians are to ... hold each other accountable to grow out of their sins (Hebrews 3:13), how much more should a husband and wife do that? (Hardcover, p. 119; paperback, p. 130)

GROW THROUGH EXHORTATION. In our culture it is easier than ever to hide from people, including your spouse. And yet there is no one who can actually see into your life better than your spouse. He or she can notice small changes in demeanor and spirit that no one else can. Hebrews 3:13 tells believers to "exhort one another every day ... that none of you be hardened by the deceitfulness of sin."[87] "Exhort" is a word that means to both sympathize and confront, to plead or implore. Our sins hide themselves from us ("deceitfulness") and so we must ask someone else to point them out. Who? There is almost no one who can carry out this biblical command better than your spouse.

Reflection: How can you hold each other accountable for small yet stubborn character flaws without falling into nagging and complaining?

Thought for prayer: Ask God for the particular traits you need to "exhort" well—winsomeness yet directness, sympathy yet insistence.

[If you are a Christian] you have an old self and a new self (Ephesians 4:24). The old self is crippled with . . . many besetting sins and entrenched character flaws. The new self is . . . you liberated from all your sins and flaws. This new self is always a work in progress, and sometimes the clouds of the old self make it almost completely invisible. But sometimes the clouds really part and [there's a] glimpse of where you are going. (Hardcover, p. 121; paperback, p. 132)

GROWTH AND THE TWO SELVES. When we believe in Christ, God gives us a whole new self (Ephesians 4:22–24). Through the gospel, that self is assured of God's unconditional approval and we are enabled for the first time to love God and others for their sake, not ours. Nevertheless the old self—that tries to earn its self-worth and get control over God and others—is still there. It does good deeds, but in order to get approval and power from God and others. The complexity and glory of the Christian life lies in this, that both selves—with their frameworks of motivation and thinking—are available to us and can assert themselves on any given day. We grow as we die more and more to the old self and live more and more into the new one.

Reflection: Briefly flesh out with your spouse the outlines of the motivations and thinking of your old self and new self in Christ.

Thought for prayer: Ask God to make you aware of the choices that we have every day, in which we can either live as our old self or the new self. Then ask him to make you happy enough in Christ to put on the new self in the trenches of daily life.

> [H]ere's what it means to fall in love. It is to look at another person and get a glimpse of the person God is creating, and to say, "I see who God is making you, and it excites me! . . . I want to partner with you and God in the journey you are taking to his throne. And when we get there, I will . . . say, 'I always knew you could be like this. I got glimpses of it on earth, but now look at you!'" (Hardcover, p. 121; paperback, p. 132)

GROW IN ANTICIPATION. Understanding a Christian's "two selves" is crucial for every stage of your relationship. When you first fall in love you are attracted by the other person's strengths rather than flaws, and so what you fall in love with is mostly the future self that God is making. During your years together you learn to love the other person as Christ loves you. You love your spouse fully with all his or her sins, yet you do not love the sins. To acquiesce and accept someone's sins is the least loving thing you could possibly do and it would be a betrayal of your spouse's true self. And ultimately, you know you *will* see your spouse transformed into glory (2 Corinthians 3:18; 1 John 3:2). Live in the anticipatory joy of that moment.

Reflection: We know that it is unloving to harshly criticize and rebuke someone for their sin. Why is it just as unloving to keep silent about it? List the ways that cowardly silence is unloving.

Thought for prayer: Ask the Lord for the crucial but elusive spiritual skill of being able to attack a problem without attacking the person, of showing yourself against their sin but *for* them. Beg God to show you how to do that, particularly in your marriage.

My wife, Kathy, often says that most people, when they look for a spouse, are looking for a finished statue when they should be looking for a wonderful block of marble. Not so you can create the kind of person *you* want, but rather because you see what kind of person Jesus is making. (Hardcover, pp. 121–22; paperback, p. 133)

GROWTH AND GOD'S WILL. As we have seen, many today insist that their spouse "not try to change them." However, Christ, our spiritual husband, worked to cleanse and beautify us, and now we should do the same in our marriages (Ephesians 5:28). But it is easy to think that we are just trying to help our spouse become "the person God is making them" when actually you are trying to make your spouse into someone who fits your personal tastes or who would bolster your self-esteem or who would please your parents more. Judge your spouse instead by God's will as expressed in his Word, by biblical standards of character like the fruit of the Spirit (Galatian 5), or godly wisdom (Proverbs), or the Sermon on the Mount (Matthew 5–7).

Reflection: Think of changes in your spouse that you have sought but which are not things that the Spirit of God necessarily creates in people. Then think of changes you have sought that are. What is the advantage of having two lists rather than one?

Thought for prayer: Ask God to help you accept the features of your spouse that may displease you personally but are not matters of spiritual character or maturity. Then ask God to help you *not* acquiesce in any sinful pattern that will grieve God and hurt your spouse.

This is by no means a naïve, romanticized approach—rather it is brutally realistic. In this view of marriage, each person says to the other, "I see all your flaws, imperfections, weaknesses, dependencies. But underneath them all I see growing the person God wants you to be." This is radically different from the search for "compatibility." (Hardcover, p. 122; paperback, pp. 133–34)

GROWTH AND GOD'S POWER. Why is the approach described above "brutally realistic"? First, it assumes that whomever you marry will be a long way from the person they need to be. Imperfections are expected. This avoids the shattering disillusionment that comes with blind romanticism. Second, however, it is *not* the enabling behavior of an alcoholic family, in which the addict is kept in his or her state so the other spouse can continually rescue them and feel noble and needed. Finally, there is the deep relief of the knowledge that changing your spouse is not, ultimately, your job at all. It is far beyond your power. You are a mere assistant to God in this great work.

Reflection: Think of other ways in which the Christian approach to change avoids the opposites of naïve romanticism and enabling behavior.

Thought for prayer: Thank God, first, for the unique wisdom of the Scriptures for understanding how people change, and, second, for the unique power of the gospel for effecting it. Then ask for both the wisdom and power of God to work in your marriage.

["Compatibility" usually] means we are looking for a partner who accepts us just as we are.... The search for an ideal mate is a hopeless quest.... [T]his is a radically different approach.... If you don't see your mate's deep flaws and weaknesses and dependencies, you're not even in the game. But if you don't get excited about the person your spouse has already grown into and will become, you aren't tapping into the power of marriage as spiritual friendship. (Hardcover, pp. 122–23; paperback, p. 134)

GROWTH AND THE GOSPEL. We might call the biblical approach "Marriage as a Vehicle for Sanctification," the word "sanctification" meaning the process of becoming holy and Christlike (cf. 1 Thessalonians 4:3). It contrasts both with the attitude "Compatibility means don't ask me to change," or, at the other end of the spectrum, "You are a mess and you need me to save you." The biblical way combines realism about our flaws with great hope for change through Christ's means of grace. It recognizes that only Christ is savior, and your spouse is not. It is similar to the combined humility and confidence that the gospel brings when it tells you that, in Jesus, you are more sinful than you dared believe but more loved than you dared hope—at the same time.

Reflection: Think of how the gospel of salvation by grace helps us be both very realistic and strongly hopeful about change at the same time.

Thought for prayer: Ask God to help you remember that you are not your spouse's savior, nor are you the Spirit of God in your spouse's life. Confess to God the specific ways you have tried to take those roles and put your spouse into God's hands.

Romance, sex, laughter, and plain fun are the by-products of this pro-cess of sanctification, refinement, glorification. Those things are important, but they can't keep the marriage going through years and years of ordinary life. What keeps the marriage going is your commit-ment to your spouse's holiness . . . to his or her beauty . . . greatness and perfection . . . honesty and passion for the things of God. That's your job as a spouse. Any lesser goal than that, any smaller purpose, and you're just playing at being married. (Hardcover, p. 123; paper-back, p. 135)

RIGHT ORDER. A by-product is something created in the manu-facture of something else. When Jesus says, "Blessed [happy] are those who hunger and thirst after righteousness," he is saying, "Happy are those who want something more than happiness, namely, righteousness." Aim at loving God and you get happiness thrown in. Aim primarily at happiness and you will get neither. Now apply this principle to marriage. Commit yourself to your spouse's good and growth into Christlikeness and you will also get romance, fun, and laughter thrown in. Aim primarily at the fun and romance, and you'll get none of it.

Reflection: C. S. Lewis wrote: "Aim at heaven and get earth thrown in. Aim at earth and you will get neither."[88] Think of the many other areas of life in which this basic principle plays out.

Thought for prayer: Meditate on Matthew 6:33. Then ask God to show you what it means particularly for you to "seek first the kingdom of God and its righteousness" so that all other things you need are added to your life.

Then Peter came to Jesus and asked, "Lord, how many times shall I forgive my brother or sister who sins against me? Up to seven times?" Jesus answered, "I tell you, not seven times, but seventy-seven times. Therefore the kingdom of heaven is like a king who wanted to settle accounts with his servants." (Matthew 18:21–23)

NO LIMIT. Peter's question implies that there is a point at which you could stop forgiving a recalcitrant person. Since "seven" was a symbol of completeness in the Hebrew Bible, Jesus's answer means we must *never* stop forgiving. He tells a story of a king who forgave a servant a debt of "ten thousand talents." Since a single talent was about ten years of wages, the amount meant something like our word "zillions."[89] Then that servant refused to forgive a fellow servant a small amount. The king angrily asked him, "Shouldn't you have had mercy on your fellow servant as I had mercy on you?" (verse 33). What God has forgiven us cannot be calculated and this can melt away our resentment toward anyone else. To the degree we grasp what he forgave us, we will be able to forgive others the infinitely smaller debts they owe us.

Reflection: How does this illustration help us emotionally to forgive others?

Prayer: Lord, how can I—who live only by your mercy—ever withhold mercy from someone who has wronged me? I have my resentments, but please shed the light of your infinite grace on them so I see them for the small-minded things they are. Help me forgive. Amen.

Then Peter came to Jesus and asked, "Lord, how many times shall I forgive my brother or sister who sins against me? Up to seven times?" Jesus answered, "I tell you, not seven times, but seventy-seven times. Therefore the kingdom of heaven is like a king who wanted to settle accounts with his servants." (Matthew 18:21–23)

THE COST OF FORGIVENESS. Jesus's parable helps motivate us to forgive, but it also helps us to understand what forgiveness is. To forgive someone a literal debt means you have to absorb it yourself. If you don't forgive them, then they will have to pay it. If you do forgive, then you will bear the cost. This is also true in nonmonetary situations. When you are sinned against, you lose something—happiness, reputation, peace of mind, or an opportunity. If you don't forgive, you hurt (or want to hurt) *their* happiness and peace. If you forgive, you bear what they did without payback. That will be painful, of course, and so we must not think forgiveness feels good. Forgiveness is a form of suffering. As Christ bore our sins in love for us without complaint, so we are to forgive one another (Ephesians 4:32).

Reflection: What does this parable add to your understanding of forgiveness? How well do *you* do at forgiveness?

Prayer: Father, make me glad to pay the price of forgiveness, so small compared to the sacrifice of your Son for me. Amen.

Do not repay anyone evil for evil. Be careful to do what is right in the eyes of everyone. If it is possible, as far as it depends on you, live at peace with everyone. Do not take revenge, my dear friends, but leave room for God's wrath, for it is written: "It is mine to avenge; I will repay," says the Lord. On the contrary: "If your enemy is hungry, feed him; if he is thirsty, give him something to drink. In doing this, you will heap burning coals on his head." Do not be overcome by evil, but overcome evil with good. (Romans 12:17–21)

OVERCOMING EVIL—THE PRINCIPLE. The word "over-come" means to overpower or defeat. When we identify *evil* too closely with the *evildoer*, thinking that to destroy evil we must destroy the wrongdoer, we unwittingly become a pawn of the evil force that is behind the wrongdoer. If, instead, we show love to the wrongdoer, there are two results. First, the spread of evil is checked in us. Hatred and pride do not infect us. Second, the spread of evil *may* be checked in the wrongdoer. He or she may wake up to what they've done wrong (thus the "burning coals" metaphor). The hostile person may be filled with remorse through the experience of kindness. Thus Jesus overcame our evil with the goodness of his life and sacrifice.

Reflection: Overcoming evil with good—have you seen this happen? Have you done this yourself? Discuss how to apply this principle to your marriage.

Prayer: Lord, I used to think that if I forgave—if I merely refrained from payback when people wronged me—that was all I had to do. Now I see I must be positively good to them. This seems beyond me! Help me, God. Amen.

Do not repay anyone evil for evil. Be careful to do what is right in the eyes of everyone. If it is possible, as far as it depends on you, live at peace with everyone. Do not take revenge, my dear friends, but leave room for God's wrath, for it is written: "It is mine to avenge; I will repay," says the Lord. On the contrary: "If your enemy is hungry, feed him; if he is thirsty, give him something to drink. In doing this, you will heap burning coals on his head." Do not be overcome by evil, but overcome evil with good. (Romans 12:17–21)

OVERCOMING EVIL—THE PRACTICE. We looked at the principle of overcoming evil, but what about the practice? First, don't avoid the person. In marriage you can't avoid your spouse physically, but you can shut down emotionally. Don't think: "I won't retaliate, but I don't want to deal with them." But that *is* retaliation, and verse 18 says that your part is to actively seek peace.[90] Don't be cold, hoping your spouse will ask, "What is wrong?" Second, it is not enough to move on (verse 19); you must express love in words and actions. (That does not mean being overly kind simply as a way of shaming them.) Verse 20 indicates that we should thoughtfully find ways to wish the person well and do helpful things and speak respectfully to them.

Reflection: When your spouse does something you have asked him and her not to do time and time again and you become angry, do you respond with these practices? Discuss how to apply them to your marriage.

Prayer: Lord, don't let me hide behind all my self-justifying excuses like "They started it. Let them come to me." Help me to see that, when our relationship is strained, it's always my move. Amen.

Do not repay anyone evil for evil. Be careful to do what is right in the eyes of everyone. If it is possible, as far as it depends on you, live at peace with everyone. Do not take revenge, my dear friends, but leave room for God's wrath, for it is written: "It is mine to avenge; I will repay," says the Lord. On the contrary: "If your enemy is hungry, feed him; if he is thirsty, give him something to drink. In doing this, you will heap burning coals on his head." Do not be overcome by evil, but overcome evil with good. (Romans 12:17–21)

OVERCOMING EVIL—THE POWER. The power for overcoming evil with good is in the gospel. When Paul tells us to think of the wrath of God (verse 19) he reminds us that all resentment and vengeance is taking on God's role as judge. But (1) only God is qualified to judge (we are imperfect and deserve judgment ourselves); (2) only God knows enough to judge (we don't know all about the offender, what he or she has faced and deserves); and (3) Jesus took the judgment of God. Christ died for us while we were his enemies (Romans 5:6–10). So don't sit in God's judgment seat. If we are to love even our enemies like this, how much more should we forgive and love our spouses, especially when we are angry at them?

Reflection: Make a commitment to one another that, when the other person angers you, you will respond with the forgiveness of Matthew 19 and the love of Romans 12.

Prayer: Lord, thank you for giving me such an array of truths that can melt my heart when it hardens toward my spouse. Help me discern the ones that affect and change me the most, and then may your Spirit use them to stir me up to love. Amen.

Is anyone among you sick? Let them call the elders of the church to pray over them and anoint them with oil in the name of the Lord. . . . Therefore, confess your sins to one another and pray for one another, that you may be healed. (James 5:14, 16)

MUTUAL CONFESSION: 1. If Christians in general should be confessing their sins to one another, spouses should be as well—and we are not talking here just about sins against the other person. They should learn to admit their failures and sins to each other, praying for each other, and graciously representing God's mercy to each other. Dietrich Bonhoeffer writes: "He who is alone with his sin is utterly alone. . . . The final break-through to fellowship does not occur because, though they have fellowship with one another as devout people, they do not have fellowship as sinners."[91] Not to be able to confess sins to your spouse is also to be alone in your marriage.

Reflection: Do you, in your marriage, have "fellowship with one another as sinners"? Discuss.

Prayer: Lord, your Word constantly says that when we hide our sin we become sick and alone (Psalm 32:3–4). We confess that we don't like showing our sins and flaws to each other. Humble our pride so we can confess and pray for each other, and be healed. Amen.

Therefore, confess your sins to one another and pray for one another, that you may be healed. (James 5:16)

MUTUAL CONFESSION: 2. Dietrich Bonhoeffer writes: "There are two dangers that a Christian community which practices confession must guard against. The first concerns the one who hears confessions. It is not a good thing for one person to be the confessor of all the others. . . . [T]his will give rise to . . . [the] spiritual domination of souls. . . . Every person should refrain from listening to confession who does not himself practice it. Only the person who has so humbled himself can hear a brother's confession without harm. The second danger concerns the confessant [the one making the confession]. . . . [L]et him guard against ever making a pious work of his confession. Confession as a pious work is an invention of the devil. . . . We can confess solely for the sake of the promise of absolution. Confession as a routine duty is spiritual death."[92]

Reflection: Put these two dangers in your own words. Which of them are dangers to you? Apply these insights to your own marriage.

Prayer: Lord, don't let us as a couple fall into the pattern of one of us always being the confessing party and the other being the one who gives out the absolution. Lead us to a true mutuality in this ministry to each other. Amen.

August 8

Paul is urging spouses to help their mates love Jesus more than them.... Only if my emotional tank is filled with love from God will I be able to be patient, faithful, tender, and open with my wife when things are not going well in life or in the relationship. And the more joy I get from my relationship with Christ, the more I can share that joy with my wife and family. (Hardcover, p. 124; paperback, p. 135)

LOVE SECOND TO LOVE WELL. If the main love of my life is my wife—if she is the person whose approval, affection, and affirmation is most valuable to me—then I will crush her with my expectations. I'll need her to always be loving me, never absorbed by her own problems or having a bad day, never sick or depressed and so unable to give me what I need. And I will be so devastated or angered by her criticism that I will make her wish she had never given it. If instead it is God's love that is my highest joy and deepest foundation, I will have the resources to love my wife when she is in need. Only if I love Jesus more than my spouse will I love my spouse well.

Reflection: Think of other ways that we will be unable to love our spouse well if we don't love Jesus more.

Thought for prayer: Ask God to open your eyes to see the specific ways that you have been blaming your spouse for failing to give you things only the Lord can give.

If singles accepted this principle, it would drastically change the way people seek a marriage partner in our day. It is typical for a single person to walk into a room and see a number of people of the opposite sex and immediately begin to screen them, not for companionship but for attractiveness. . . . The problem is many of your best prospects for friendship were likely among those you ruled out because they were too tall or too short, too fat or too skinny. (Hardcover, p. 125; paperback, p. 137)

THE FILTERS: 1. A spouse is a romantic lover, an economic partner, and a co-parent. When a single person in our culture looks for someone to marry, these roles are preeminent in their minds. Therefore, looks and financial capacity tend to be the standards for assessment. They are like two filters by which many candidates of stellar character—but who are ordinary in the physical and financial categories—are screened out. However, if we realize that spiritual friendship is at the core of marriage, and is the thing that sustains us through the ups and downs of the other roles and pursuits, it will give us a new set of eyes to see great potential in people who otherwise would be virtually invisible to us.

Reflection: You may yourself be looking for someone to marry or you may know someone well who is doing so. Take off the filters and look again at the people you know. Who now shows up on the list?

Thought for prayer: Pray that singles (especially in the church) would not unnecessarily delay marriage or miss great prospective partners because of these "filters" given to us by our culture. Pray secondly that they would not have a residual negative effect on you yourself in your marriage.

We think of a [mate] as primarily a lover . . . and if [they] can be a friend on top of that. . . . [Instead] look for someone who understands you better than you do yourself, who makes you a better person just by being around them. And then explore whether that friendship could become a romance and a marriage. So many people go about their dating starting from the wrong end, and they end up in marriages that aren't really about anything and aren't going anywhere. (Hardcover, pp. 125–26; paperback, pp. 137–38)

THE FILTERS: 2. We have said that most people in our culture simply screen out any prospective spouses on the basis of looks and finances. A healthier approach is to not merely want a lover but also want a friend. Nonetheless, we still tend to screen out anyone who is not very sexually attractive to us, leaving us with a set of (pretty good-looking) persons. Then we evaluate that group to see which ones we could also make into friends. We propose you reverse the order. Look first for persons of wisdom and sympathy, who show the ability to really "get" you. Then see if you can become attracted to them, because romance is also important. Romanticism based on admiration for character is much longer lasting than romanticism based on a once beautiful but now aging body.

Reflection: Do you think that it is possible to find someone sexually attractive as much or more for their character and heart as for their body?

Thought for prayer: Pray that the romantic aspect of your marriage would only increase as you age, and ask the Lord for both the wisdom, self-knowledge, and attitudes of heart necessary in both of you for that to happen.

If you see your spouse as mainly a sexual partner or a financial partner, you will find that you will need pursuits outside of marriage to really engage your whole soul. . . . Your marriage will slowly die if your spouse senses that he or she is not the first priority in your life. But only if your spouse is not just your lover and financial partner but your best friend is it possible for your marriage to be your most important and fulfilling relationship. (Hardcover, p. 126; paperback, p. 138)

BEST FRIENDS. Every person needs a variety of friends who can provide intellectual stimulation and sage advice that no one person can offer, including your spouse. But unless we put spiritual friendship at the heart of our marriage, we will have to look for our deepest counsel and best affirmation elsewhere. While that does not break the covenant in the same way as sexual infidelity, it makes it hard to give your marriage the priority it should have. No marriage can be healthy if some other personal relationship has become significantly more important to you than the one you have with your spouse.

Reflection: Would you say you have struck this balance—having good friends and yet a uniquely close friendship with your spouse?

Thought for prayer: Examine your friendships before the Lord in prayer. If one of them has become more valuable than that with your marriage, ask God for help not to withdraw from that friend but to grow the depth of spiritual companionship with your spouse.

August 12

[R]ight in the midst of these patriarchal cultures, and in the face of these realities, God says, "I didn't put a parent and a child in the Garden, I put a husband and a wife. When you marry your spouse, that must supersede all other relationships, even the parental relationship. Your spouse and your marriage must be the number one priority in your life." Your marriage must be more important to you than anything else. (Hardcover, p. 127; paperback, p. 139)

IDOLS OF THE CULTURE. The biblical vision for marriage challenges the idols of every culture. It subverts the individualistic, transactional culture of the West, insisting that the good of the spouse and of the relationship must come before selfish individual benefits. On the other hand, biblical marriage also contradicts the heavily family-oriented traditional cultures. In those societies your spouse is explicitly or implicitly chosen for you by your parents, and your marriage stays largely under the authority of them while they live. But as Jesus says, quoting Genesis 2, we must "leave" our parents to unite with our spouse, a countercultural idea. We will explore what that means in the following days.

Reflection: Which of the two basic cultural views of marriage most affects you? What do you think it should mean that we "leave" our parents in order to be united to our spouse?

Thought for prayer: Ask God to show you ways in which the values of your family and culture may be affecting your marriage. Ask him also to ground you increasingly well in the Scriptures over the years so you see things more and more as he sees them.

August 13

Sometimes I heard a wife say, . . . "Pleasing [his parents] is far more important to him than pleasing me." Or I would hear a husband say, . . . "Being a mother is much more enjoyable to her than being a wife." I could also hear . . . "His (or her) career is what's really important. The career is the real spouse." . . . If your spouse does not feel that you are putting him or her first, then by definition, you aren't. And when they feel that way, your marriage is dying. (Hardcover, pp. 127–28; paperback, p. 140)

THE PRIORITY OF YOUR MARRIAGE. The quote above extends the Genesis 2 metaphor of "leaving" to mean establishing the priority of your marriage relationship. You must not put your job, your parents' wishes, or even your children ahead of your wife or husband. You must "leave" them for your spouse—who must take precedence in regard to time, emotional satisfaction, and loyalty over every other human relationship. For example, if your job gets the lion's share of your creative energy and intellectual engagement, leaving little for your marriage—then you have not "left" your career to be united to your spouse. What is the acid test to determine where you are on this? "If your spouse does not feel that you are putting him or her first . . . you aren't."

Reflection: Do you feel that the acid test is a fair one? Why or why not? Ask each other if you are passing the test.

Thought for prayer: Ask God for the self-control you need to give your spouse and marriage first place ahead of other pursuits and relationships that might provide a more immediate emotional satisfaction and payoff.

[Y]ou can also fail to leave your parents if you resent or hate them too much. . . . [Y]ou may say, "I can't marry him—he reminds me of my father." So what if a man resembles your father? You should be judging him on what he is *in toto* and how he relates to you. Don't let your bad relationship with your father control how you relate to your partner. You must leave it behind. (Hardcover, p. 128; paperback, pp. 140–41)

LEAVING FLAWED PARENTS. The first way to fail to "leave" your parents when you marry is to be residually angry at them. There are many bad parents in the world, and they can inflict long-term suffering and grief on their children. But if you resent them, they ironically will still be controlling you. There may be many things that would be good to do in your new family, but you refuse to do because they remind you of your parents or family of origin. It may seem counterintuitive to the modern mind, but the only way for the evil they may have done to you not to triumph over you is to forgive them from the heart (Mark 11:25) as God has forgiven you (Matthew 18:33).

Reflection: Think of ways your parents wronged you, by omission or commission. Have you forgiven them?

Thought for prayer: Ask God to at least begin the long work of forgiving your parents for where you feel they have failed you. Ask God for help in what can never be a quick and easy process.

Maybe your family's way of operating was wise in a particular regard, but you should only carry it into your new family if it makes sense to your spouse, too.... When you marry, you commit to becoming a new decision-making unit, and to developing new patterns and ways of doing things. But if you rigidly impose the patterns that you saw in your own family rather than creating your own new dynamic, you haven't left home yet. (Hardcover, pp. 128–29; paperback, p. 141)

LEAVING GOOD PARENTS. A second way that you can fail to "leave" your parents is if you make your marriage and your new family a virtual extension of the old one. If you are constantly insisting that your husband or wife act in such and such a way because "that's how my mother (or my father) did it," then you are creating a kind of straitjacket for your spouse. Instead of designing new patterns of behavior and relation, based on your marriage's particular needs, gifts, and aspirations, you are forcing your spouse and yourself into the mold of your family of origin. That is both unwise and unloving.

Reflection: List the ways that overattachment to your family's ways is (a) unwise and (b) unloving.

Thought for prayer: Ask God to help you put your spouse's needs and desires ahead of your parents' needs and desires. Ask him for the wisdom you need to devise new ways of life that fit you as a couple rather than simply holding to older, comfortable patterns.

Over-commitment to parents is one problem . . . over-commitment to children is even more of a problem. . . . [Y]our children do need you desperately. . . . [I]t is right to consider parenting a very high and important calling in life. [However,] if a marriage cools, it is natural to get your primary need for love and affection met through the parent-child relationship rather than the husband-wife relationship. But if you love your children more than your spouse, the entire family will be pulled out of joint and everyone will suffer. (Hardcover, p. 129; paperback, pp. 141–42)

APPROVAL. A third way you can fail to "leave" your parents is to look more to your parents or even to your children for approval and love than you do to your spouse. Your spouse is in the best position to see your weaknesses and tell you about them. Parents and children may offer more uninterrupted adulation and praise. So the temptation to look away from your spouse to parent or child relationships can be strong. But neither of these important relationships can offer you the spiritual friendship, the "iron sharpening iron" in truth and love, or, of course, the deep oneness of romantic love. If you put your spouse second in your life, all of those avenues of love and growth will be diminished.

Reflection: Which temptation—toward parents or children—are you more prone to? Are you giving in to either?

Thought for prayer: Pray together that you would be affectionate and affirming enough to each other daily and that you would not be tempted to look to best friends, parents, or children too much for approval and love.

August 17

"The best way for you to be a great mother to your daughter is by being a great wife to your husband. That is the main thing your daughter needs from you." (Hardcover, pp. 129–30; paperback, p. 142)

YOUR MARRIAGE AS A GIFT. Why is it true that one of the best ways to be a good parent is to be a great spouse? First, it creates a profound sense of security for your children. It gives them a confidence that the world is a safe place to live, and this has enormous implications for emotional and character development. Second, it provides a sustained, concrete, practical lesson for children on how the genders can relate to each other well despite their deep differences. This removes much of the fear and loathing that so many young people otherwise have toward the other gender or even their own. Finally, it will teach children the irreplaceably valuable skills of repenting and forgiving, without which no one can navigate life.

Reflection: Can you think of other reasons that a healthy marriage is the first ingredient in good parenting? What are the implications of this truth for your family?

Thought for prayer: Thank God for saving you from the penalty of all your sins through Jesus, and ask him to save you from the *power* of your sins, especially your failures as spouse and parent. Then ask that he would empower you to give your children the gift of an increasingly strong marriage.

Jesus asks for nothing that any spouse doesn't ask for. "Put me first," he says, "have no other pseudo-gods before me." Same with marriage. Marriage won't work unless you put your marriage and your spouse first, and you don't turn good things, like parents, children, career, hobbies, into pseudo-spouses. (Hardcover, p. 130; paperback, p. 143)

PROTECTION AGAINST ABUSE. No other *human* relationship should take precedence in time or emotion over your marital relationship. But your relationship with God must come first, taking priority even over your marriage. What does that mean? First, it means his love needs to be more grounding to you than any other so that you can bear the ups and downs of every human relationship, including your marriage. Second, "We must obey God rather than human beings" (Acts 5:29). We must not disobey clear commands of Scripture in order to please our spouse. That protects us against abuse, among other things. It is wrong to allow your spouse to sin against God by abusing you.

Reflection: What if a husband tells his wife that she may not go to church, despite Hebrews 10:24–25. What should she do in that situation? Discuss.

Thought for prayer: Ask God for both the discipline to mount a prayer life that draws closer to him and also for the courage to confront your spouse if he or she is contradicting God's Word in some way.

The reason [marriage] must have priority is because of the power of marriage. Marriage has the power to set the course of your life as a whole. If your marriage is strong, even if all the circumstances in your life around you are filled with trouble and weakness, it won't matter. You will be able to move out into the world in strength. (Hardcover, p. 131; paperback, p. 144)

THE POWER OF MARRIAGE: 1. How does this principle work? If "your marriage is strong," that is, if your spouse, next to God, is the most important source of love and wisdom and affirmation for you, then troubles and failures out in the rest of life will be discouraging but they won't touch your fundamental self-regard and identity. This is because it is rooted primarily in God and is reinforced powerfully, though secondarily, by your spouse. If, instead, you have largely drawn your self-worth, say, from your career or some other kind of achievement, then a job loss or major setback will inflict a wound that can't be healed. Don't make yourself vulnerable to that.

Reflection: Sometimes it takes "troubles and weakness" to drive you more into the arms of God and your spouse for strength and healing. Most Christians have had that experience to some degree. Can you remember any of yours?

Thought for prayer: Thank God for some specific failures or times of weakness that drove you to ground your identity more in his salvation. Ask him for the grace to continue that process until the end of your life.

However, if your marriage is weak, even if all the circumstances in your life around you are marked by success and strength, it won't matter. You will move out into the world in weakness. Marriage has that kind of power—the power to set the course of your whole life. It has that power because it was instituted by God. And because it has that unequalled power, it must have an unequalled, supreme priority. (Hardcover, p. 131; paperback, p. 144)

THE POWER OF MARRIAGE: 2. You may get a great deal of applause and affirmation from the world. You may be popular and successful. However, your spouse is the one person in the world who knows you the best, sees you most intimately, and knows more about your sensitivities and fears and flaws than anyone else. If *that* person is constantly showing you your sins without any concomitant words of grace and forgiveness, or of praise and appreciation, then that will be like a wound that can't be healed. Your heart will be like a bucket with a hole in the bottom. No matter how many accolades are poured into the top, they won't fill you with satisfaction.

Reflection: Look back over today's and yesterday's devotionals. Summarize in your own words the answer to this question: Why does marriage have the power to set the whole course of your life?

Thought for prayer: Ask God to help you to avoid ever criticizing your spouse without accompanying it with words of appreciation and grace. Ask forgiveness for the times when you failed to do that.

[T]he key to giving marriage that kind of priority is spiritual friendship. . . . Many Christians congratulate themselves that they have married another believer, but they look at their prospective spouse's faith as simply one more factor that makes him or her compatible, like common interests and hobbies. But that is not what spiritual friendship is. It is eagerly helping one another know, serve, love, and resemble God in deeper and deeper ways. (Hardcover, pp. 131–32; paperback, pp. 144–45)

SPIRITUAL FRIENDSHIP. We are using the term "spiritual friendship" along the lines of the description in the classic twelfth-century book by Aelred of Rievaulx.[93] Spiritual friendship has all the basics of any friendship. There must be sharing—especially of one's feelings (transparency), of one's time (being there for one another). But the common loves and interests that make for *spiritual* friendship have to do with Christian discipleship. Spiritual friends love the same Savior, share an experience of amazing grace, love the same Scripture, and hold each other accountable to grow into Christ (Hebrews 3:13) and into a profound knowledge of his Word (2 Peter 3:18). At the simplest level, that means that spouses who are spiritual friends study the Bible and Christian theology together, and pray together.

Reflection: Do you read the Bible and Christian literature together and discuss it? Do you pray together? Christian couples have good intentions here, but so often it doesn't happen. If you aren't doing this as much as you should, what are the barriers or reasons for it?

Thought for prayer: Don't just pray in general that you'll "be better at reading and praying together." Instead, identify the reasons you are not doing it and ask God to help you remove them.

[M]arriage is to make us "holy . . . without stain or wrinkle or any other blemish. . . ." ([Ephesians] verses 26–27). . . . Does this mean "marriage is not about being happy, it's about being holy?" [No,] that is too stark a contrast. . . . [R]eal happiness is on the far side of holiness, not the near side. Holiness gives us new desires, and brings old desires into line with one another. So if we want to be happy in marriage, we will accept that marriage is designed to make us holy. (Hardcover, pp. 132–33; paperback, pp. 145–46)

THE CHIEF END. The Westminster Shorter Catechism asks, "What is the chief end [purpose] of man?" and answers, "To glorify God and enjoy Him forever." Is it saying that if we glorify God by loving him and obeying him that it will result in great joy? Yes. But is it also saying that we only truly glorify God *if* we enjoy him? That too, because it is only if we are obeying him just for his sake, just for the greatness of our love of him, that we are truly obeying for his glory and not ours. Happiness and holiness have the same interdependent relationship in marriage. The more we grow spiritually, the more unselfish we can become, and the more we can find our happiness *in* the happiness and growth of our spouse.

Reflection: Have you seen holiness and happiness relate interdependently in your marriage?

Thought for prayer: Praise God for being so glorious and beautiful. Adore him until you feel something of his greatness. Then confess that you go to him too much for *things* instead of just more of God himself. Ask for a heart that seeks him like that.

[T]he in-love phase . . . includes the illusion that the beloved is perfect in every aspect that matters. . . . The in-love experience passes when the flaws in the other person come home to us. Things that seemed small and inconsequential now loom large. . . . And this presents us with the challenge of loving a person who, at the moment, seems in large part a stranger, not the person you remember marrying. . . . Just as distressing will be . . . that your spouse finds *you* a stranger and . . . [produces] a list of your serious shortcomings. (Hardcover, pp. 135–36; paperback, pp. 148–49)

DISENCHANTMENT. The disillusionment that can come early in marriage is so prevalent that the saying "the honeymoon is over" has entered our language. But it's no laughing matter. Having sex during dating can ramp up the romantic infatuation so that the realistic friendship never gets started by the time you are married. The disenchantment may therefore be intensified in the modern model of spouse as sexual partner/soul mate rather than the spouse as spiritual friend. Nevertheless, you ordinarily can't see all of the sins and flaws of your spouse before you are married, and so you should expect times of disenchantment in any case.

Reflection: Did you have a "honeymoon over" time of disappointment? How did you deal with it?

Thought for prayer: Ask God to help you not look to any thing or relationship—not even marriage—to give you the joy and love and peace that only he can give. Ask God to make himself real enough to your heart that you can worship only him.

What are the "tools" for this work? . . . As a divine institution, marriage has several inherent "powers" that we must accept and use—the power of truth, . . . of love, and . . . of grace. As we use each power in the life of our spouse, we will help him or her grow into a person who not only reflects the character of Christ, but who also can love us and help us . . . [especially] when we find it hard to love the semi-stranger to whom we are married. (Hardcover, pp. 136–37; paperback, pp. 149–50)

MARRIAGE WITHOUT GRUMBLING. So what do you do when you discover the "honeymoon over"? In the short term you need some good theology. Fundamental is the humility that comes from the gospel. When disillusioned with your spouse, think of your own flaws and weaknesses that did not put God off from loving you. Also remember the wise and good plan of God, who "makes all things work together for the good of those who love him" (Romans 8:28). You are in this marital relationship by God's design. Don't be like the children of Israel who, when the going got tough, thought God was out to hurt them and grumbled constantly against him (Exodus 14:10, 16:2, 17:3). Use these two "theological tools" to help you learn to love an imperfect person.

Reflection: Have you used the two theological resources mentioned here? Can you think of any others?

Thought for prayer: Meditate on the stories of Exodus 16 and 17. Then ask God to help you avoid a spirit of quiet grumbling in your heart against him. Ask, instead, for a sense of constant gratitude.

Marriage brings two human beings into closer contact than any other relationship can bring them. . . . The merged life of marriage brings you into the closest, most inescapable contact with another person possible. And that means not only that you see each other close up, but that you are forced to deal with the flaws and sins of one another. (Hardcover, pp. 137–38; paperback, p. 151)

A UNIQUE VANTAGE POINT. Your spouse has a unique vantage point on you—closer than anyone else, but still outside. Have you ever heard a recording of yourself and thought, "That doesn't sound like me at all"? You can't really hear how you sound on the outside to others, since you hear yourself to a large degree through your own body. In the same way we may know about our flaws in the abstract but be oblivious to their impact on others. Marriage prevents us from "screening out" things in our character that don't fit in with our self-image. For all these reasons our spouse may be able, in some ways, to see us better than we see ourselves.

Reflection: Make a short list of flaws that your spouse has pointed out that you did not see well on your own.

Thought for prayer: Thank God for the criticism you get from your spouse. And also ask for the ability to receive it gratefully from him or her.

What are the flaws that your spouse will see? You may be a fearful person, with a tendency toward great anxiety. You may be a proud person, with a tendency to be opinionated and selfish. You may be an inflexible person, with a tendency to be demanding and sulky if you don't get your way. You may be an abrasive or harsh person, who people tend to respect more than they love. (Hardcover, p. 138; paperback, pp. 151–52)

BLEMISHES: 1. It is easy to talk about "flaws" and "defects" in very general terms, but let's not do that. For the next three days let's consider the kinds of blemishes on our character that marriage can reveal. Here are four blemishes to consider: Are you what *you* call a "detail person" but what others call anxious and prone to worry too much? Are you selfish, so that you find sacrificing your rights for someone else to be very difficult? Are you what you call "very particular about things" but what others call rigid and prone to always insist on doing things in your favorite way? Are you what you call a "straight talker" but what others call brusque and sharp-tongued?

Reflection: Discuss these traits with your spouse. To what degree, if any, do they characterize you? Assuming they do not all apply, which ones do?

Thought for prayer: Ask God for inner peace rather than anxiety, for a spirit of liberality to overcome stinginess, for graciousness rather than rigidity, and for gentleness instead of abrasiveness.

You may be an undisciplined person, with a tendency to be unreliable and disorganized. You may be an oblivious person, who tends to be distracted, insensitive, and unaware of how you come across to others. You may be a perfectionist, with a tendency to be very judgmental and critical of others, and also to get down on yourself. You may be an impatient, irritable person, with a tendency to hold grudges or to lose your temper too often. (Hardcover, p. 138; paperback, p. 152)

BLEMISHES: 2. Let's continue our look at the kind of character faults and failings that our spouse may discover. Here are four more: Are you what *you* call a "laid-back" person but what others call unreliable and undisciplined? Are you what you call "a bit absentminded" but what others call thoughtless and insensitive to others' impressions and feelings? Are you what you call a "perfectionist" but what others call hypercritical? Are you what you call "impatient" but what others call short-tempered?

Reflection: Discuss these traits with your spouse. To what degree, if any, do they characterize you?

Thought for prayer: Ask God for self-control rather than an undisciplined spirit, for wise attentiveness rather than obliviousness, for a readiness to praise rather than a critical spirit, and for patience rather than constant frustration.

You may be a highly independent person, who does not like to be responsible for the needs of others, dislikes having to make joint decisions, and most definitely hates to ask for any help yourself. You may be a person who wants far too much to be liked, and so you . . . shade the truth . . . can't keep secrets, and . . . work far too hard to please everyone. You may be thrifty but at the same time miserly with money. (Hardcover, p. 138; paperback, p. 152)

BLEMISHES: 3. This is the final part of our list of character blemishes that create problems in marriage. Are you what *you* call a "self-reliant" person, but others see that you are proud and cannot ask for help? Are you what you call an "independent" person, but friends see that you hate it when others want a say in your decisions? Are you so eager to please that you shade the truth rather than upset them? Out of this need to please, do you have trouble saying no and so end up starting many more things than you can get done, which then fills you with self-pity and resentment? Are you what you call "thrifty" but what others call ungenerous?

Reflection: Discuss these traits with your spouse. To what degree, if any, do they characterize you?

Thought for prayer: Ask God to prevent you from being a proud, controlling, duplicitous person *or* a needy, guilt-ridden, self-pitying person.

[W]hile your character flaws may have created mild problems for other people, they will create major problems for your spouse and your marriage. For example, a tendency to hold grudges could be a problem within friendships, but within marriage it can kill the relationship. No one else is as inconvenienced and hurt by your flaws as your spouse is. And therefore your spouse becomes more keenly aware of what is wrong with you than anyone else ever has been. (Hardcover, p. 139; paperback, p. 153)

FEELING THE BLEMISHES. Your spouse may be wiser and more insightful than most people.[94] But that is not necessary for him or her to know your faults better than anyone else, including you. A spouse is uniquely positioned to see into our hearts. While others may have seen your tendency to self-pity or resentment, your spouse not only sees it but feels it. Why? Because in marriage our sins are so often against our spouses. If you have a tendency to hold grudges, your spouse will not only learn about it, she or he will experience it personally. Even when we stay angry at someone else, it indirectly effects our spouses because it saps us of joy at home. Without seeking it, your spouse is the world's expert on how you need to change.

Reflection: Talk candidly with your spouse about the ways in which your sins, even when not directed at him or her, still indirectly affect and hurt.

Thought for prayer: In one another's presence, ask God's forgiveness and your spouse's forgiveness for all the ways your blemishes of character have hurt him or her and grieved God. Thank God for assured forgiveness in Jesus Christ.

[I]t isn't ultimately your spouse who is exposing the sinfulness of your heart—it's marriage itself. . . . Marriage shows you a realistic, unflattering picture of who you are and then takes you by the scruff of the neck and forces you to pay attention it. This may sound discouraging, but it is really the road to liberation. Counselors will rightly tell you that the only flaws that can enslave you are the ones that you are blind to. (Hardcover, p. 140; paperback, p. 154)

ROAD TO LIBERATION. One of the greatest temptations in marriage is this—we blame our spouse for the conflicts rather than marriage itself. When two naturally self-centered persons are brought into the closest daily contact with someone, it inevitably brings about clashes of will. Even living with parents or children is less demanding, since they are not on the same plane—there is a hierarchy of authority. Nothing gives another human being a clearer sight of your inner life more than does marriage. Marriage inherently brings out and shows the worst in you. Don't blame the spouse—it's the marriage. But the only way to grow and change your flaws requires this kind of hard-won self-knowledge. So the conflicts of marriage are the road to liberation.

Reflection: Can you think of other reasons or ways that marriage brings out and reveals our dark sides?

Thoughts for prayer: First, ask God to help you to be grateful for the conflicts with and criticisms from your spouse. Then, relying on his help, thank him for them, and ask his aid in learning and growing through them.

Marriage brings out the worst in you. It doesn't create your weaknesses (though you may blame your spouse for your blow-ups)—it reveals them. This is not a bad thing, though. . . . [No one says,] "Oh, I wish the doctor had never found that lump" [of cancer, for] . . . the consequences of being "spared all the trouble" would have been, in the end, far more deadly, far more trouble, than finding and treating the cancer while it was small and confined. (Hardcover, pp. 139–40; paperback, pp. 153–54)

DON'T FEAR MARRIAGE. "In my marriage we are always fighting." That sounds bad and certainly marriage shouldn't be all conflict. But would you say, "Doctors' examinations kept revealing things that needed treatment—so I stopped going"? That is certainly unpleasant, but no, you wouldn't say that. In the same way, marriage could be thought of as God's way to give you a spiritual examination in order to see what needs to be treated. Since many people get married in the earlier part of their lives, these sins are less entrenched and may be easier to address. Don't fear or resent marriage for its power to show you where you are "sick"!

Reflection: Think of some recent or ongoing conflict with your spouse. How does it help to think of this as a kind of "exam," revealing something in your heart and character that needs to be treated?

Thoughts for prayer: Meditate on 1 John 4:18, which teaches that the opposite of love is not hate but fear. Ask God to help you to sense his love for you and your spouse's love for you so that you don't fear the difficulties of marriage.

September 1

"I have the right to do anything," you say—but not everything is benefi-cial. "I have the right to do anything"—but I will not be mastered by anything. . . . Now for the matters you wrote about: "It is good for a man not to have sexual relations with a woman." (1 Corinthians 6:12; 7:1)

SEX AND THE CULTURE. Corinth offered a smorgasbord of sexual practices of all sorts.[95] Some Christians there responded that since they were saved by grace, what they did sexually didn't matter to God. "I have the right to do anything," they are quoted as saying. Another party taught, on the contrary, that sexual relations are never good and should be avoided altogether (1 Corinthians 7:1). In his letter Paul steered a middle course between these extremes, but he was not merely splitting the dif-ference.[96] Both approaches let the culture rather than the gospel shape sexual behavior. Even the seemingly conservative approach assumed that the culture's definition of sex—that it is a mere physical appetite and release—was the true one.[97] It is the great-est challenge, in any cultural moment, to let biblical theology shape our vision and practice of sex.

Reflection: In what specific ways has your attitude toward sex been more influenced by the culture's practices than by biblical teaching?

Prayer: Lord—my friends, my culture, and even my body are all, as it were, "speaking" to me about sex. How hard it is to listen to your Word and what the gospel says about it. Give me ears to hear you. Amen.

September 2

"I have the right to do anything," you say—but not everything is beneficial. (1 Corinthians 6:12a)

SELFISH SEX. Some Christians thought they were free to have sex as they wished. Our culture is even more intensely committed to personal freedom in sex. "What I do in the privacy of my bedroom is my business" is nearly a national motto! But Paul says sex must be *beneficial*, a word that means to build up others and especially to seek the common good (cf. 1 Corinthians 12:7).[98] Wendell Berry argues that communities can only happen when people bind themselves to each other, voluntarily giving up much freedom. He says sex is a "nurturing discipline" or glue that binds two people together to provide long-term stability in a relationship that not only helps children to thrive, but also affects the larger community's need for families. So our use of sex *is* other people's business. We can use it to create community or simply for self-fulfillment.[99]

Reflection: Think of all the ways that how you have sex *does* in fact have an effect on the society in which you live, and therefore is not strictly your business alone.

Prayer: Lord, I thank you for this reminder that I should not be thinking about sex preoccupied with my needs and what brings me pleasure, but how our love-making can build up my spouse. If you give us *both* this same mind, how our marriage will sing! Amen.

"I have the right to do anything"—but I will not be mastered by anything. (1 Corinthians 6:12b)

ENSLAVING SEX. Paul gives a second reason we are not free to have sex with whomever we wish. He says literally, "I have the power to do to anything, but I won't let anything have power over me."[100] How can sex put us under its power? There are so many ways. We can become sexually intoxicated by someone of flawed character who leads us into an unwise relationship. We can have sex with different people out of a need for approval or as a way of proving ourselves. Having sex outside of marriage can weaken its natural "commitment apparatus" so that sex no longer enables us to give ourselves as deeply to someone (see March 5). All these quite common ways of having sex are hardening, disempowering, and enslaving.

Reflection: Make your own list of the ways that sex can master you if you think that it is merely something you are doing for your own enjoyment.

Prayer: Lord, help me see the things that spiritually enslave me even as they pose as empowerment. Remind me daily that only faithful service to you through your Word is perfect freedom.[101] Amen.

September 4

> You say, "Food for the stomach and the stomach for food, and God will destroy them both." The body, however, is not meant for sexual immorality but for the Lord, and the Lord for the body. By his power God raised the Lord from the dead, and he will raise us also. (1 Corinthians 6:13–14)

THE IMPORTANCE OF THE BODY. The Greeks and Romans believed that sex, like eating, was not a matter of morality but only an appetite that had to be satiated. Food and body were temporary, unlike the soul ("God will destroy them both") and so were of no spiritual consequence. Paul differs strongly. He argues that the body is *not* temporary—it will be redeemed and resurrected. And so what we do with our body is all-important. Our body belongs to the Lord and, as we will see in the next two days, how we love with it must align with how God loves.[102] Paul's teaching is relevant in our culture, which has in some measure reverted to this older view.

Reflection: Modern culture thinks that, because of our more strict sexual ethic, Christians have a "lower" view of the human body. In your own words, give a counterargument.

Prayer: Lord, I praise you that you promise to redeem not just our souls but our bodies, too. Above all I thank you, Lord Jesus, for taking a body in order to save us. For all these reasons, I want to honor you with my body. Help me to do that. Amen.

Do you not know that your bodies are members of Christ himself? Shall I then take the members of Christ and unite them with a prostitute? Never! Do you not know that he who unites himself with a prostitute is one with her in body? For it is said, "The two will become one flesh." But he who unites himself with the Lord is one with him in spirit. (1 Corinthians 6:15–17)

THE MEANING OF THE BODY. Ancient cultures saw the body as a discardable container of the soul. Christianity taught, on the contrary, that it was the soul's integral expression, a crucial part of who we are, and so to fit your bodies together physically should always be part of uniting your lives in every aspect. In 1 Corinthians 6 Paul is saying that it is a monstrous incongruity to activate the "one flesh" apparatus of sex and then not follow through by giving everything else. "Paul . . . here displays a psychological insight into human sexuality which is altogether exceptional by first-century standards . . . he insists that it is an act which . . . engages and expresses the whole personality in such a way as to constitute a unique mode of self-disclosure and self-commitment." [103]

Reflection: Modern culture has reverted to the ancient belief that the body is the prison house of the soul and not its integral expression. What are other implications of this view for our understanding of sex and gender?

Prayer: Lord, in this sinful world our bodies are flawed, subject to weakness, and nothing like what they will be in the resurrection. Help me to see my body as the a great gift from you, and help me to honor you in all the ways I treat it and use it. Amen.

September 6

Do you not know that your bodies are members of Christ himself? Shall I then take the members of Christ and unite them with a prostitute? Never! Do you not know that he who unites himself with a prostitute is one with her in body? For it is said, "The two will become one flesh." . . . Do you not know that your body is a temple of the Holy Spirit, who is in you, whom you have received from God? (1 Corinthians 6:15–16, 19)

THE SIGNPOST OF SEX. While Christianity's sex ethic seemed more restrictive, its underlying vision was infinitely higher. Paul taught it was "something of transcendent significance. The body is a temple, a site of sacred communication. The [ancients] urged self-control, on the grounds that physical pleasure was . . . distraction from the virtuous life. Paul does so because sex implicates us in something with sacred significance."[104] In Christ God has given himself to us and we to him so wholly that even our body parts are one with him. And so when we give ourselves in body to another human being, it must imitate God's saving love in an exclusive, permanent, whole-life union. Sex anticipates the unimaginable bliss of full union with the Lord in love.[105]

Reflection: In our culture, Christianity's sex ethic again seems too restrictive and many of your friends certainly think so. How can you communicate to them and your children not just the sex ethic but also the underlying vision?

Prayer: Lord, help us to remember, amidst the joy and even playfulness of sex, its solemn importance and the great thing of which it is but a foretaste. And let that only enhance our joy. Amen.

Flee from sexual immorality. (1 Corinthians 6:18)

PORNEIA. The Greek word *porneia* is translated "sexual immorality." Commonly it meant prostitution, but in the Greek Old Testament it was used to refer to spiritual adultery, the worship of other gods besides the Lord. Paul took it and filled it with distinctively Christian content. It meant any sexuality that did not reflect the divine, saving love, one that brought about union between two deeply different beings—God and humanity—and one that brought about an exclusive, permanent relationship. The word *porneia*, then, meant that any sex outside a covenant of marriage between a man and a woman was a "religious betrayal" of God.[106] Both in their sexual practices and in their view of the deep significance of sex (see yesterday's devotional) were one of the main ways in which Christians differed from those around them.[107]

Reflection: For the early Christians sex was a witness to the world, signifying care and community rather than glamour, performance, and self-fulfillment. Could it be that way again? Discuss together.

Prayer: Lord, thank for you for what you've taught us this week. Let our sexual life together be a witness to your character and love, particularly for our friends and our children. Amen.

[It's typical to say,] "I need to find someone better than this." But . . . [in] Christian marriage . . . the "someone better" you can think of [is] the future version of the same person to whom you are already married. . . . (Hardcover, p. 144; paperback p. 159) It will help a great deal to say, "I hate it when he does that, but that is not truly *him*. That is not permanent." (Hardcover, p. 143; paperback, p. 158)

NO TURNING BACK. When we argue with our spouse over certain issues it can be tempting to think that, if we had a better, more thoughtful, more insightful, kinder, [fill in the blank] spouse, we would not be fighting. But there are two problems with that thinking. First, if it is marriage itself that reveals our dark side, then another spouse will not eliminate the conflicts. If anything, changing spouses may mean starting all over on the same issues. So make progress and change now. Second, while you might possibly reap benefits from a "better" spouse, assume that your improved spouse is the future version of your current one. Marriage is about a journey together toward the better selves God is making us. Don't turn back.

Reflection: Think of an issue that causes periodic, repeated conflicts. Now, together, think of one significant change *both* of you could make that might lessen or eliminate the fights.

Thought for prayer: Remember Abraham, who was given a promise of a family that did not come true for decades, yet he remained faithful in his confidence that it would be fulfilled. Ask God for the same patience and pray that both of you will grow into the people he wants you to be.

You come into marriage with a self-image, an assessment of your worth. It is the sign of many verdicts passed upon you over the years by a great variety of people . . . [who have] called you good and bad, worthy and unworthy, promising and hopeless. . . . If it were made visible it might look something like the Frankenstein monster, with many disparate parts. However, perhaps the most damaging statements that have ever been said about us are those things we have said and do say about ourselves to ourselves. (Hardcover, pp. 146–47; paperback, p. 162)

A WORD FROM OUTSIDE. Our culture tells us to decide who we want to be, to "live our own truth," and to affirm and validate ourselves. "Don't care what anyone else thinks," we are told. But that is impossible. We are irreducibly relational creatures, and we need a word of affirmation from outside. But when we look for it, we discover that people can't agree on even basic definitions of good and evil. Some people will praise you and others condemn or mock you. While we quickly forget the praise, the criticism tends to stick. Our self-image is, therefore, a patchwork of internalized, contradictory assessments from different people over the years. Whose view of us gets to overrule everyone else's?

Reflection: Think of the various "layers" of your self-image—the layer put there by parents and siblings, by friends, by teachers and coaches, by the popular culture and media, by politics, by your faith. Which of these layers is the most dominant?

Thought for prayer: Meditate on Psalm 86:11: "Unite my heart to fear your name."[108] Then ask God to heal and unite the contradictory feelings you have about yourself, bringing them together in the gospel, which tells you that you *are* a great sinner but also a loved child.

Marriage puts into your spouse's hand a massive power to reprogram your own self-appreciation. He or she can overturn anything previously said about you, to a great degree redeeming the past . . . [and healing] you of many of the deepest wounds. Why? If all the world says you are ugly, but your spouse says you are beautiful, you feel beautiful. To paraphrase a passage of Scripture, your heart may condemn you, but your spouse's opinion is greater than your heart. (Hardcover, p. 147; paperback, p. 163)

THE ULTIMATE SOLUTION. Our self-image is the aggregation of many "verdicts" that have been passed on to us over the years. Some were good and some were bad and your heart is deeply divided over which verdicts to believe and how to assess yourself. The ultimate solution to this identity problem is the gospel. Christ covers all your sins and gives a final verdict of "not guilty—and fully loved, in me" (cf. Galatians 3:10–14; Romans 8:1). But the wonderful fact is that a good spouse can provide a foreshadowing and a representation of that amazing love. He or she can say, "I see all your sins but I love you fully, forever." As a spouse, do you see the power for good that you have?

Reflection: Recall a time in which your spouse affirmed you and lifted you up despite the counterevidence of your flaws and failures.

Thought for prayer: Meditate on John 19:30 (Jesus's cry, "It is finished!") and Romans 8:1: "There is now no condemnation for those who are in Christ Jesus." In light of these promises, praise God, thank him, and confess ways you fail to accept these truths.

[B]ecause marriage . . . brings you into the closest possible contact, a positive assessment by your spouse has ultimate credibility. If someone I know a little comes up to me and says, "You are one of the kindest men I know," I will certainly feel complimented and pleased. But . . . he doesn't really know me. . . . But if my wife, after years of living with me, says, "You are one of the kindest men I know," . . . [t]hat affirmation is profoundly comforting . . . [b]ecause she knows me better than anyone. (Hardcover, p. 148; paperback, pp. 163–64)

THE PENULTIMATE SOLUTION. A spouse's uniquely intimate knowledge can and often does lead to painful critique and conflict. But when he or she, despite seeing all that is wrong with you, nevertheless praises and affirms you, the effect is powerful. Criticism always stays with us longer than commendations. Why? All human beings have a primordial sense that we are not what we should be (cf. Genesis 3:7). It is not easy to overcome that baseline sense of shame. Yet spouses can do it, because when they compliment you, they do it with full knowledge of your flaws. When the thoughtful, sincere praise comes, deep down you can't help but think something like, "If *she* says that, I guess it's true."

Reflection: Think of other reasons that the testimony of your spouse to your gifts and growth is so formative and powerful.

Thought for prayer: In each other's presence, thank God for the ways that the affirmation of the other has comforted you deeply, and ask God for the ability to use well and wisely your power to bless the other.

September 12

And if, over the years, you have grown to love and admire your spouse more and more, then his or her praise will get more and more strengthening and healing. As Faramir says to Sam Gamgee in *The Lord of the Rings: The Two Towers*: "The praise of the praiseworthy is above all rewards." To be highly esteemed by someone you highly esteem is the greatest thing in the world. (Hardcover, p. 148; paperback, p. 164)

ADORED BY THE ADORED. One reason that we find spouses' affirmation so powerful is that they know us. Here is a second reason: a compliment from an admirable person is always more uplifting than approval from a person you don't respect. You marry a person that you admire, and so right from the start his or her approval means a lot. But as the years go by, if you both grow in grace and Christlike character and you come to admire and adore your spouse more and more, then the effect of any praise from the other becomes transformative. To be adored by someone you adore is like heaven. And that *is* what heaven will be like (1 John 3:2).

Reflection: Discuss with your spouse the place in your life where you need his or her encouragement and affirmation more.

Thought for reflection: Realizing that your power to bless and build up your spouse depends in part on his or her respect for *your* growth and character, ask God to help you grow in grace (2 Peter 3:18) so your ability to affirm and bless your spouse will have the greatest effect.

In Christ, God sees us as righteous, holy, and beautiful (2 Corinthians 5:21). . . . Jesus has the ability to overcome everything anyone has ever said about or to you. . . . Sometimes your spouse points you directly to Jesus's love. Sometimes your spouse's affirmation . . . stimulates us to more fully believe and accept the love we have in Christ. So, more than any other human relationship, marriage has a unique power to heal all hurts and convince us of our own distinctive beauty and worth. (Hardcover, p. 149; paperback, pp. 164–65)

THE POETRY OF THE HEART. Certainly the primary relationship of love we need is with God. But remember that though Adam was sinless, there was an emptiness that a relationship with God alone could not satisfy—a need for human love that the Creator had put into him. When Adam looks at Eve for the first time, he says, in the first poetry in the Bible: "This is now bone of my bones and flesh of my flesh" (Genesis 2:23). This was at the same time a covenant commitment as well as an explosive outburst of lyrical joy for her.[109] The power of our spouse to give us a Christlike approval and healing love is vividly foreshadowed here. Know the power you have to build up your partner.

Reflection: Discuss with your spouse an additional place in your life (see yesterday's devotional) where you need his or her encouragement and affirmation more.

Thought for prayer: Ask God to keep you from being too busy, tired, and distracted to accomplish one of your main callings in life—the edification of your spouse in love. Ask him or her to help you keep this in the forefront of your mind and attention.

A radio signal may be sent out on one frequency, but the radio receiver . . . is tuned to another. . . . [So] a husband may be . . . very sensual and romantic toward his wife, but that might not be where her love receiver is tuned. He doesn't listen sympathetically to her when she wants to talk about the things that discourage her. . . . [S]he tells her husband, "I don't feel you love me!" He retorts, "But I do love you!" Why . . . ? He is sending his love over a channel to which she is not tuned. (Hardcover, p. 153; paperback, p. 169)

LOVE LANGUAGES: 1. We have seen that the love and affirmation of your spouse can be healing and transformative. But how do you communicate love to your spouse? Let's introduce the concept of "love channels" or "love languages." The idea is that you think you are conveying love and affirmation to your spouse, but you may be doing so in a way that can't be heard, because it is not emotionally valuable to him or her. The metaphor of a radio is helpful. You may be sending love on one channel but your partner doesn't listen to that channel. Learning our spouse's love languages is crucial. It requires coming to understand much about his or her temperament, history, and identity.

Reflection: Before doing any more reading or study, answer this very general question: In what ways can you express love in a way that pleases your spouse the most?

Thought for prayer: Meditate on Proverbs 27:14, that tells us our efforts to bless—if poorly expressed—can be "counted . . . as a curse." Ask God for wisdom, not just good intentions, for how to love your spouse skillfully.

There are many different ways to express love. You can buy a present, say, "I love you" out loud, give a compliment, be romantic and tender physically, abide by your loved one's wishes, and spend time in focused attention. That's just the beginning of the list. . . . The Greeks had . . . affection (*storge*), love between friends (*philos*), erotic love (*eros*), and service (*agape*). . . . All forms of love are necessary, and none are to be ignored, but all of us find some forms of love to be more emotionally valuable to us. (Hardcover, p. 153; paperback, p. 170)

LOVE LANGUAGES: 2. Let's look at the first of the four broad categories of love languages. "Affection" includes what has often been called edifying or blessing the other. To do this means, on the one hand, eliminating many practices that undermine your spouse. Do you use cutting humor? Do you use sarcasm and belittling words when making points? Do you criticize him or her in front of others? Are you far less courteous in little things toward your spouse than you are toward a guest in your home? Do you brighten up for others and engage, but shuffle around in an emotionally unresponsive, distracted way when you are home with just your partner? This is a list of *dis*affecting behaviors and attitudes. Eliminate them.

Reflection: Evaluate yourself and each other according to the list above.

Thought for prayer: Unaffectionate behavior comes from a heart hardened with self-pity and resentment. Ask God for a heart softened so you are neither sharp-tongued nor emotionally distant in your daily dealings with your spouse.

You could, like Kathy and I, have an intractable conflict over child-care responsibilities. But it could be that the husband is thinking (as I did), "If you love me like my mother loved my father, you'd not ask me to change diapers," and the wife could be thinking (as Kathy did), "If you love me like my father loved my mother, you'd volunteer." Instead of thinking about the other person, "He (she) is so selfish," each should think, "He (she) is feeling particularly unloved." (Hardcover, p. 155; paperback, pp. 171–72)

LOVE LANGUAGES: 3. Let's look at the positive side of showing affection. To do that well, think of everyday behavior or traits you respect in your spouse. Do you identify them and speak of them? Then, standing back, think of the work and accomplishments of your spouse. Do you identify them and speak of them? Study your partner, looking for the areas where your spouse "feels a lack" and think of ways to encourage him or her specifically in those areas.[110] Finally, take thought for how to create loving climates, creatively arranging for situations in which focused attention is easier. Walks, scenic drives, and eating out (or cooking for one another) are only a few examples. These are the best settings in which your work of edifying and blessing can really sink in.

Reflection: Evaluate yourself and each other according to the list above.

Thought for prayer: Ask God to give you constant remembrances of his mercy and grace to you, so you can be regularly and instinctively kind and warm to your spouse.

[R]ealize you have a "filter" on. You tend to only "hear" certain kinds of love language. For example, your spouse may be working hard to provide you with material things, but you wish he were more verbal. There is a tendency to say, "He doesn't love me!" because he is not communicating love in your most valuable language. Take off your filter and recognize the love your spouse is giving you. (Hardcover, p. 154; paperback, p. 171)

GIVING, HELPING, LISTENING, TALKING. Judson Swihart wrote a book called *How Do You Say "I Love You"?* that provided a number of specific ways to show love that stretched over all four categories.[111] We've teased these out into twelve specific ways to show love. We will look at four each day. Some say "love me . . ." (1) by giving me things, from thoughtful gifts to meeting my material needs and wants; (2) by helping me, by giving priority to helping me accomplish my responsibilities; (3) by listening to me with focused attention when I want to talk, by being understanding; (4) by talking to me and letting me know what you are really thinking and feeling—your joys, hopes, worries, and fears.

Reflection: Which of these four love languages are the most emotionally valuable to you? Before asking—which do you think is the most valuable to your spouse? Now compare your answers.

Thought for prayer: Ask God that over these three days that you and your spouse can get more clarity about how to communicate love to each other in ways that fit your particular needs.

September 18

Learn the primary languages of your spouse and send love over those channels, not over the channels you prefer for yourself. We tend to give love through the channels in which we like to receive it. (Hardcover, p. 155; paperback, p. 172)

TOUCHING, LIKING, POINTING, STANDING. Consider the following kinds of love languages. Some say "love me . . ." (5) by being physically warm, tender, affectionate and playful, and not just when you are interested in sex; (6) by telling me what you like about me, affirming my strengths, helping me find my gifts; (7) by telling me where I need to grow—in a context of affirmation—and pointing out where I need to change; (8) by standing up for me in front of others, and always being on the same side when we are dealing with others, including our children.

Reflection: Which of these four love languages are the most emotionally valuable to you? Before asking—which do you think is the most valuable to your spouse? Now compare your answers.

Thought for prayer: Ask God for the continual attentiveness it takes to discern the particular ways that your spouse both needs and wants love expressed to him or her.

September 19

Remember that improper love languages can be "heard in reverse." For example, if you give material gifts to a person who wants some other form, she may say, "You are trying to buy my love!" (Hardcover, p. 155; paperback, p. 172)

CHANGING, SHARING, PRAYING, AND SPACE. Finally, consider these love languages. Some say "love me . . ." (9) by volunteering to change your habits, attitudes, and other things that bother me, by being open to my criticism; (10) by spending time with me doing and sharing activities that I like, by sharing each other's worlds and growing together intellectually and emotionally; (11) by praying and reading the Bible and talking about our spiritual lives together; (12) by giving me freedom or privacy to pursue my interests, by not being too smothering and possessive.

Reflection: Which of these four love languages are the most emotionally valuable to you? Before asking—which do you think is the most valuable to your spouse? Now compare your answers.

Thought for prayer: Ask God for the wisdom to know the differences and balances—between being too smothering or too detached, between being only affirming or only critical, between only listening or only talking. Ask for the ability to love skillfully and well.

Never abuse the primary love language. Never withhold it to hurt the other, for the hurt will go deep. A man who greatly values getting respect from his wife in public will not be able to take it when she mocks him in front of their friends. A woman who needs lots of verbal affirmation will be devastated by the silent treatment. (Hardcover, p. 155; paperback, p. 172)

THE ABUSE OF THE LANGUAGES. If we are angry with our spouse we may instinctively get back at them by withholding a love language we know is valuable to them or even by giving them the very opposite behavior as a way of hurting them. But wounds inflicted in this way can be hard to heal. God did not do that to us. When the Israelites complained that they could not bear listening to his voice on Mount Sinai directly, God sent his word through a human prophet (Deuteronomy 18:15–19). God adapted his communication to our capacities. Jesus himself is God's way of giving us love in a form to which we could relate (John 1:14). So love your spouse as God in Christ has loved you.

Reflection: Think of a time in which you were tempted to use your spouse's love language against him or her.

Thought for prayer: In God's presence, think of how he did not merely send us a prophet to tell us about his love, but he gave us his Son to embody it and his Spirit to feel it, so we could know his love. Ask God to help you love your spouse in the same way.

September 21

> [T]here's the Great Problem of marriage. The one person in the whole world who holds your heart in your hand, whose approval and affirmation you most long for and need—is the one who is hurt more deeply by your sins than anyone else on the planet. . . . When we see how devastating truth-telling . . . can be . . . [w]e may then decide that our job is to . . . shut up [and] . . . stuff and hide what we really think and feel. We exercise . . . love, but not . . . truth. (Hardcover, pp. 162–63; paperback, pp. 180–81)

THE NEED FOR GRACE. We have been looking at two "powers" of marriage: truth and love. But these two powers create a tension. Our spouses, as we have seen, do not merely learn the truth about our sin in an abstract way. We sin against our spouses and we hurt them. How will they, in spite of that, be enabled to use their power to love and edify? How can you affirm someone whose sins you see so painfully well? We may choose to only tell the truth or only be loving—but it takes both to bring about change. The powers of truth and love will only work together if they are joined by a third—the power of grace and forgiveness.

Reflection: It is difficult to be truthful and loving at the same time. We tend to choose one over the other. Which one do you tend to choose?

Thought for prayer: Thank the Lord that he is not merely a demanding and just God or one of indiscriminate beneficence. Thank him for the grace of the Cross, which reveals how he can both be infinitely just to punish sins and infinitely merciful to forgive sins at the same time.

Truth without love ruins the oneness, and love without truth gives the illusion of unity but actually stops the journey and the growth. The solution is grace. The experience of Jesus's grace makes it possible to practice the two most important skills in marriage: forgiveness and repentance. Only if we are very good at forgiving and very good at repenting can truth and love be kept together. . . . Spouses either stay away from the truth . . . or else they attack one another [with it]. (Hardcover, pp. 163–64; paperback, p. 182)

UNITING TRUTH AND LOVE. When a couple learns the moves of grace—to both repent and forgive—it unites the other two powers—of truth and love—in such a way that it leads to personal growth for all. To repent is to *admit* the truth *because* you are confident that in love your spouse will forgive you. If you weren't assured of your spouse's love, you couldn't admit the truth, you would merely justify and defend yourself. To forgive is to *insist* on truth (not making excuses for your spouse) *because* you love them too much to let them continue in their sin. In these and many other ways, repenting and forgiveness make truth and love interdependent, not contradictory.

Reflection: "Loving without telling the truth is not really love. Truth-telling without love is not really conveying the truth." Defend these two statements.

Thought for prayer: In each other's presence, thank God for times in which you have been able to extend grace to each other through repentance and forgiveness, and ask for increasing abilities and opportunities to do the same.

September 23

The Bible says we are supposed to forgive people and *then* go and confront them . . . almost always because . . . *we confront people who have
wronged us as a way of paying them back . . .* getting revenge. . . . The
person you are confronting knows you are doing payback and he or
she will either be devastated or infuriated—or both. You are not really
telling the truth for [truth's sake or for] their sake; you are telling it for
your sake. (Hardcover, p. 164; paperback, p. 183)

"TRUTH" WITHOUT LOVE. Truth-telling without love dishonors the truth. We say we are only telling our spouse the truth
when we are really trying to punish them. They made you feel
bad and you want to make them feel bad, using the truth as a
club. In such cases the so-called "truth" is usually unbalanced,
one-sided, and crafted to hurt. The response to truth-without-
love is seldom repentance and seeing the truth clearly. The other
person will either be decimated or angered, because they will
know you are not so much committed to truth as to payback. If
you really care about people realizing the truth, you will convey
it in love so it is possible for them to do so.

Reflection: When was the last time you used truth-without-love
on each other?

Thought for prayer: Meditate on Galatians 6:1, that you should
only correct someone if they are, first, "caught" in a sin, doing it
repeatedly, and second, if you can do it gently and humbly. Now
ask God for the ability to only ever criticize along these lines.

[W]ithout . . . the power of forgiving grace in your life—you will use the truth to hurt [and punish when you are wronged]. The other person [then] will either attack you back or withdraw. Your marriage will go either into a truth-without-love mode, with constant fighting, or a shallow love-without-truth mode, in which both partners simply avoid the underlying problems. (Hardcover, pp. 164–65; paperback, p. 183)

"LOVE" WITHOUT TRUTH. Just as truth without love doesn't really honor truth, so love without truth isn't really love. Proverbs 13:24 says that if parents fail to discipline a wayward son, they "hate" him. If you allow a child to grow up lying, stealing, and abusing others, it is the most unloving thing you can do. Many parents fail to discipline their children because, they say, they "love" them too much to make them unhappy. The reality is that you want to avoid the experience of your children's displeasure more than you want their growth and their good. It's the same in marriage as in parenting. To shrink from truth-telling because it will be painful for you is selfishness, not love.

Reflection: When was the last time you indulged in love-without-truth-telling? What were you avoiding?

Thought for prayer: Thank God for his transforming love for you, how his love refuses to allow you to acquiesce in your flaws and sins, but insists on your growth. Remember how painful it was for Christ to love you. Now ask God for the courage to love others and your spouse like that.

This does not mean you cannot express anger. In fact, if you never express anger, your truth-telling probably won't sink in. But forgiving grace must always be present, and if it is, it will, like salt in meat, keep the anger from going bad. Then truth and love can live together because, beneath them both, you have forgiven your spouse as Christ forgave you. (Hardcover, p. 165; paperback, p. 184)

REPENTING. Forgiveness (see tomorrow's devotional) is far easier to give if there is repentance. How do you repent? First, say what you think you have done wrong. Second, ask your spouse to add to your list and then listen receptively to the criticism you've invited. Don't be too quick to defend or explain yourself. Show respect for your spouse's concerns. Third, ask forgiveness and at the same time offer a concrete plan for change that avoids the same thing happening again (cf. Luke 3:7–14). If you feel some of your spouse's complaints are unjustified, wait until you've freely confessed the justified ones, and then humbly offer your perspective. This is all hard to do, so pray silently and assume God is speaking to you through this whole process.

Reflection: When was the last time you repented and asked forgiveness from your spouse? Look at the list above and evaluate how well you did this.

Thought for prayer: Confess to Jesus that though he humbled himself without the obligation to do so, when we humble ourselves and repent, we *do* have an obligation—yet we find it tremendously hard. Cry out for help to become a better repenter.

September 26

What does it take to know the power of grace? First it takes humility. If you have trouble forgiving someone, it is at least partly because deep in your heart you are thinking, "*I* would never do anything like *that*!" As long as you feel superior to someone, feel like you are a much better kind of person, you will find it very hard if not impossible to forgive . . . [so] truth will eat up love. (Hardcover, p. 165; paperback, p. 184)

FORGIVING. How do you forgive someone? First, forgive your spouse in your heart even before you talk to them (Mark 11:25). That way you avoid what we have discussed—using the truth to pay back rather than to lovingly correct. Second, go and say what was done wrong, but be open to the possibility that you aren't seeing things clearly. Say something like: "It looks to me like you did this _____ and it affected me like this _____. Correct me if I'm wrong." Attack the problem, not the person. If your spouse apologizes, express forgiveness; if not, keep talking. Finally, remember that forgiveness is granted before it's felt. Forgiveness is a promise not to keep bringing up the past to your spouse, to others, or to yourself.

Reflection: When was the last time you confronted and offered forgiveness to your spouse? Look at the list above and evaluate how well you did this.

Thought for prayer: Meditate on Colossians 3:12–13. Confess your lack of "compassion, kindness, humility, gentleness and patience" in light of how "the Lord forgave you." Ask for a forgiving heart.

But speaking the truth in love requires . . . also "emotional wealth," a fundamental inner joy and confidence. If you are very down on yourself . . . then it may be far too important for you to have your spouse always pleased with you. You will not be able . . . to criticize your spouse or [receive criticism]. . . . You will stay resentful but will hide it. . . . In this case, we have love eating up truth. (Hardcover, pp. 165–66; paperback, p. 184)

THE GOSPEL AND FORGIVENESS. The experience of the gospel gives us the two prerequisites for a life of forgiveness: First, it provides *emotional humility.* Those who won't forgive show they have not accepted the fact of their own sinfulness. To remain unforgiving means you remain unaware of your own need for forgiveness. Second, it provides *emotional wealth.* You can't be gracious to someone if you are too needy and insecure. If you know God's love and forgiveness, then there is a limit to how deeply another person can hurt you. He or she can't touch your *real* identity, wealth, and significance. The more we rejoice in our own forgiveness, the quicker we will be to forgive others. No heart that is truly repentant toward God can be unforgiving toward others.

Reflection: Which of the two requirements for forgiveness do you lack most often?

Thought for prayer: Meditate on Psalm 130:4: "with you there is forgiveness, that you may be feared." God's free grace for us should lead us to awe and wonder ("fear") before him. Think about that until you can praise him for his forgiveness from the heart.

September 28

We are so evil and sinful and flawed that Jesus had to die for us. . . . But we are so loved and valued that he was glad to die for us. The Lord of the universe loved us enough to do that! So the gospel humbles us into the dust and at the very same time exalts us to the heavens. We are sinners, but completely loved and accepted in Christ at the same time. . . . [This] gives you both the emotional humility and wealth to exercise the power of grace. (Hardcover, pp. 166–67; paperback, pp. 185–86)

THE CROSS AND FORGIVENESS. On the cross Jesus fulfilled the law and justice's demands *and* procured mercy and forgiveness for us at the same time. We, too, are also required to forgive in a way that honors both justice and truth. "Christians are called to abandon bitterness, to be forbearing, to have a forgiving stance even where the repentance of the offending party is conspicuous by its absence; on the other hand, their God-centered passion for justice, their concern for God's glory, ensure that the awful odium of sin is not glossed over."[112] Love, but speak the truth. Speak the truth, but always in love. That's how to show grace to your spouse.

Reflection: Did your upbringing teach and support this idea of forgiveness and repentance? In what ways does your family background help you? Hinder you?

Thought for prayer: Today think first of how your family background has either oriented you toward moralism or toward relativism in viewpoint. If there are any ways in which your past shackles you, ask God to break them and free you for truth and love.

> [U]nder the influence of the curse in Genesis, every human culture has found a way to interpret male headship in a way that has marginalized and oppressed women, and it's usually the women who notice, and object, to this treatment first. (Hardcover, p. 170; paperback, p. 191)

INTRODUCING "HEADSHIP." With tremendous ingenuity and creativity, sin has found ways in every time and place to twist the headship of men, prescribed in the Bible (Ephesians 5:23) and intended for good, into culturally approved ways to push women to the margins, rather than partnering together for the health of the family, the church, and the world. In order to nourish our God-starved sense of self, we oppress and exploit those who cannot resist. Instead of deploying strength and power to nurture and protect, as Jesus did, we "lord it over" others for our own comfort and benefit. We see men doing this to women and read that back into the term "head" in the Bible and reject the whole idea. We should not do this.

Reflection: Would both you and your spouse say that you are partners in the marriage and in the shared life to which God has called you? If not, which of you feels unappreciated or under-utilized?

Thought for prayer: In each other's presence pray for your ability as a couple to hear the biblical teaching amid the cacophony of cultural voices around this subject.

September 30

There's no denying that the subject of gender roles in marriage is a contentious and controversial one. . . . I have seen Bible verses used as weapons of both oppression and rebellion. I have also seen the healing and flourishing that can happen in a marriage when hot-button words like "headship" and "submission" are understood correctly, with Jesus as the model for both. (Hardcover, p. 171; paperback, p. 192)

SUBMISSION. In these times, one can almost provoke a riot by using the words "headship" and "submission." To many they mean oppression from men and willing subservience from women. This stems in part from a lack of understanding of the headship/submission dynamic in the ministry of Jesus. Also, some of it is willful misconstruction in the service of political agendas. Further, bad experiences with authority lead us to the conclusion that it is bad in all its forms. In Matthew 20:26–28 Jesus explained to his disciples that authority is to be used to serve, not to "lord it over" others, something Paul elaborated on in Ephesians 5:22–33. We see Jesus as the husband who sacrifices everything to bring his bride to perfection (verse 25).

Reflection: Husbands, ask your wives if your exercise of headship makes them feel secure, loved, and cared for, or bullied and oppressed. Pray first to be able to receive the answer with grace, whether it is offered lovingly or not. Wives, are you ready to imitate Jesus, who set aside his glory as a gift to his Father in the accomplishment of our salvation (and then was glorified even further as a result)?

Thought for prayer: Pray that the pride and fear in both of your hearts would be suppressed by God's Spirit, so that headship and submission in your marriage would be life-giving and not painful.

October 1

> Now for the matters you wrote about: "It is good for a man not to have sexual relations with a woman." But since sexual immorality is occurring, each man should have sexual relations with his own wife, and each woman with her own husband. (1 Corinthians 7:1–2)

CELIBACY. The Bible everywhere assumes that if they are not married, Christians must be celibate (see October 4). Yet some in Corinth taught that the ideal was for Christians not to have sex at all.[113] This view, however, was based on a view of the body as inferior to the soul or spirit. That belief can lead to indiscriminate sexual activity, since what you do with the body would be spiritually inconsequential (see September 1). But it could also lead to seeing bodily pleasure as sinful in itself and something to be avoided.[114] Paul did not see singleness and celibacy as an inferior life, but he would not teach it was the ideal either. Both of these views rejected the Christian sexual revolution, which saw sex not as just an appetite but something of cosmic significance.

Reflection: Which of these views—that sex is somewhat dirty, or that it is "no big deal"—has had an influence on you in the past? How might it be affecting your marriage?

Prayer: Lord, I thank you for the wisdom of your Word, especially as it tells me about the purpose of your gift of sex. Its lofty vision keeps us from being either afraid of sex or addicted to it. Shape my mind and heart by this biblical wisdom about sexuality. Amen.

The husband should fulfill his marital duty to his wife, and likewise the wife to her husband. The wife does not have authority over her own body but yields it to her husband. In the same way, the husband does not have authority over his own body but yields it to his wife. Do not deprive each other except perhaps by mutual consent and for a time, so that you may devote yourselves to prayer. (1 Corinthians 7:3–5)

THE BIRTH OF CONSENT. In ancient times wives could not commit adultery, but husbands were free to have sex with others, and especially with women of lower social rank who had little choice in the matter. Paul condemned the double standard—adultery was equally a sin for the husband and wife—but he went far beyond that. He said that *both* husband and wife have "authority" over the other person's body; even in marriage sex had to be a matter of mutual agreement. The modern idea that sex must be consensual came from Christianity.[115] But Paul, by insisting that sex also be always within marriage, argued that it had to be *super*-consensual. Both the Christian ethic for sex and its high vision for sex were exponentially better for women. Arguably, in the midst of today's hookup culture, it still is.

Reflection: Think of the thesis that the Christian ethic for sex and its underlying vision for sex's cosmic significance is better for women. Is that true? How?

Prayer: Lord, I thank you for the health that comes into our world through your Word, even if it only reaches our world partially. And let this loving consent be the principle in our marriage. Don't let one of us bully the other with regard to sex or to anything at all. Amen.

October 3

> The wife does not have authority over her own body but yields it to her husband. In the same way, the husband does not have authority over his own body but yields it to his wife. (1 Corinthians 7:4)

NO CONSENT TO "GHOST." In *The New York Times* a woman described having sex with a boyfriend, but afterward, when she texted the man, he wouldn't answer—he "ghosted." She told her roommates, "[H]e asked for my consent, over and over. So sex felt like a sacred act, and then he disappeared." They laughed at her, but she argued: "[C]onsent doesn't work if we relegate it exclusively to the sexual realm. Our bodies are only one part of the complex constellation of who we are." She was experiencing the biblical truth that giving our bodies without giving our whole lives fails to recognize that the physical is an integrated part of one's self. If we forget this it is dehumanizing. "I don't think many of us would say yes to the question "Is it O.K. if I act like I care about you and then disappear?"[116] Sex must be superconsensual.

Reflection: Even in sex within marriage, it is possible at a particular moment to give your body but not your mind and heart. Consider how important it is to give your whole self when you have sex.

Prayer: Lord, I never thought I'd be in prayer thanking you for the sex act—but I am! It is a way we can give ourselves wholly to each other in the most powerful possible way. Help us to use it as such. Amen.

October 4

I say this as a concession, not as a command. I wish that all of you were as I am. But each of you has your own gift from God; one has this gift, another has that. Now to the unmarried and the widows I say: It is good for them to stay unmarried, as I do. But if they cannot control themselves, they should marry, for it is better to marry than to burn with passion. (1 Corinthians 7:6–9)

PREMARITAL SEX. People often ask, "Where is there a verse that says it's wrong to have sex before marriage?" The answer is twofold. First, the Greek word *porneia* (translated "sexual immorality") means, specifically, any sex outside marriage between a man and a woman (see September 6). But second, the Bible everywhere assumes that sex outside of marriage is wrong, even when it is not stated directly. For example, here Paul says that if unmarried people "cannot control themselves" they should marry rather than going around "burning with passion." In other words, Paul simply assumes that a single person will be celibate. The number of biblical texts forbidding *porneia* or sex outside of marriage is remarkable.[117]

Reflection: Imagine someone said to you, "I know that it's a sin to commit adultery, but where does it say that you can't have sex before marriage—if you are both unmarried—as long as you love each other?" On the basis of what you have learned in this devotional this year, what would your answer be?

Prayer: Lord, you are a covenant God, because you love us enough to bind yourself to us and us to you. Renew us in your image, so that more and more our love becomes self-giving. Amen.

October 5

> I think that it is good for a man to remain as he is. Are you pledged to a woman? Do not seek to be released. Are you free from such a commitment? Do not look for a wife. But if you do marry, you have not sinned. . . . But those who marry will face many troubles in this life, and I want to spare you this. (1 Corinthians 7:26–28)

MARRIAGE AND THE KINGDOM. Christianity was perhaps the first religion or worldview that held up single adulthood to be a viable adult life.[118] Society recognized no long-term economic security apart from children. And who would remember your name and your legacy? But Paul pressured no one to marry and even made financial provision for widows so they did not have to marry unless they wanted to (1 Timothy 5). Why? "The 'sacrifice' made by singles was not . . . 'giving up sex' but in giving up heirs. . . . This was a clear [sign to the world] that one's future is not guaranteed by the family, but by [the kingdom of God]."[119] Christians choose to marry—or not—not on the basis of personal fulfillment, but on which way we can best serve as a sign of the kingdom to the world.

Reflection: When you married did you think at all about how, together, you could better be a sign of the kingdom to the world? Think more about it now with each other.

Prayer: Lord, many of our friends who don't believe in you think we were crazy to get married. Let the quality of our marriage impress them in such a way that they don't simply credit us but they become more interested in your Word and grace. Amen.

What I mean, brothers and sisters, is that the time is short. From now on those who have wives should live as if they do not; those who mourn, as if they did not; those who are happy, as if they were not; those who buy something, as if it were not theirs to keep; those who use the things of the world, as if not engrossed in them. For this world in its present form is passing away. (1 Corinthians 7:29–31)

THE TIME IS SHORT. Behind the phrase "the time is short" is a sophisticated view of history. The kingdom of God—the spiritual power to renew the world—is here to a substantial degree, but only partially (Romans 13:11–14). It means we should not be too elated by success or too cast down by disappointment—because our true success is in God (Colossians 3:1–4). Though we have possessions, we should live as if they weren't really ours—for our real wealth is in God (Luke 16:1ff.). We should "sit loose" to everything. Paul says we should be neither overelated by getting married nor overdisappointed by not being so, because Christ is the only spouse who can truly fulfill us and God's family the only family that will truly embrace and satisfy us (Ephesians 5:21ff.).

Reflection: Take this principle and apply it to other parts of your life. Can you refuse to tie your joy too much to your career? How? What about the success of your children?

Prayer: Lord, sometimes you "break our schemes of earthly joy" so that we can "find our all in you."[120] Help us—without needing trials and disappointments—to rest our hearts so much in you that we have an abiding peace in the world. Amen.

A woman is bound to her husband as long as he lives. But if her husband dies, she is free to marry anyone she wishes, but he must belong to the Lord. (1 Corinthians 7:39)

MARRYING "IN THE LORD." The biblical directive that a Christian must marry another believer is seen by some as mere prejudice, like saying you must marry someone of the same race or class. But in the context of this chapter, we see the reasons. The Bible forbids you to wittingly marry someone who doesn't share your faith. Because one of the main purposes of marriage is *to build kingdom-exhibiting community*—to show the world how Christ transforms everything, including marriage. You can't do that if both spouses aren't believers. A Christian who deliberately marries a nonbeliever shows that his or her motive is not mission or kingdom-exhibition. One of the main ways that married Christians witness to Christ is to show the difference Christ makes in marriage.

Reflection: For the same reasons that spouses should both be Christians, they should also be Christians who are both growing together, becoming more and more mature in their understanding of the Word and practice of the faith. Is one of you falling behind the other?

Prayer: Lord, help us to together "grow in the grace and knowledge" of you (2 Peter 3:18). Don't let either of us fall behind the other, so we can love each other such that others will know you came into the world (John 17:20–23). Amen.

October 8

Tim and I . . . have found that in submitting to our own divinely assigned gender roles that we discovered one of God's great gifts for getting in touch with our deepest selves, as well as entering into the Great Dance of the universe. And no, this did not involve me developing a taste for frilly clothing, nor Tim taking up car maintenance. (Hardcover, pp. 171–72; paperback, p. 193)

GENDER TYPICAL? Neither Tim nor I would describe ourselves as "gender typical." I, Kathy, am more blunt, forceful, and aggressive; Tim is more conciliatory, seeking consensus rather than conflict. God has not called us to change our temperaments to resemble stereotypical male and female behavior. In particular we are not to imitate the characteristic sins of each gender. Indeed, we have been called to step into biblical marital roles that do not come automatically or easily to us. Tim is not temperamentally eager to be a leader. However, we follow the Scripture in order to model before the world the way Jesus loves his Bride, the Church. In order to submit to our roles we have had to rely more deeply on God's grace than if it came naturally to us.

Reflection: Husbands, can you take on the "Jesus role" of loving your wife as Christ loves the Church? Wives, can you take on the role of the submissive servant, as Jesus did in Philippians 2, still aware of your equality, but setting it aside in order to glorify God?

Thought for prayer: Together, share with each other the particular ways in which each of you struggles with these biblical guidelines. Then pray for each other.

[Genesis 1:27] means that our maleness or our femaleness is not incidental to our humanness but constitutes its very essence. God does not make us into a generic humanity that is later differentiated; rather from the start we are male or female. Every cell in our body is stamped as XX or XY. This means I cannot understand myself if I try to ignore the way God has designed me or if I despise the gifts he may have given to help me fulfill my calling. (Hardcover, p. 172; paperback, p. 194)

GENDER DISCOMFORT. Some people become uncomfortable with their physical birth sex and cannot feel at home in their bodies. To have your feelings sharply out of accord with your body is a life-dominating grief. As Christians, we of all people should be able to show understanding and compassion, knowing how the fall (Genesis 3) has twisted what God pronounced "good" when he made humanity into a binary-gendered reflection of his nature. But we also know that only through being in Christ's Body—through the change in identity that comes from being a child in his family—does anyone find ultimate relief from their sense of dislocation in the world (Ephesians 1:9–10, 22). So be understanding, and yet point people—and your own heart—to God, "our eternal home" (John 14:1–4).

Reflection: Do you know anyone who expresses gender discomfort? Have you shown understanding and compassion? Do you love them enough to talk to them about Jesus and identity in him?

Thought for prayer: Pray for anyone you know in this situation, and all those you don't. Ask God to give them relief in the way most aligned with wisdom and compassion.

At the same time, Genesis shows us that men and women were created with absolute equality. Both are equally made in the image of God, equally blessed, and equally given "dominion" over the earth. This means that men and women together, in full participation, must carry out God's mandate to build civilization and culture. Both men and women are called to do science and art, to build families and human communities. (Hardcover, pp. 172–73; paperback, p. 194)

GENDER DIVERSITY. It's common to say that diversity always makes a team stronger. The difference in viewpoints leads to creativity; the variance in abilities means the whole group is far stronger than any one member. Rather than creating two identical humans, God created two humans *equally* in his image and gave each of them a diverse spectrum of gifts and abilities. Since they express themselves differently in various cultures and personalities, the diversity is even greater. God meant us to utilize the insights and effectiveness that men and women produce when working together—in marriage, family, church, and community. In order to care for his creation and be "subcreators" under his kingship, men and women must strive to bring out the best in one another, valuing and praising each person's distinct contribution.

Reflection: Do you value the contributions your spouse makes to your marriage? Do you treat his or her ideas, work, sacrifice, and critiques as being as valuable as your own? Are there ways you could do this even better?

Thought for prayer: Ask God for the patience and humility it takes to receive this gift of gender diversity, and not to wish the person you loved was not so deeply different.

God tells us to be "fruitful" and "fill the earth." Here God gives the human race the mandate to procreate . . . a reflection of his own boundless life-giving creativity. But, obviously, this wonderful gift of creating new human life is something we can only carry out together. . . . [T]he sexes, while equal in dignity and worth, are complementary. . . . Genesis 2, in which a piece of the man is removed to create the woman, strongly implies that each is incomplete without the other. . . . Each sex is gifted for different steps in the same Great Dance. (Hardcover, pp. 173–74; paperback, pp. 194–96)

GENDER AND GOD'S IMAGE. We live in a world of color, not one of all shades of black and white. Music depends on the harmony of parts for its most beautiful expression, and the fecundity of plant and animal life is astonishing. Only this variety can "tell of the glory of God" (Psalm 19:1). No single tree, flower, note, or creature can capture the full creativity and joy of the Creator. In the same way, one gender could not have reflected the image of a personal God, who has been Creative Love from all eternity (Genesis 1:26–27). Apparently the paired polarities of male and female reflect the richness of the Triune God in a way that no one person or gender could do.

Reflection: Do you value the ways in which your spouse differs from you, or do you find it annoying? Whether you have children or not, do you as a couple support the development of the next generation? How could you do more?

Thought for prayer: Thank God that he has prescribed gender diversity for marriage. Admit that you can hardly grasp how it is possible, but thank him for the privilege of reflecting his character to the world through your relationship.

[In] Genesis 3 . . . both man and woman sin against God and are expelled from the garden of Eden. We immediately see the catastrophic change in the unity between man and woman. The air is filled with blame shifting, finger pointing, and accusation. Rather than their Otherness becoming a source of completion, it becomes an occasion for oppression and exploitation. (Hardcover, p. 174; paperback, p. 196)

THE CURSE ON GENDER: 1. When Adam and Eve disobeyed God, they overturned what had been pronounced "good" and turned it sour, corrupted, and corrosive. Partnership turned into oppression, declarations of ecstatic love became accusation, and toxic masculinity was born in the first moments of a broken new world. One of the results of sin is that husbands will seek to tyrannize their wives and women in general (Genesis 3:16).[121] Jesus is lifted up as the authority who never dominates, only serves (Luke 22:27). Yet the image of God remains in every human being, no matter how debased by sin it may have become. Nor should we think that sin has affected one gender more than the other.

Reflection: Talk together, candidly and graciously, about the ways in which the husband's masculine personality needs to be refined or changed.

Thought for prayer: Together pray that Jesus—with his sacrificial love for the church—could be an inspiration for the husband in your marriage, in order to make the changes that are necessary.

October 13

In Jesus Christ's person and work we begin to see a restoration of the original unity and love between the sexes. Jesus both elevates and underlines the equality of women as co-bearers of the image of God and the creation mandate, and he also redeems the roles given to man and woman at the beginning by inhabiting them, both as servant-head and *'ezer*-subordinate. (Hardcover, p. 174; paperback, p. 196)

THE CURSE ON GENDER: 2. Read through the Gospel of John, noting all the places where Jesus calls himself *equal* with God, as well as the places where he claims that he has come only to do *God's* will, not his (5:17–18, 19–23, 30; 6:38; 7:16–18; 8:16, 19, 28–29, 54–58; 10:29–30; 12:49–50; 13:3; 14:31; 16:15; 17:1–5, 10, 24–25). Well, which is it? Is Jesus equal with God from all eternity, or is he submissive to the Father's words and executing the Father's plans? Yes! Jesus is both equally God, and also the submissive servant. With him as our model neither should the wife use submission as an excuse for weakness, nor should the husband use submission as an excuse for domination.

Reflection: Talk together, candidly and graciously, about the ways in which the wife's feminine personality needs to be refined or changed.

Thought for prayer: Together pray that Jesus—with his willingness to submit to the Father—could be an inspiration for the wife in your marriage, in order to make the changes that are necessary.

In [Philippians 2:5–11] we see taught both the essential equality of the First and Second Persons of the Godhead, and yet the voluntary submission of the Son to the Father to secure our salvation. Let me emphasize that Jesus's willing acceptance of this role was wholly voluntary, a gift to his Father. I discovered here that my submission in marriage was a gift I offered, not a duty coerced from me. (Hardcover, p. 175; paperback, pp. 196–97)

GENDER MENTORS. So husbands and wives acknowledge equality and celebrate difference. More importantly, each one mentors the other. While the Bible does not give us detailed lists of gender differences, because in each culture and couple they express themselves somewhat differently, nevertheless in each case there will be things each of you, in your gender, is weaker at and so you will need the other's help. In heaven we will all (men and women) be God's sons, as well as (men and women) his beloved Bride. These things are mysteries beyond our understanding, but in living them out in our marriages we experience some small measure of the joy we will receive when all is fully known.

Reflection: Husband, how do you celebrate your wife's full equality with you? Wife, how do you voluntarily offer your submission as a gift?

Thought for prayer: Together ask the Lord to show you the particular ways in which you can mentor each other.

The Father's headship [1 Corinthians 11:3] is acknowledged [by the Son with] mutual delight, respect, and love. There is no inequality of ability or dignity. We are differently gendered to reflect this life within the Trinity. Male and female are invited to mirror and reflect the "dance" of the Trinity, loving, self-sacrificing authority and loving, courageous submission. The Son takes a subordinate role, and in that movement he shows not his weakness but his greatness. (Hardcover, p. 176; paperback, p. 198)

THE DANCE OF GENDER. Dancing is a good metaphor for understanding gender differences. Usually, one person is moving forward and the other backward so that the couple can execute the dance steps. There is also traditionally one partner who is the lead. If both parties fought to be the lead, there would be no dance. When you dance well, it is a joy. Most of everyday life is more like running a marathon. There are chores, careers, housing crises of various kinds, financial decisions, and too little time to get everything done. It becomes easier to do all our tasks beside one another instead of with one another. When we fail to work cooperatively we lose the dance.

Reflection: How can you bring back "dance" in your marriage? Think of ways to do things together rather than separately. Think of ways to experience intimacy in order to recover the dancing in your life.

Thought for prayer: After making the lists through the reflection above, pray to God to give you the wisdom and self-control to follow through, to reinject both cooperation and joy into your marriage.

Jesus redefined—or, more truly, defined properly—headship and authority, thus taking the toxicity of it away, at least for those who live by his definition rather than by the world's understanding. . . . [A Christian] husband has been called to . . . submit [to the role of] servant-leader, who uses his authority and power to express a love that doesn't even stop at dying for the beloved. In Jesus we see all the authoritarianism of authority laid to rest, and all the humility of submission glorified. (Hardcover, pp. 177–78; paperback, pp. 199, 201)

THE SERVANT. On the way to Jerusalem to lay down his life for his people, Jesus made it clear that power and authority in the world were forever redefined by his actions. In Matthew 20:25–26 and 28 Jesus called them together and said, "You know that the rulers of the Gentiles lord it over them, *Not so with you.* Instead, whoever wants to become great among you must be your servant . . . just as the Son of Man did not come to be served, but to serve, and to give his life as a ransom for many." This statement demands that leaders sacrifice their own interests and good for those they serve.

Reflection: Together, honestly and gently assess where the husband may be failing to sacrifice his interests and good for his wife.

Thought for prayer: In each other's presence, pray that in assessing the husband's headship you may be of one mind, that you will see things the same and therefore be able to work on them together.

[H]ow does this authority work out in the context of mutually serving persons equal in dignity and being? The answer is that a head can only overrule his spouse if he is sure that her choice would be destructive to her or to the family. He does not use his headship selfishly, to get his own way about the color of the car they buy . . . whether he has a "night out with the boys" or stays home to help with the kids when his wife asks him. (Hardcover, p. 242; paperback, pp. 278–79)

BARRIERS. There are barriers to taking up Jesus's model of the servant-leader husband. First, there's your own heart. It's hard to serve when one would rather kick back and think of no one but oneself. But second, you will have to swim against the strong tide of cultural views. Most people see marriage as two identical individuals who negotiate with each other for the meeting of needs. The idea that one is a leader and therefore should be surrendering his interests to meet his wife's needs is completely foreign. Husbands aspiring to this could get pushback from friends. In that, they are standing with their Savior, and there is no higher calling.

Reflection: Husbands, how often do you think about ways to help your wife grow? What costs are you willing to pay to see that happen? Wives, do you appreciate and encourage your husband when he, trembling, exercises his headship on your behalf?

Thought for prayer: In one another's presence, thank God for each other's sacrifices and efforts in this area of headship and submission. Be specific.

October 18

But in a marriage, where there are only two "votes," how can a stale-mate be broken without someone having to give way? In the vast majority of cases, the stalemate is broken because each will try to give the other his or her pleasure. The wife will try to respect the husband's leadership, and the husband will in turn try to please his wife. If this dynamic is in place, in the course of a healthy biblical marriage, "over-ruling" will be rare. (Hardcover, p. 243; paperback, p. 279)

SELF-DECEPTION. We have such a capacity for self-deception that what starts out as well-meant management can so easily turn into accumulating power in order to enjoy the perks of hav-ing others serve you. The novelist Patrick O'Brian put into the mouths of one of his characters his distaste for this kind of authority: "I am opposed to authority. . . . I am opposed to it largely for what it does to those who exercise it."[122] But in Jesus's model, power is utilized to serve others, not oneself. Husbands must never, never say, "My needs before yours" but "Yours before mine." When a wife sees a husband handling his role with godly fear and using his authority only to serve instead of oppress, she can rejoice in his leadership.

Reflection: Does the above describe the way authority is exer-cised in your relationship? What changes could be made?

Thought for prayer: Together, with both of you praying for the husband, ask God to prevent this self-deception about authority from operating in your marriage at any level.

What of a case where both parties cannot agree, but some kind of decision must be made? Someone must have the right to cast the deciding vote. . . . When it happens, both people "submit" to their role. . . . (Hardcover, p. 243; paperback, p. 279) A servant-leader must sacrifice his wants and needs to please and build up his partner (Ephesians 5:21ff.). . . . A wife is never . . . merely compliant but . . . her husband's most trusted friend and counselor (Proverbs 2:17). . . . Completion is hard work and involves loving contention (Proverbs 27:17) with affection (1 Peter 3:3–5). (Hardcover, pp. 241–42; paperback, pp. 277–78)

STRONG HELP. To be any kind of a helper—an *'ezer*—a wife must bring all her gifts and abilities to bear on the problems and issues she and her husband face together. You are not a helper if you withhold wise counsel, even rebuke, when it is meant to inform and correct a decision. I (Kathy) have found through the decades that Tim appreciates my vigorous input, but I must also know when I have said all that can be said and it is time to allow him to make the choice. Let no one forget that I was the one who strongly opposed our move to New York City to start a new ministry! But in supporting Tim in making a decision he knew I dreaded, our family and many other people were blessed.

Reflection: Do stalemates in which the husband must make the final choice occur routinely or rarely in your marriage? Why? And remember that sometimes the debate resolves with the husband deferring to the wife's desires, as a way to serve her.

Thought for prayer: Pray for the wisdom to know when—in the good debates and contentions you will have—you should stop pushing your point of view.

Both women *and* men get to "play the Jesus role" in marriage—Jesus in his sacrificial authority, Jesus in his sacrificial submission. By accepting our gender roles, and operating within them, we are able to demonstrate to the world concepts that are so counterintuitive as to be completely unintelligible unless they are lived out by men and women in Christian marriages. (Hardcover, p. 179; paperback, pp. 201–2)

THE CHARACTER OF GOD. "Jesus knew that the Father had put all things under his power, and that he had come from God and was returning to God; so . . . he poured water into a basin and began to wash his disciples' feet, drying them with the towel that was wrapped around him" (John 13:3–5). That could be paraphrased: "*Because* I am the all-powerful God, I wash your feet as your servant." Jesus humbling and self-giving was not an exception but an expression of the character of God. Then he added: "I have given you an example, so that you may do as I did" (verse 15). Jesus was emphasizing, on the eve of his arrest, torture, and death, that power is to be used for servanthood, and that submission reveals glory. Here both husbands and wives have their model and power to fulfill it.

Reflection: Husbands, use the example of Jesus as the basis for you to serve those over whom you have authority, even to death. Wives, act as *'ezer*-helpers with the knowledge of your identity in Christ.

Thought for prayer: Praise God for the mystery of his glory, that it is *because* he is God, and *because* he has all authority, that he gives up power to serve. Then ask him to let this same kind of love and glory characterize your marriage.

Since God called woman specifically to be a "helper" suited for her husband, it would be strange if he did not endow both men and women with distinguishable abilities to better fulfill their distinguishable calls. The most obvious are physical characteristics that enable women to bear and nurture children, but more subtle emotional and psychological endowments would be natural accompaniments to those physical differences, albeit on a spectrum. (Hardcover, p. 179; paperback, p. 202)

FORM AND FREEDOM. The Bible lays down the roles of headship and submission in marriage, using Jesus as a model for both. But then it does not provide a specific list of jobs, chores, or employment for husbands and wives in all times and all places. We have here "form yet freedom." There are unchangeable commands, but freedom within that framework to express our obedience in ways that are culturally intelligible and personally appropriate. It is not a case of "that was then, this is now." What the Bible says, we follow in all times and places (allowing for the progress of redemptive history, i.e., the things Jesus has fulfilled, such as the sacrificial system). But the Bible offers enough flexibility so in every century and culture we can find ways to obey whatever is clearly commanded in Scripture.

Reflection: Men, do your personality traits gravitate toward or away from traditional masculinity? How does studying Jesus refine for you what "masculine" means? Women, what do you think of when you encounter the word "feminine"? Is your definition informed by stereotypes or by Scripture?

Thought for prayer: Thank God for the consummate wisdom of his Word, that it is always relevant, never dated, always applicable, a solid foundation for life in any time.

Using all the qualifiers in the world, in general, as a whole and across the spectrum, men have a gift of independence, a "sending" gift. They look outward. They initiate. Under sin, these traits can become either an alpha male individualism, if this capacity is turned into an idol, or dependence, if the calling is utterly rejected and the opposite embraced in rebellion. The first sin is hypermasculinity, while the second sin is a rejection of masculinity. (Hardcover, p. 180; paperback, p. 203)

REFUSING GOD'S GIFTS: 1. Rejecting God's gift of gender can be done in many ways. There can be outright denial of the truth that God made human beings two binary genders. There can also be subcultures that exaggerate God's good gift into hypermasculininty or hyperfemininity, which many people rightly feel to be like a straitjacket. All of these depart from God's intention of making us "in his image" (Genesis 1:27), "like-opposite," male and female persons. While sin has twisted and contaminated the content of what it means to live together as male and female people, we cannot walk away from being made in God's image any more than we can decide to grow a third eye or sprout wings.

Reflection: Men, have you adopted an understanding of your biological sex and gender that is nonbiblical? In what ways? Women, have you been molded by the world's expectations of behavior and thought, rather than God's? In what ways?

Thought for prayer: Thank God for the freedom you have in the gospel not to be constrained by rigid gender stereotypes. But ask God to show you the particular ways in which he has called you to be a man or a woman.

Using all the qualifiers in the world, on the whole and across the spectrum, women have a gift of interdependence, a "receiving" gift. They are inwardly perceptive. They nurture. Under sin, these traits can become either a clinging dependence, if attachment is turned into an idol, or individualism, if the calling is utterly rejected and the opposite embraced in rebellion. The first sin is hyperfemininity, while the second sin is a rejection of femininity. (Hardcover, p. 180; paperback, pp. 203–4)

REFUSING GOD'S GIFTS: 2. When God created humanity in two genders he pronounced it very good (Genesis 1:28, 31). Today there are some who, contradicting God, argue that the binary of male and female is bad or at least incomplete. Because our world is broken, "groaning" under the effects of human sin (Romans 8:20–22), it should not be a surprise to believers that humans are sometimes born with physical and mental conditions that don't fit with God's original design. After all, death itself was not part of God's world. However, it is not a good argument to say that exceptions disprove the existence of the rule. We help with all compassion those who do not feel they "fit," but it does not help them or us to deny that the two genders are a wonderful gift of God.

Reflection: Men, looking at Jesus, what ways can you think of to change the way in which you have been using your gendered gifts? Women, looking at Jesus, what ways can you think of to change the way in which you have been using your gendered gifts?

Thought for prayer: Ask God to help you as Christians to steer the "middle course" in our culture between those who see gender in stereotypes and those who see the idea of two genders as oppressive. Look to Jesus to model this middle course for your marriage.

[O]ur sinful drive for self-justification often leads us to despise those who think, feel, and behave differently than we do. Personal, racial, and class pride naturally grow out of the human heart's alienation from God and therefore our need to prove ourselves and win an identity based on our specialness, superiority, and performance. One of the main places where "exclusion of the Other" happens is between the sexes. Loving someone of the other sex is *hard*. (Hardcover, p. 181; paperback, pp. 204–5)

REFUSING GOD'S GIFTS: 3. The diverse gendered giftedness of men and women has often become a source of scorn and mocking, even oppression and violence. The Other is not our completion, but our competition. Indeed, when Genesis 3:16 describes the results of sin, of women "desiring" the man and the man "ruling over" the woman, the likely meaning is that both are trying to dominate and control the other, though using different ways of manipulation.[123] Since our gendered humanity is one of the ways we most closely mirror the image of God, this harms not only we ourselves as individuals, but also those close to us, and the world at large.

Reflection: Men, are there ways in which you mentally demean or physically treat women as made less in God's image than yourself? Women, are there ways in which you nurture anger and plot revenge against men for their failure to appreciate your equality?

Thought for prayer: Ask God to forgive you for the ways in which you struggle with your spouse for power in the marriage, rather than deferring to and serving each other. Ask him for the wisdom to discern these hidden power plays in the future.

However, this is where the Christian understanding of marriage comes in. Marriage, in the biblical view, addresses the chasm between the sexes. Marriage is a full embrace of the other sex. We accept and yet struggle with the gendered "otherness" of our spouse, and in the process, we grow and flourish in ways otherwise impossible. Because, as Genesis says, male and female are "like-opposite" each other—both radically different and yet incomplete without each other. (Hardcover, p. 182; paperback, p. 205)

GENDER BLAMING. A marriage will inevitably have hurt feelings, anger, resentment, and conflicts. Sometimes we respond by saying we married the wrong person, but another way to respond is to conclude we are married to the wrong gender. That is, some blame the conflict on the alienation we often feel from the other gender and they seek refuge with someone of their own sex. But this reasoning is mistaken. In general, the fights within marriage are due to you both being sinners. The proof of this is that they will continue, no matter who else you turn to. With the tools of repentance and forgiveness, the Holy Spirit can use a marriage as a primary setting for healing our alienations.

Reflection: Men, have you identified the places that your wife is hurt? How have you sacrificed to bring healing to her? Women, can you see your husband's needs before he can himself? Do you use that knowledge to criticize and belittle, or to minister to him?

Thought for prayer: Pray to God first that you have enough love and wisdom not to grieve your spouse. Then pray that, when you do, you both will have the grace to reconcile and become stronger through the hurt.

But God's plan for married couples involves embracing the otherness to make us unified, and that can only happen between a man and a woman. Even at the atomic level, all the universe is held together by the attraction of positive and negative forces. The embrace of the Other, as it turns out, really *is* what makes the world go around. (Hardcover, p. 182; paperback, pp. 205–6)

GENDER BLESSING. The world is built to a great extent on paired polarities. There are protons and electrons, carrying positive and negative electric charges that run from the atomic level to the interstellar magnetic field. There is light and darkness, heat and cold. Some religions have even enshrined these polarities as *yin* and *yang*. On the biological level sperm and egg, pollen and ovule, account for the vast majority of complex reproduction. Only with this uniting of difference—of what only male and female can produce together—has God bestowed the blessing of the creation of new human life. Written both small and large is God's vision for the embrace of the Other, the most glorious example of which is his holy embrace of his people, his Bride.

Reflection: Married couples, have you ever thought of your sexual union as a sacred witness to God's final plan for the universe? Would it change the way you embrace your spouse if you did? Would there be more joy, more freedom, more kindness, more sacrifice?

Thought for prayer: Together, answer the questions in the Reflection section above, and when you are done, sit before God in wonder at how sex participates in his plan. Praise and thank him for it.

It is not simply that the other gender is different; it's that his or her differences *make no sense*. And once we come up against this wall of incomprehensibility, the sin in our heart tends to respond by assigning moral significance to what is simply a deep temperamental difference. . . . Husbands and wives grow distant from one another because they allow themselves to engage in a constant, daily drumbeat of thoughts of inner disdain for the gendered difference of their spouse. (Hardcover, pp. 182–83; paperback, p. 206)

GENDER DISDAIN. One of the ways we justify ourselves is to bolster our self-esteem by disdaining people who are different. So more punctual people despise those who are less so as "irresponsible." More talkative people dismiss quieter folks as unfriendly. We do the same thing with gender differences. When men or women are with their own sex, they often mock the other gender even though the differences are just that—different. Such a moralizing, self-justifying approach to gender can be toxic in marriage, make real friendship with your spouse hard, and make the raising of children a minefield. Be humble instead.

Reflection: Husbands, make a list of the things about women that you have mocked in the past. Wives, make the same list about men. Share the lists and, if possible, explain your gender a bit more to your spouse.

Thought for prayer: Confess to God the ways typical to you in which you build yourself up by criticizing and disdaining other persons or types of persons.

Christ embraced the ultimate "Other"—sinful humanity. He didn't exclude us . . . [but] embraced us by dying on the cross for our sins. To love the Other, especially an Other . . . means sometimes experiencing betrayal, rejection, and attacks. The easiest thing is to leave. But Jesus did not do that. . . . Knowing this kind of gracious, sin-covering love gives believers in the gospel of Christ the basis for an identity that does not need superiority and exclusion to form itself. (Hardcover, pp. 183–84; paperback, p. 207)

ATTACKS. The quote from *The Meaning of Marriage* above, if taken in isolation, could be read as counsel that one remain in a marriage even when there has been physical or sexual abuse. Physical abuse and rape in marriage are not only sins, which must be confronted (Matthew 18: 15–17), but they are also crimes (Romans 13:1–5), and Christians are called to submit to the governing authorities. So do not acquiesce in this kind of abuse. Having said that, our culture has lowered the bar to include as a reason for leaving a relationship many things that are not wrong or dangerous, but merely the clashes and struggles that sinners experience when living in close community. Marriage needs deep and abiding commitment that "covers over a multitude of sins" (1 Peter 4:8).

Reflection: In your marriage, do you cover over your spouse's unthinking sinfulness, or is everything an occasion for an argument?

Thought for prayer: Pray for the wisdom—both for you in your marriage and friends in their marriages—to know the difference between crimes that must be confronted and reported and clashes that must be resolved through repentance and forgiveness.

This has nothing to do with who brings home the biggest salary or makes the most sacrifices to care for the children. . . . The external details of a family's division of labor may be worked out differently across marriages and societies. But the tender, serving authority of a husband's headship and the strong, gracious gift of a wife's submission restore us to who we were meant to be at creation. (Hardcover, p. 184; paperback, p. 208)

THE WONDER OF GENDER. The awesome mystery of God's love for us is beyond our wildest imagination. We can only resort to metaphor and symbolism, and the one most frequently chosen by God himself is that of gender—the union of husband and wife. God is the tender loving Bridegroom, Husband, and Lover of our Souls; we, the church, are his Bride, for whom he will die, and has died, to save. With that as our template, Christian marriages can enact an allegory of God's love for his people by "playing the roles" of servant-leader husband and joyfully submissive wife. In the words of Eowyn Stoddard, the Church is the Second Adam's (Jesus's) Second Eve, meant to bear his fruit into the world.

Reflection: Is this language of metaphor and allegory any earthly, practical good? Does it have any concrete, daily-life implications for how you conduct your marriage?

Thought for prayer: Remember that when we have been the recipient of great help or of a great gift from someone, there is a desire to imitate it. Ask God to show you how you can imitate his spousal love for you in your marriage.

[Y]ou have to find a very safe place to practice headship and submission. I say this because I am not unaware of God's warning that sin will lead men to try to dominate women. . . . Therefore it is crucial that women who want to accept gender-differentiated roles within marriage find a husband who will truly be a *servant*-leader to match her as a strong helper. (Hardcover, pp. 184–85; paperback, p. 208)

CHOOSE WISELY. The first of the curses to be visited on human beings after sin entered the world was the blighting of the relationship between men and women (Genesis 3:16), but the Bible gives us tools for healing the relationship. We have the toolbox of truth, love, and grace that is made operational in repentance and forgiveness. This bridges the gap between any two sinful people. We also have the tools of biblical gender roles. We are neither to adopt the stereotyped roles of traditional culture that diminish the equality of male and female nor the view of modern culture that gender is just socially constructed and there are no roles in marriage. What does this mean? It means we must choose our spouses wisely. Unite with someone who wants the same thing, who has the same vision.

Reflection: Discuss how much more work the "biblical toolbox of gender roles" entails, since you must work out the details of your roles for yourself. Have you done this work? How much of it?

Thought for prayer: In each other's presence, thank God for the gifts of your genders, and ask him to help you receive those gifts. Ask for help to understand what it means for you in particular to be a man or a woman in your marriage, and in your time and place.

No human being should give any other human being unconditional obedience. As Peter said, "We must obey God rather than men" (Acts 5:29) . . . [A] wife should not obey or aid a husband in doing things that God forbids, such as selling drugs or physically abusing her. If . . . he beats her, the "strong help" that a wife should exercise is to love and forgive him in her heart but have him arrested. It is never kind or loving to anyone to make it easy for him or her to do wrong. (Hardcover, p. 242; paperback, p. 278)

ALL OR NOTHING. Nuance is often lost in a culture that only sees Them or Us, Good or Bad, Woke or Oppressor. We really do not believe in something that can be good and yet misused. If something can be misused, well, we should have nothing to do with it. But everything is capable of being used wrongly. The teaching that there are distinct roles to which the genders are called is routinely blamed for encouraging oppression and abuse. I (Kathy) have no doubt that in the name of "biblical teaching" there have been abuses and evil. Nevertheless, God's gifts to us are good and meant for our joy. When those gifts are put to use in the service of sin we must *never* believe the lie that it was the fault of the gift, rather than the wrong use of it.

Reflection: Is your view of gender roles more determined by your past experiences (either good or bad) or more determined by the Bible?

Thought for prayer: Meditate on Colossians 3:16, on having the message of Christ—the biblical gospel—"dwell in you richly." Ask God to show you what that means for you, how to have his Word shaping not only your thinking but your desires.

"[She:] Let him kiss me with the kisses of his mouth—for your love is more delightful than wine. (Song of Solomon 1:2–3)

THE BIBLICAL LOVE SONG. Paul McCartney noted that people "want to fill the world with silly love songs."[124] A love song is more of an outburst than a teaching. It celebrates love and romance. It is notable that the Bible contains a book that is one sustained love song. The Song of Solomon tells us the story of two lovers who seek and find one another, and then consummate their love in marriage. Many interpreters have sought to find "deeper meaning" in the story. Of course *every* loving marriage points to our union with Christ through his love. But this book in itself is a celebration of love and marriage as a good in itself. And that tells us a lot. "The Song intends to teach us that sex is good and pure within marriage and is the appropriate object of longing and desire before marriage."[125]

Reflection: What does the Bible tell us about marriage when it gives us one book that is a love poem and romantic story? What are the implications for your marriage?

Prayer: Lord, how wonderful that your Word does not only regulate sex and romance—it powerfully celebrates it, and calls us to enjoy it. I praise you that you are a God of joy who wants us to have it too. Amen.

[She:] Let him kiss me with the kisses of his mouth—for your love is more delightful than wine. Pleasing is the fragrance of your perfumes; your name is like perfume poured out. No wonder the young women love you! Take me away with you—let us hurry! Let the king bring me into his chambers. (Song of Solomon 1:1–4)

COUNTERCULTURAL ROMANCE. Biblical scholar Iain Duguid writes: "The Song sketches a paradigm for male-female relationships that is neither traditionalist nor radical." She urges him, "Take me away with you," a term that sounds very traditional. Yet she is not "emotionally dependent . . . waiting forever for the man to make the first move." She takes her own initiative. There is no "macho model of male-female relationships" in which the only sexual desires are his, and she merely acquiesces to them.[126] Biblical figures in some ways, of course, reflect the cultures of their time, but in important ways they also subvert cultural norms and provide readers of God's Word with directions for all times and places. The woman here is not just the object of male attention. She has her own designs.

Reflection: How could this paradigm both challenge and yet fit into various cultural models for male-female relationships?

Prayer: Lord, thank you for the abiding truth and profound insight of your Word. Thank you that it is not the product of any one culture but rather it critiques every culture and my own heart, too. Amen.

[She:] Dark am I, yet lovely, daughters of Jerusalem, dark like the tents of Kedar, like the tent curtains of Solomon. Do not stare at me because I am dark, because I am darkened by the sun. My mother's sons were angry with me and made me take care of the vineyards; my own vineyard I had to neglect. (Song of Solomon 1:5–6)

BEAUTY FEARS. The woman's fear is that she will be rejected because she does not match the culture's view of beauty. The rich were able to stay indoors and the poor had to work out in the fields—so darker skin in that culture represented the working class. So did slenderness because it meant you did not eat well. The fact that today slenderness and a nice tan mean the opposite should remind us how fleeting and ultimately unimportant cultural views are! Instead, the Bible speaks of inward character as the only "unfading beauty" (1 Peter 3:3–4). Breaking stereotypes, the woman asserts that she is lovely. This is not shyness. She calls for her lover to find her attractive. Yet the text reminds us of how we wrestle with conformity to the culture's image of beauty. We should not.

Reflection: In your marriage, how can you help each other in this area? How can you both support stewardship of the body but also reinforce the concept of "unfading beauty"?

Prayer: Lord, there *is* such a thing as ugliness and as beauty, but your Word shows me that it is more a matter of spirit than of body. Help me not to be captive to any other definition of beauty than yours. Amen.

November 4

[Friends:] [M]ost beautiful of women. . . . [He:] Your cheeks are beautiful with earrings, your neck with strings of jewels. We will make you earrings of gold, studded with silver. (Song of Solomon 1: 8, 10–11)

MUTUAL ATTRACTION. For the first time we hear the man speak. He answers her call, naming her the "most beautiful of women." Such a statement is always, literally speaking, an exaggeration, but subjectively it is absolutely authentic. It is the way one feels in love. "If the only biblical advice on seeking a spouse were Proverbs 31:30 ("Charm is deceitful, and beauty is vain, but a woman who fears the Lord is to be praised"), we might not think that chemistry matters in relationships." The point of Proverbs is that physical attractiveness must not be the decisive factor in choosing a mate. If it is, and you inevitably change and lose your looks as you age, then your marriage will be in a bad way. But the Song of Songs brings us the balance, that "mutual attraction is important."[127]

Reflection: How can you honor the Proverbs 31 principle and the Song of Songs 1 principle together?

Prayer: Thank you, Lord, for making it possible to be "outwardly wasting away" while being inwardly renewed in the likeness of our Savior (2 Corinthians 4:16). Give me eyes to see this inner person in my spouse and be attracted to it. Amen.

November 5

[She:] Dark am I, yet lovely, daughters of Jerusalem, dark like the tents of Kedar, like the tent curtains of Solomon." [He:] Your cheeks are beautiful with earrings, your neck with strings of jewels. We will make you earrings of gold, studded with silver. (Song of Solomon 1:5, 10–11)

GOD'S EYES. "There is more of a hint of insecurity in the woman's defiant claim to be beautiful." But the man responds . . . "by affirming her beauty and enhancing it through his gifts of jewelry." There is an echo here of the nakedness and shame that both Adam and Eve felt when they fell. Deep down we know that to God's eyes we are not spiritually beautiful but disfigured by sin. Yet like this man—though with infinitely more power—God "chose us, in spite of who we are, and disfigured his own Son on the cross in order to pay for our sins. He now clothes us in the glorious royal robes of his righteousness, adorning us with a breath-taking beauty."[128] Some of our insecurity about our looks will be lessened by the knowledge that we are beautiful, in Christ, to the only eyes in the universe that count.

Reflection: Do you affirm each other's inner and outward attractiveness? How would you be different if you believed and grasped more deeply how you look to God in Christ?

Prayer: Lord, it overwhelms my reason and even my imagination that you love us even as you love Jesus, so that in your eyes we are more beautiful than all the jewels beneath the earth. But help me to grasp even a small part of this truth, that I might be forever changed by it. Amen.

> [She:] "I am a rose of Sharon and a lily of the valley." [He:] "Like a lily among thorns is my darling among the young women." [The woman] "Like an apple tree among the trees of the forest is my beloved among the young men." (Song of Solomon 2:2–3)

AFFIRMING UNIQUENESS. When the woman calls herself a "lily of the valley" she describes a very common wildflower that blooms widely in the desert. It is like saying, "I'm no one special." But the man counters that "she is uniquely attractive" and compared to others around her she is like a flower "among thorns." The woman responds in kind, saying he is like a unique apple tree among the ordinary trees of the wood. This is how it should be. "One way of keeping the flame burning in our marriages is to affirm repeatedly what it was about the other person that drew us to them uniquely in the first place and that we continue to see in them now."[129]

Reflection: Do you do this? Take time to speak to your spouse about what you find unusually or singularly attractive about him or her.

Prayer: Lord, all things work together for our good (Romans 8:28) and that includes the spouse you have given me. Help me to regularly affirm my spouse's distinct and unique gifts and qualities because that will honor you as well, and will enhance our joy. Amen.

Strengthen me with raisins, refresh me with apples, for I am faint with love. His left arm is under my head, and his right arm embraces me. Daughters of Jerusalem, I charge you by the gazelles and by the does of the field: Do not arouse or awaken love until it so desires. (Song of Solomon 2:5–7)

THE POWER OF LOVE. The woman is overwhelmed, literally *sick* with love. Love has often been described as an experience of insanity or drunkenness, in which we do things that afterwards we regard with horror or shame. So the woman warns "those who are as yet unmarried about the dangers of stirring up such feelings before their time." Here then is another perspective on not having sex before marrying. She urges them not to allow such feelings to rise to great height before marriage "not because sex is dirty or insipid, but precisely because it is so beautiful and potent" and is "intended to bond two people inseparably together for life by its unique and overwhelming power."[130]

Reflection: Considering either your own experience or those of friends, think of ways that the unleashed power of sexual love led to foolish behavior or other wrong decisions.

Prayer: Lord, you made our feelings, yet they often cloud judgment. Don't let my feelings and attractions—and repulsions—keep me from loving and serving you and my spouse. Amen.

November 8

While the principle is clear—that the husband is to . . . have ultimate authority in the family—the Bible gives almost no details about how that is expressed in concrete behavior. . . . Should women take primary responsibility for daily child care while men oversee the finances? [Some] are tempted to nod yes . . . until it is pointed out that nowhere does the Bible say such things. The Scripture does not give us a list of things men and women must and must not do. It gives no such specific directions at all. (Hardcover, pp. 185–86; paperback, pp. 209–10)

A MIXTURE. The Proverbs 31 woman is often held up as a model for "biblical womanhood," either in approval or in mocking rejection. She makes real estate investments and launches a clothing business (verses 16–19). Yet she cooks and clothes her family, decorating the home (verses 15, 21–22). She also does this under her husband's authority (verses 11 and 23). This is a mixture of both traditional and progressive visions for activities appropriate for women. Again we see that what the Bible says about gender roles is basic enough to apply to all cultures, pointed enough to critique every culture, and flexible enough to have different expressions in each. The Bible provides no one-size-fits-all list of pursuits that women can and cannot do.

Reflection: Christian married couples today reflect a "mixture of traditional and progressive" ways to live. How does your marriage reflect this?

Thought for prayer: Pray that God would give you the spiritual freedom to devise patterns of married life that are not constrained by cultural prejudices but are informed by your own gifts and the Scripture.

[R]igid cultural gender roles have no biblical warrant. Christians cannot make a scriptural case for masculine and feminine stereotypes. Though social scientists have made good cases about abiding gender differences . . . different individual personalities and different cultures will express those distinctions in somewhat different ways. . . . We must find ways to honor and express our gender roles, but the Bible allows for different freedom in the particulars, while still upholding the obligatory nature of the principle. (Hardcover, p. 186; paperback, p. 210)

FLIPPED TASKS, NOT ROLES. Elisabeth Elliot reported about her time living among the Waorani people, a small, isolated body of people who lived deep in the Amazon rain forest, completely cut off from modern civilization. There "everyone knew" that it was women's work to go out into the field to plant and harvest food, while it was men's work to make poetry and decorative objects. Nevertheless, the basic idea of a husband's leadership was still discernible.[131] The roles were there, but the cultural incarnation through tasks can differ widely. God has made us to bear his image, and we do so with glorious variety.

Reflection: Are there any ways our culture still acknowledges gender roles as good? Think of some. What evidence do you see that Western culture would rather erase gender distinctions?

Thought for prayer: Meditate on Revelation 7:9, which shows that racial and cultural differences are so important that they will extend into God's renewed universe. Now thank God for the cultural flexibility of our faith, its wise and gracious openness to difference, even while affirming truths that are true for everyone.

[S]ome women might [say]: "I agree that men and women are profoundly different according to their sex, but why does the *man* get to lead? If men and women are equal in dignity but different, why is the husband the head?" I think the truest answer is that we simply don't know. Why was Jesus, the Son, the one who submitted and served (Philippians 2:4ff.)? Why wasn't it the Father? We don't know, but we do know that it was a sign of his greatness, not his weakness. (Hardcover, p. 187; paperback, pp. 211–12)

ACCEPTING GOD'S ASSIGNMENT. There comes a time when parents give their children an assignment they don't want and the parents know there is no way to explain it in a way that they will understand. The child has nothing to go on but to trust the parent's heart and authority. Has God given us a full explanation of why the husband gets to lead? No. But acceptance and thanksgiving are the appropriate responses, even when he sends us assignments we don't understand and/or don't want. Even difficult "assignments" such as illness or loss will one day be revealed as God's wisdom operating in love for our glory. Fixing our eyes on Jesus is the only way I know to calm my heart when I would rather struggle and fight for "MY will" to be done rather than "THY will be done."

Reflection: Is there anything God has shown you about your life, or altered in your life, that you find mysterious or upsetting? Has Jesus, with his death, earned your trust that he has your best interests in view at all times?

Thought for prayer: Meditate on Luke 22:42, in which Jesus accepts a painful death that he doesn't want, but embraces it in full trust. Remembering Jesus saved you by embracing hard things from God as gifts of his wisdom, ask the Father to give you the same mind and spirit toward your own hard assignments.

[Kathy writes:] In some ways Tim is under–gender typed (such as in his desire not to offend others). But in other ways he's quite frustratingly masculine. . . . I will think, "How can an *adult* be that out of touch with his feelings?" He tends to look outward; he doesn't look inside his own feelings very well. Over the years, I have needed to respectfully teach him. (Hardcover, p. 189; paperback, p. 214)

THE STRENGTH OF "HELP." When Lydia *persuaded* Paul to use her home as his church planting base in Philippi (Acts 16:15) and when Priscilla and Aquila *showed Apollos a better way* (Acts 18:26), we see women being the *'ezer*. See what a strong thing it is! Lydia changed the mind of an apostle! In sports there is such a thing as a "player coach," which is someone who plays but also coaches the other players. Be that for one another—sometimes even in the middle of a fight, calling a time out and saying, "Here, let me tell you how you can win me over to your point of view." Or "Let me help you see why I am getting so angry." Then, back to the field!

Reflection: To "help" is not merely to assist in something but to question the whole enterprise, to *show a better way*. Married people, what do you wish you could tell your spouse about your relationship? With prayer, do so.

Thought for prayer: Thank God for this highly nuanced, biblical understanding of how husband and wife can strongly guide, critique, and affirm each other, all within the framework of loving leadership and submission.

Submission to God's pattern in marriage gets you more in touch with . . . your primary maleness or femaleness, yet marriage balances you and broadens you, too. . . . Tim [says] he often finds himself in situations where he is about to respond, but he knows instinctively what I would say or do if I were there . . . "and now I have a greater range of responses and a greater likelihood of doing the right thing." Therefore, marriage is for both the overly gender typed and the under–gender typed. It broadens us and deepens us. (Hardcover, pp. 188–89; paperback, p. 213)

SUBMISSION ALL AROUND. As we have said, the one-flesh union of marriage is not just a reference to sex and the physical. It means the complex of two entire selves—physical, emotional, social, spiritual—uniting. As we live with one another, our ideals, our hopes, our thoughts begin to wrap around one another and we become a new thing. That changes us both and so, in a sense, both spouses submit their desires and interests to the marriage. I knew a man who cold-bloodedly set out to find a marriage partner because he realized he was becoming a selfish, rigid person, and he needed someone to balance and sharpen him. He was in love when he married her, but his motivation at first was to course-correct who he was becoming.

Reflection: Consider who you would be if you had not spent time married to your spouse. What kind of person do you think you would be?

Thought for prayer: Ask God to help you both embrace the submitting, merging, and changing that marriage naturally entails, and not to let your natural selfishness and pride keep you from the love and changed lives that can result.

The result of completion is personal ease. Adam and Eve were naked and unashamed with each other before the Fall. There was no anxiety, no hiding. There was a sense of a primordial, ancient unity and accord that Adam and Eve had then that we've not experienced since, because sin entered and disrupted the unity that they had. When you see marriage as completion, submission finds its place. (Hardcover, p. 190; paperback, pp. 214–15)

ROLES AS BALLET. What I enjoy about ballet, Tim appreciates in basketball—the sheer physical mastery and grace, the split-second timing, the hours of practice behind the effortless maneuvers. For your marriage to reclaim the dance, it will take the same level of commitment and effort, but the beauty, the deference to one another's needs, the solid sense of being in touch with a reality beyond oneself is worth the investment. Headship and submission in a marriage should be as grace-full as that of two dancers or two players on a team—always submitting one's desire to be center stage to the overall pattern, the goal, the achievement of family life, ministry to the world, and (not to be too overblown about it) the continuation of civilization.

Reflection: Do the roles of servant-leader and servant-helper play out gracefully in your marriage, as a submission of both spouses to their calling from God?

Thought for prayer: One reason for both spouses submitting to gender roles is out of obedience to God's Word. But another reason is that it is a natural, glad, and humble response to God's grace. Ask God to stir up and make both motives strong in you.

[S]uppose a husband in a putatively Christian marriage has a wife who wants no part of a gender role that requires her to be "submissive" to her husband, the "head"? Or a wife whose churchgoing husband uses a misreading of the Bible to dismiss and marginalize her opinion, her contribution, even her person? (Hardcover, pp. 190–91; paperback, pp. 215–16)

DON'T WAIT FOR PERMISSION. It is understandable that you would like your spouse to be every bit as eager to grow and make changes to improve your marriage as you are. But you should not wait for the other person before doing what you know you should do. Since the role of "headship" is one of servant-leadership, the husband needs no permission to *serve* his wife. And wives who have husbands who do not understand their role as servants can best help ('*ezer*) their husbands by gently but firmly standing their ground and "showing him a better way." She may be the most help by insisting on counseling (or going by herself, if necessary). Don't wait for permission. Making your own changes is the best way to encourage the other to do the same.

Reflection: Men, are you convinced of Jesus's definition of leadership being a servant role like the one he took himself? Women, are you confident enough in the teaching of Scripture to take your stand on it and not be bullied or dismissed?

Thought for prayer: Honestly assess where you are not on the same page and either share those areas and pray together about it, or pray yourself that God would help you "be of the same mind."

You can change no one's behavior but your own. If a man or a woman wishes to bring him- or herself more fully into the biblically defined gender roles, it does not actually require assent from the other person. Since both the headship role of a husband and the submission role as a wife are *servant* roles, one can always begin to serve without waiting for permission. Often this will be an invisible change of attitude before it is ever visible in action. (Hardcover, p. 191; paperback, p. 216)

THERE'S ALWAYS HOPE. The truth that you cannot change anyone's behavior but your own should be subject to one huge caveat: God can change the hearts of anyone. When (not if) your marriage is at a difficult place, concentrate on prayer for your own heart to have the necessary courage, self-knowledge, forgiveness, love, and wisdom to proceed. Problems in a marriage, even severe ones, are not reasons to give up hope (though we have discussed biblical grounds for divorce elsewhere). God can resurrect relationships like he can resurrect people. So stick with your covenant vow, and do whatever it takes to solve the problems in your marriage.

Reflection: Have you lost hope in your marriage? Even if you don't fear its demise, have you settled for too little love and joy in your marriage?

Thought for prayer: Meditate on Romans 15:13 and then ask God to give you hope for growth in your marriage.

[S]ingle people cannot live their lives well as singles without a balanced, informed view of marriage. If they do not have that, they will either over-desire or under-desire marriage, and either of those ways of thinking will distort their lives.... [In 1 Corinthians 7] Paul says ... that [w]e should be neither over-elated by getting married nor over-disappointed by not being so—because Christ is the only spouse that can truly fulfill us and God's family the only family that will truly embrace and satisfy us. (Hardcover, pp. 192, 194; paperback, pp. 219–20, 222)

JESUS OUR SPOUSE. Singles get tired of hearing "Jesus is your true husband" from their well-meaning married friends. But clumsy (and often ill-timed) articulation doesn't make it untrue. Jesus is the true husband of each of us, man or woman, married or single. We are his Bride, for whom he died to win. In a culture that has largely removed a relationship to God from the list of things humans should aspire to, the supposed raptures of romantic love have become the substitute experience. It was not made for that, and no human relationship can carry the weight of that level of need and expectation. Every Christian is in the greatest marriage and the greatest family—the family of God.

Reflection: If you are a couple not yet married, is your relationship with Christ such that it is a corrective to your single and married friends who expect romance to fulfill all their needs?

Thought for prayer: Ask God to make your church a genuine family, and not one only in name, in which all members feel adopted and cared for and protected as the members of any strong family do.

> In non-Western . . . cultures, there continues to be strong social pressure to build one's hope on family and heirs. . . . Western culture [gives us] innumerable Disney-style . . . narratives [that] begin telling life stories only when two parties are about to find True Love and then, once they do, the story fades out. The message is that what matters in life is finding romance and marriage. Everything else is prologue and afterword. So both traditional and Western cultures can make singleness seem like a grim and subhuman condition. (Hardcover, p. 197; paperback, pp. 225–26)

THE ULTIMATE FAMILY. In Mark 3:33–34 Jesus said his true family was not his biological relatives but "whoever does God's will," those united to him by faith. This radical principle means that being married and having children—wonderful divine gifts—are not things that everyone needs to know love and lead a fulfilled life. The only spouse we *must* have is Jesus and the only family we *must* be in is the community of believers. The institutional church has to find ways to live out this reality. We cannot allow our churches to be just a club, a school, or a community service center. All of these things fall short of being a family, with unconditional love, the sharing of living space and finances, suffering and burdens. Both singles and married persons need the church to be a true family if we are to thrive.

Reflection: Married couples, do you include single members of the church in the life of your family? Church leaders and pastors, are your programs and sermons all slanted towards families, leaving singles feeling invisible and excluded? Is your church a family?

Thought for prayer: Meditate on 1 Timothy 5:1–2. Praise God that the church is capable of being much more than an institution but also a life-giving, life-changing family. Ask God to help you realize this capability in your own church community.

November 18

Christianity was the very first religion that held up single adulthood as a viable way of life. . . . In ancient cultures, long-term single adults were considered to be living a human life less than fully realized. But Christianity's founder, Jesus Christ, and leading theologian, St. Paul, were both single their entire lives. Single adults cannot be seen as somehow less fully formed or realized human beings than married persons because Jesus Christ, a single man, was the perfect man (Hebrews 4:15, 1 Peter 2:22). (Hardcover, pp. 194–95; paperback, pp. 222–23)

CHOOSING THE SINGLE LIFE. Men and women may deliberately choose a single life, as did St. Paul, in order to give more time and energy to God's kingdom. For this they will need the gift of chastity, as marriage is the "only innocent context" for our sexuality. Those who find themselves single unwillingly should not think of themselves as repressing or denying a crucial part of their identity, but as offering their sexual capacity back to God as a sacrifice. In this Jesus, their elder brother, will be of help, as he has made the same sacrifice.

Reflection: Single men and women should pursue chastity as outlined in 1 Thessalonians 4:3–8. Married men and women, are you chaste in mind and body, thought and behavior, in your marriages?

Thought for prayer: Pray for the single adults you know, that they might be able to have the gift of chastity, and that they may find a church in which they know the intimacy and love of spiritual friendship.

> Paul's assessment . . . is that singleness is a good condition blessed by God, and in many circumstances, it is actually better than marriage. . . . The Christian gospel and hope of the future kingdom de-idolized marriage. . . . Having children was the main way to significance for an adult, since children would remember you. They also gave you security, since they would care for you in old age. Christians who remained single, then, were making the statement that our future is not guaranteed by the family but by God. (Hardcover, pp. 195–96; paperback, p. 223)

TEMPTATIONS ON BOTH SIDES. The New Testament has a remarkably balanced view of singleness and marriage. 1 Corinthians 7 (see the week of October 1–7) recognizes the disadvantages of each. Singles may perhaps be more subject to sexual temptations, but married people have their own challenges. John Newton claimed that the biggest danger of a happy marriage was idolatry. Idolatry of the perfect family leads to fear and anxiety if anything appears to threaten that idol. Love of family is not a sin, of course, but *inordinate* love of family easily can insinuate itself into otherwise strong Christian families. Married and single Christians need to welcome each other and aid and assist one another with their distinctive spiritual challenges.

Reflection: Married men and women, in what ways could your family become an idol? Has it done so already? If you are an unmarried couple, do you realize that new challenges lie ahead?

Thought for prayer: Ask God to remind you that idolatry, the primary sin (Exodus 20:3, the first of all the commandments), is not doing bad things but rather making good things into God-substitutes. Ask God to help you to put away all idols, and to not make your own marriage into one.

Single adult Christians were bearing testimony that God, not family, was their hope. God would guarantee their future, first by giving them their truest family—the church—so they never lacked for brothers and sisters, fathers and mothers, in Christ. But ultimately, Christians' inheritance is nothing less than the fullness of the kingdom of God in the new heavens and new earth. (Hardcover, p. 196; paperback, p. 224)

INEXPLICABLE BELIEVERS. Our modern culture is deeply conflicted about sex and love. It pities married people who have constrained themselves so they are not free to have sex with others. It pities singles who are unattached because it sees sexual love as the main way to get intimacy. When Christians actually live the truth that their citizenship is in heaven and the community of believers is their truest family, the watching world is bemused, confused, and yet attracted (1 Peter 2:11–12). Humans clutch so desperately at the happiness *this* world offers that anyone contentedly living out of the riches of the world to come disrupts their worldview in a powerful way.

Reflection: Married or single, how does your life display your ability to be content with whatever your life holds? Are there ways in which you are *not* content? What, like Paul, do you need to learn in order to be content?

Thought for prayer: Meditate on Philippians 4:11–13. Then pray that God would give you the same "secret of contentment" that Paul spoke about.

[Christian authors have] point[ed] out that Christian hope not only made it possible for singles to live fulfilled lives without spouse and children, but also was impetus for people to marry and *have* children and not be afraid to bring them into this dark world. "For Christians do not place their hope in their children, but rather their children are a sign of their hope . . . that God has not abandoned this world." (Hardcover, p. 196; paperback, p. 224)

THE MULTIPLE USES OF HOPE. Fewer married couples are having children. Many say we shouldn't bring new people into a darkening world. Others simply don't want the limitations on freedom that children bring into your life. But everywhere in Scripture that children are mentioned they are called a "blessing" from God. I (Kathy) had to rely on God's word, as I was one of the people who never enjoyed babies and resented the time children seemed to take from their parents. How much I would have missed if I had not moved into motherhood simply because I trusted God! Trusting in God's promise—that we will all live forever in love in a new, renewed universe—gives both singles hope that their future is secure without children, and married people hope that their children's future is secure as well.

Reflection: Elisabeth Elliot's definition of suffering is "Having what you don't want or wanting what you don't have." Some people want children (singles or the infertile); others have them and are at their wit's end. How does God's word address each group?

Thought for prayer: Meditate on Romans 8:18–25 for our hope in a restored future world. Ask God to fill you with joy at this prospect, and make it a baseline of peace in your life, regardless of how things are going at the present time.

> The Christian church in the West . . . has labeled [singleness] "Plan B for the Christian life." . . . Beneath [this statement] is the premise that single life is a state of deprivation for people who are not yet fully formed enough for marriage. [Paige Benton Brown says:] "I am not single because I am too spiritually unstable to possibly deserve [a spouse] . . . nor . . . too spiritually mature to possibly need one. I am single because God is so abundantly good to me, because this is his best for me." (Hardcover, pp. 196–97; paperback, pp. 224–25)

NOT A DEPRIVATION. If you are single, or if you want to be good brothers and sisters to Christian single adults, I know of no better place to direct your thoughts than to Paige Benton's article, "Singled Out for Good," the article from which the quote above was taken.[132] Whether our life circumstances are of singleness or marriage, sickness or health, happiness or grief, they all give us an opportunity to bear witness to God's wisdom and his love by serving him gladly where we find ourselves, rather than thinking we could serve him so much better if only he would change things. Singleness is no deprivation, and all of us in the Christian community must understand that if we are to be brothers and sisters together in each local church family.

Reflection: Do you think that God has been unloving to you in designing the circumstances of your present life? What consolation is it to you that you can glorify him in those circumstances? Or that the fullness of God's glory awaits you?

Thought for prayer: Meditate on Genesis 50:20, in which Joseph says that all the circumstances of his life, even those that his brothers designed for his harm, were places in which Joseph was able to serve God. Pray for this same mindset of patient, gracious acceptance of circumstances.

Ephesians 5 tells us that marriage is not ultimately about sex or social stability or personal fulfillment. Marriage was created to be a reflection on the human level of our ultimate love relationship and union with the Lord. It is a sign and foretaste of the future kingdom of God. But this high view of marriage tells us, then, that marriage is penultimate. It points us to the Real Marriage that our souls need and the Real Family our hearts were made for. (Hardcover, p. 198; paperback, p. 226)

IMAGES OF GOD EVERYWHERE. Only human beings are made in the image of God (Genesis 1:26–27) and yet all sorts of things in his creation "tell of him," reflecting something of his glory (Psalm 19:1). God made sure that there were sheep, shepherds, sons, gates, bread, and Brides and Bridegrooms—all things he would use to tell us things about himself and his relationship to us. This is not us "anthropomorphizing" God, but rather God filling his world with types and signs and allegories that would teach us about our Creator and Redeemer. The book of Revelation ends with the presentation of the Bride, pure and spotless, God's people joined to him forever. Our earthly marriages are meant to give us (and the world) a hint and a taste of what that eternal union will be like.

Reflection: Does your marriage give you and those who see you a foretaste of the heavenly marriage?

Thought for prayer: Meditate on Psalm 119:64. Thank God for a world filled with his love, with signs and images of his saving grace and care for us. Ask him to remind you of him during the day, so that your daily life can be lived out against a background of constant, quiet, grateful praise.

Married couples will do a bad job of conducting their marriage if they don't see this penultimate status. Even the best marriage cannot by itself fill the void in our souls left by God. Without a deeply fulfilling love relationship with Christ now, and hope in a perfect love relationship with him in the future, married Christians will put too much pressure on their marriage to fulfill them, and that will always create pathology in their lives. (Hardcover, p. 198; paperback, p. 226)

WAYS TO CRUSH. We have been saying that no human being can ever provide you with the love you need and that only God can give. To look for it in a person is to crush them—but how? One way is that we can't allow them to have times of difficulty in which they are understandably somewhat self-absorbed and not as attentive to your needs. Chronic illness is an example. Another way we crush them is because we cannot bear their displeasure at all, so we fail to lovingly critique them. A third way is that we overcorrect them, because we need them to have a practically perfect life. Only if filled with a sense of God's love for you can you risk relationships with imperfect people (and there are no other kind!).

Reflection: Assess whether you have put pressure on each other in any of these three ways, to any degree at all. Forgive and talk about how to improve.

Thought for prayer: Meditate on Ephesians 3:17–19. Ask God to help you not just know about his love but to *know* it.

If single Christians . . . develop a deeply fulfilling love relationship with Jesus, they will . . . be able to handle single life without a devastating sense of being unfulfilled and unformed. And they might as well tackle this spiritual project right away. Why? Because the same idolatry of marriage that is distorting their single lives will eventually distort their married lives if they find a partner. So there's no reason to wait. Demote marriage and family in your heart, put God first, and begin to enjoy the goodness of single life. (Hardcover, p. 198; paperback, pp. 226–27)

LONELINESS WITHIN MARRIAGE. There are many possible reasons that you may feel very alone even if you are married, so many that we can't even list them in this short devotional. But here is one not usually noticed. The same prioritizing of God's love over all human loves is necessary both for married people and singles. Otherwise single people might approach marriage thinking something like, "Finally, this is going to heal me of all my problems and sadness." You have no idea of how lonely you can be in a marriage that is not what you expected it to be—nor can it be. Reorder your hopes for happiness so that they rest on Jesus or, whether inside or outside of marriage, you will never be ready for it.

Reflection: How can a person become a dispenser of God's love, rather than a needy person who needs constant human validation? How can you?

Thought for prayer: Ask God to keep you from either expecting too much out of marriage, forgetting its limits; or too little from marriage, forgetting its cosmic significance.

How can we claim that long-term singleness is a good condition in light of the . . . argument that males and females are in some ways "incomplete" without the other? The answer is the same. It has to do, again, with our hope in Christ and our experience of Christian community. Just as Christian singles find their "heirs" and family within the church, so do brothers find their sisters and sisters find their brothers. (Hardcover, p. 199; paperback, p. 227)

INTIMATE COMMUNITY. First Timothy 5: 1–2 exhorts us to treat Christians as family, as brothers and sisters. That means to look for the same kind of support and friendship you would expect from a good biological sibling, but with spiritual understanding and support added in. As evidence that he wants our relationships with believers to be extremely intimate, Paul adds "in all purity" (cf. 1 Thessalonians 4:1–8). Our hearts are deceitful and we must be on guard, but this little phrase is testimony to how wonderfully close our friendships in Christ can be. One safeguard is to remember our brother-sister relationships should always be in community, and not isolated and exclusive.

Reflection: We are commanded to treat one another as brothers and sisters, knowing the pitfalls that sin can introduce into those relationships. How can you obey God's command, reap the rewards of supportive relationships, and still remain pure?

Thought for prayer: Spend a moment thinking of two Christian brothers or sisters who have been a major help and influence on you. Now thank God for them and ask him to turn you into the same kind of friend, not only to your spouse, but to others.

Gospel beliefs and experience create a bond between Christians that is stronger than any . . . blood relationship, or racial and national identity (Ephesians 2; 1 Peter 2:9–10). . . . I love my biological siblings, my neighbors, and the other members of my ethnic or racial group, yet we no longer share in common our deepest instincts and beliefs about reality. . . . This means that single people within a strong Christian community can experience much of the unique enrichment of cross-gender relationships within a family, particularly the sibling relationships between brothers and sisters. (Hardcover, pp. 199–200; paperback, pp. 227–28)

"COMPLETION" IN COMMUNITY. Christians talk loudly about how marriage to another gender "completes" us, and how our spouses are our better halves. This implies that unmarried people are incomplete half persons. However, while Genesis 1 and 2 do indicate that men and women reflect God's glory together, and that both have unique glories and strengths that the other gender does not, marriage is not the only way for the genders to help and complete each other. Because the church is a family—and because our bond in Christ is deeper than any biological, racial, or cultural tie—singles in a good church can know the "unique enrichment" (see above) of cross-gender relationships in a family.

Reflection: Did you have good sibling relationships? Do you have sibling relationships within the church? Have you ever had difficulties to overcome? What were they and how was God's grace brought into that relationship?

Thought for prayer: Thank God for the ways in which you and your spouse help and complete each other as man and woman, and ask the Lord for opportunities to establish strong family ties within your church, so that corporately you can complete each other as men and women.

[Christian marriage] . . . forces you over the years to learn how a person of the other sex habitually looks at and reacts to people and situations. . . . [C]all this "cross-gender enrichment." . . . But . . . in a strong Christian community, where the sharing of our hearts and lives goes beyond the superficial down to what God is teaching us and how he is forming and growing us . . . in . . . mutual "one-another" ministry, a kind of cross-gender enrichment happens naturally. (Hardcover, pp. 200–201; paperback, pp. 229–30)

DIFFERENT DIFFERING GIFTS. The Bible tells us that Christians have differing gifts—no one can do everything well (1 Corinthians 12:4–7). But churches often fail to recognize that a man and a woman who share the same gift will exercise it somewhat differently, with diverse insights often reaching and helping different persons. So often we need both men and women doing the same ministry in partnership side by side. Since we all have one Creator who made us, male and female, in his image, it would be wrong to neglect the gifts he has given to men and women to strengthen his Body. We must honor one another as we each inhabit the roles he has given us in which to exercise our gifts.

Reflection: Men, do you honor the gifts that women bring to a meeting, a conversation, or a task? Women, do you honor the gifts that men bring to a situation? How could you do better?

Thought for prayer: Take time to think about at least one man and one woman who ministered to you in different but profound ways. Thank God for them both, and ask God to help your church fully use the gifts of men and women together.

Of course it is less intense than in marriage. And yet the more corporate experience is not a "poor second" to marriage, since in marriage you are put together with just one member of the opposite gender, which does and should limit the extent of friendships with others of the opposite sex. In Christian community . . . singles can have a greater range of friendships among both sexes. (Hardcover, p. 201; paperback, p. 230)

ORGANIC COMMUNITY. If the church is to be our truest family we must recognize that it is not just an organization, but an *organism*, a Body. In a body every part supports the other, and every part feels the others' pain. (Have you ever noticed that when you hurt your toe or finger, suddenly it becomes the center of attention?) Your church is becoming an organic community when it is the best possible place to be when you are going through a time of suffering. If you are hurting, are you noticed? Cared for? Nuclear families—and singles—are often going through too much pain to make it without help from God's family.

Reflection: The point of these recent devotionals is to see the "penultimacy" of marriage; that being married does not furnish you with all you need and you must be a part of God's family. Have you been convinced of this? If you have, what does that mean concretely for you in your marriage?

Thought for prayer: Ask God to pour out his Spirit on your church and churches in general, so they might truly become the family of God.

Unlike traditional societies, Christianity sees singleness as good because the kingdom of God provides the most lasting possible legacy and heirs. Unlike sex-and-romance-saturated Western society, Christians see singleness as good because our union with Christ can fulfill our deepest longings. And yet, unlike our commitment-averse, postmodern society, Christianity does not fear or avoid marriage either. Adults in Western society are deeply shaped by individualism, a fear and even hatred of limiting options for the sake of others. (Hardcover, p. 201; paperback, p. 230)

BEING FRIENDS. I have known women and men who can't commit to marrying someone they really love because of FOMO (fear of missing out). They hesitate just in case a better prospect comes along. Married people should be good friends to singles by neither pushing them toward marriage nor allowing them to acquiesce in such a consumerist attitude. Singles in turn have much to offer married friends. They may direct married people, too often absorbed in family maintenance, to what is happening in the wider world. From our differing vantage points we all come to know an aspect of the goodness of God that no one else has ever seen, and in heaven we will never tire of telling one another of his goodness to us.

Reflection: Think of how your friends who are married and friends who are single enrich your life in different ways. What are those ways? Do you need to add more of one kind of friend to your relationships?

Thought for prayer: Ask God to increase in you the candor, wisdom, willingness to be vulnerable, and willingness to dedicate time—all the things that it takes to be a good friend.

December 1

[He:] You have stolen my heart, my sister, my bride; you have stolen my heart with one glance of your eyes, with one jewel of your necklace. (Song of Solomon 4:9)

UNION. Here in the Song of Solomon, for the first time the woman is called "my bride," and so the lovers have at last been married. However, she is not only called bride but "my sister." In ancient times "the relationship . . . between a brother and a sister was the closest bond of friendship . . . possible with a person of the opposite gender."[133] This is one more biblical way to say "sexual union was never intended to exist by itself." It should be part of a complete union of body *and* soul that includes "mutual care, respect, and self-giving to each other in every area of life."[134] Sex is meant to make you one flesh and to knit you to each other as completely as an arm is knit to a body.

Reflection: What does the Bible tell us when it says your spouse should not only be a lover and friend, but like a sibling? What does that add to our understanding of marriage?

Prayer: Lord, thank you for giving us in marriage the closest possible relationship two human beings can have in this life. Console us both with each other, healing as much as possible the loneliness that afflicts us all spiritually. Thank you for my lover, friend, and sister (or brother) in Christ. Amen.

December 2

[He:] How delightful is your love, my sister, my bride! How much more pleasing is your love than wine, and the fragrance of your perfume more than any spice! (Song of Solomon 4:10)

MATURE WINE. In the intervening chapters the man likened the woman's body to a vineyard in blossom (1:6; 2:13), and now he speaks of their sexual consummation as the best wine. The extended metaphor is instructive. You don't harvest a vineyard when it is in bloom but rather when its fruit is completely ripe.[135] Until your love has brought you to full, thoughtful willingness to commit your whole life to the other in marriage, the wine of your relationship is not yet mature. "Now on their wedding day, the couple's love is fully mature, like a fine wine, ready to be consummated."[136] Again we see the Bible's insistence that sexuality be integrated with all the rest of one's life in self-giving, rather than isolated as a consumer good to be partaken at one's leisure.

Reflection: What does this image—of love as mature, fine wine—teach us about marriage?

Prayer: Lord, your goal for me is that I become "fully mature in Christ" (Colossians 1:28). I also want that for our marital love. Enrich our love with wisdom and discernment, with mercy and grace, and with to-the-death commitment so that we can rejoice in the gift of each other and in you, the Giver. Amen.

[He:] How beautiful you are and how pleasing, my love, with your delights! Your stature is like that of the palm, and your breasts like clusters of fruit. I said, "I will climb the palm tree; I will take hold of its fruit. May your breasts be like clusters of grapes on the vine." (Song of Solomon 7:6–8)

DELIGHT IN THE BODY. In the first three chapters of the Song of Solomon the lovers pursue and long for each another, yet there is a repeated exhortation to self-control, to "not arouse or awaken love until it pleases" (2:7, 3:5). Finally comes the wedding in chapter 4. Now the man takes hold of his wife's breasts in sexual embrace. No longer is he merely admiring them—now he will partake. "God invented our bodies and delights in them, and would have us do the same."[137] The Bible is subversive to both hedonism and asceticism. In it we see a bare-faced rejoicing in sexual beauty and pleasure—no prudishness here. And yet, as we have seen, the man and woman have waited on sex until their love has made them capable of whole-life investment in each other.

Reflection: Is there a celebratory note in your sexual relationship? Do you ever let your spouse feel that you rejoice in his or her body?

Prayer: Lord, protect me from either the semiworship of sex, as in pornography, or a discomfort with it entirely. Instead, in my marriage, show me how to delight in touch and physicality, as I love my spouse as you loved us. Amen.

[He:] How beautiful you are, my darling! Oh, how beautiful! Your eyes behind your veil are doves. . . . [Y]ou have stolen my heart with one glance of your eyes, with one jewel of your necklace. (Song of Solomon 4:1, 9)

CAPTIVATED BY THE INNER PERSON. For all the Song of Solomon's rejoicing in physicality, the part of the body that gets the most attention is, interestingly, the eyes. Of course a person's eyes can be attractively shaped, but in verse 9 it is the *glance* of the eyes that reveals the inner life of the heart. To be captivated by the eyes is to be captivated by all the person is. Here again we have a biblical concept of romantic attraction that does not ignore physical beauty but does not make it the most important component. Indeed, aging spouses have learned that even when bodies are slowly losing their loveliness, the eyes can become more attractive. Why? Because behind them are deepening wells of joy and wisdom, of love for God and for each other.

Reflection: It takes a beautiful heart to capture a heart. What do you find beautiful about your spouse's inner person? Share your answer.

Prayer: Lord, as my spouse and I age, help us to find each other more and more delightfully attractive, even as our outward bodies waste away. Amen.

[She:] My beloved is radiant and ruddy, outstanding among ten thousand. . . . His arms are rods of gold set with topaz. His body is like polished ivory decorated with lapis lazuli. His legs are pillars of marble set on bases of pure gold. . . . This is my beloved, this is my friend, daughters of Jerusalem. I belong to my beloved and his desire is for me. (Song of Solomon 5:10, 14, 16; 7:10)

SEXUAL ASSERTIVENESS. "The role of the woman . . . is truly astounding, especially in light of its ancient origins. . . . In Song 5:10–16 she boldly exclaims her physical attraction. . . . ["His abdomen is like a polished ivory tusk, decorated with sapphires" (verse 14).] The Hebrew is quite erotic, and most translators cannot bring themselves to bring out the obvious meaning."[138] Yet in 7:10 this sexually assertive woman expresses her submission to her husband: "I belong to my beloved." As in the book of Proverbs, the woman depicted does not fit into either the traditional model of wife as possession or servant, or with the modern view of husband and wife as interchangeable partners without distinct roles.

Reflection: Are you clear on your roles within the marriage and the family? Do those roles reflect the balance depicted here?

Prayer: Lord, your Word puts all sorts of hedges around sex, but it also exults in it. It shows us sex as neither a good nor an evil in itself, but as either consecration or desecration, depending on whether we offer it to you. Help us as a couple, and help Christians as a people, to offer it to you. Amen.

December 6

[Friends:] Where has your beloved gone, most beautiful of women? Which way did your beloved turn, that we may look for him with you? (Song of Solomon 6:1)

MARITAL REALISM. In the Song of Solomon, no sooner is there marital union (3:6–5:1) than there is separation. The man is gone and the woman is again searching for him with the help of her friends (6:1), but by 6:3 they are reunited. The particular reasons for this losing and finding are not obvious, but the message is clear. The Bible never sees marriage as a "and they lived happily ever after" story. As the premarital relationship had its ups and downs so will the marriage. In fact, if spouses do not continue to constantly pursue one another, they will drift apart. Why? Because marriage is giving all you know of yourself to the other—and that is constantly changing. Marriage is like riding a bicycle—you either go forward or you fall off.

Reflection: What significant things have you learned about yourself since you were married? How has that affected your marriage? Are you still "pursuing" one another?

Prayer: Lord, we thank you for making marriage a covenantal union, and for how it has held us together through trials and brought us to a place of richer love than we could have otherwise known. Amen.

> [She:] Place me like a seal over your heart, like a seal on your arm; for love is as strong as death, its jealousy unyielding as the grave. It burns like blazing fire, like a mighty flame. Many waters cannot quench love; rivers cannot sweep it away. (Song of Solomon 8:6–7)

LOVE OVERCOMING DEATH. The woman claims that nothing—not floodwaters, death, or the grave—will be able to end their love. But don't even marriage vows acknowledge "till death do us part"? Isn't this poetic hyperbole? Yes, but the text also hints at something. The Lord's love is literally stronger than death, and it protects us from both water and flames (Isaiah 43:2). So the subtle references in these verses "point us beyond this life to the greater love [of the Lord] who will never let us go, triumphing even over death, the last enemy."[139] What if spouses love each other *in Christ*, with Christ's love that cannot end? Then while at the wedding we say, "till death do us part," on our deathbeds we can say, "See you later."

Reflection: How can you and your spouse be more ready for death—not just financially and practically but emotionally and spiritually? Have you discussed it candidly?

Prayer: Lord, how we praise you for giving us a love that is stronger than death—a love that will survive the grave. What greater comfort could there be? And we thank you for the price you paid for that comfort when you went to the cross for us. Amen.

December 8

While traditional societies tend to make an idol out of marriage [and] . . . of the family and tribe, contemporary societies tend to make an idol of independence [and] of individual choice and happiness. While the traditional motive for marriage was social duty . . . the contemporary motive for marriage is personal fulfillment. Both of these motives are partially right, of course, but they tend to become ultimates if the gospel has not changed your mind and heart. (Hardcover, p. 202; paperback, pp. 230–31)

ALWAYS OUT OF STEP. The Gospel challenges every human culture at some point, so Christians will always be somewhat out of step. As to sex and marriage, they will be too traditional for modern people and too lax for traditional cultures. This can create suspicion and mistrust on the part of nonbelievers if we allow ourselves to act self-righteously. If, instead, we are able to warmly welcome into our homes and lives those who don't believe and allow them to witness us repenting and forgiving one another, the power of the Gospel to change lives can make those same differences attractive and intriguing.

Reflection: Would your marriage intrigue a nonbeliever if he or she were to witness it closely? Would your dating life as a single create curiosity and interest among your friends?

Thought for prayer: Ask God to help you be neither resentful and disdainful toward the values of the surrounding culture nor too influenced by it.

December 9

[Traditional culture says to singles,] "You aren't a whole person until you are married." . . . [Modern culture says to those who aren't married,] "You shouldn't marry until you have professionally made it big and you find the perfect partner who won't try to change you in any way." . . . Their first culture [makes us] over-desirous of marriage. Their second culture [makes us] over-afraid of marriage. (Hardcover, p. 202; paperback, p. 231)

TRUSTING GOD FOR MARRIAGE. It's natural to be nervous about making a marriage commitment. Sometimes we want to have complete assurance that if we marry, everything in life will be wonderful. But decoded, this translates into a fear of trusting God when moving into uncharted territory. Don't give in to that. Even if a person remains unmarried they will have to trust God for their future, because they don't know what lies ahead—health or sickness, success or failure, happiness or sorrow. So remaining single is not a protection against the unknown. God will have to be your guide, protector, and Father in any case.

Reflection: Have you avoided marriage because of a fear of the complications marriage might bring into your life? Did marriage ever scare you because you thought it would complicate your life? Conversely, as a married person, do you ever long for the single life, thinking it would be simpler and therefore happier than your married state?

Thought for prayer: Meditate on Proverbs 3:5–6. Then ask God to help you trust him completely, putting your times in his hands (Psalm 31:15).

December 10

[E]mpirical studies show that males will look for near perfection in physical looks while women will look for partners who are financially well off. . . . [S]exual and financial factors dominate the thinking. As a result, modern dating can become a remarkably crass form of self-merchandising. You must look good and make money if you are to attract dates, a partner, or a spouse. And the reason you want a good-looking or affluent partner is for your own self-esteem. (Hardcover, pp. 202–3; paperback, pp. 231–32)

YOU NEED JUST TWO THINGS. Successful, happy marriages must be built on a much more stable foundation than physical appearance or financial solvency—both of which are subject to changes, even sudden ones. What, then, do we need? Two things. First, we need two people who love one another enough to make a promise to each other. Life has so many unexpected twists and turns that anything not grounded in a common covenantal life before God will always be fragile. A wedding is not a declaration of *present* love as much as it is a promise of *future* love, when the exhilaration of feelings may have abated. Second, we need two people who believe and understand the gospel well enough to solve problems with it, to repent, forgive, and change.

Reflection: Unmarried couples, what are you looking for in a spouse? A traveling companion who will join you in seeking a life pleasing to God? Or something else? Married people, in what ways have your wedding vows supported and enriched your love in the rough patches?

Thought for prayer: If the flourishing of your marriage is dependent on the strength of your promise and the ability to repent and forgive, ask God to stir up his grace so you grow in both.

Many singles are looking for a highly compatible, brilliant, and beautiful partner. For others, singleness is at best a purgatory, where you live waiting for your real life to begin, or at worst a misery. The first kind of single looks right past all sorts of good prospective spouses because of fear and perfectionism. The second kind of single can scare people away because of his or her neediness, and sometimes can make terrible choices in marital partners out of desperation. (Hardcover, pp. 203–4; paperback, p. 233)

MARRIAGE SEEKING. Both the single state and marriage have their spiritual advantages and disadvantages, as St. Paul points out at length in 1 Corinthians 7. Should you decide to seek marriage, you must use wisdom to choose the person with whom you will share your life, your ministry, and your heart. How do you assess a person for those qualities? Not by using numbers, either of body stats or financial bottom lines, and not from a distance. Instead, throw yourself into ministry and the service of others. Someone you serve with (missions trip, evangelism outreach, mercy effort, prayer team) is someone you will get to know from the inside out. Meanwhile, you will be filling your life with activities in obedience to God, rather than obsessing about with who or when you might be married.

Reflection: Unmarried couples, have you gotten to know each other in the context of serving others together? If you have, you will learn much more about each other. Married couples, how can your home and family provide unpressured occasions for singles to meet one another?

Thought for prayer: Remember that you and your spouse are not just lovers, or even just friends, but builders of Christian community and witnesses to the gospel and kingdom. Confess to God where you are weak, and ask him to strengthen your marriage in each area.

December 12

How different seeking marriage would be if . . . we were to fall in love especially with the glorious thing God is doing in our spouse's life? Ironically, this view of marriage eventually does provide unbelievable personal fulfillment, but not in the sacrifice-free and superficial way that contemporary people want it to come. Instead, it gives the unique, breathtaking fulfillment of visible character growth (Ephesians 5:25–27) into love, peace, joy, and hope (Colossians 1, Galatians 5, 1 Corinthians 13). (Hardcover, p. 203; paperback, pp. 232–33)

MOTIVES FOR CHANGING. This vision is very different from marrying a person with the expectation of *you* changing *him* or *her* into what you conceive to be their "best self." You must be able to see into a potential spouse's life enough to know something of the gifts and calling that God has given them, and to desire to support them in growth in those areas. It takes great wisdom to know yourself well enough to discern the difference between "supporting your spouse's growth" and "manipulating your spouse into becoming the person YOU want him or her to be." Humility, a reasonable self-distrust (am I suggesting this because it benefits *me*, or because it will benefit *him* or *her*?), and prayer together are vitally necessary.

Reflection: Do you pray together enough to know one another's hearts? Is there a better way to become more intimate with one another than to have a prayer life together?

Thought for prayer: Meditate on 1 Samuel 12:23 to see that it is a sin against both God and your spouse to fail to pray with and for them regularly. Confess to God your lack of a sufficient marital prayer life and ask him for his great help.

December 13

[What is the "gift" of singleness in 1 Corinthians 7:7?] It is fruitfulness in life and ministry *through* the single state. When you have this gift, there may indeed be struggles, but . . . God is helping you to grow spiritually and be fruitful in the lives of others despite them. That means a single gift is not just for a select few, and it is not necessarily lifelong, though it may be. It may [also] be a grace given for a finite period of time. (Hardcover, p. 208; paperback, p. 238)

YOUR LIFE, A SACRIFICE. God has redeemed us and given us everything. In return, we give him our lives, acknowledging him as Lord over all. As we yield the circumstances of our lives—singleness, married with children, infertile, widowed, healthy, sick, perplexed, struggling—he will use them as he did the five loaves and two fish to do greater things than what we can imagine. Often the only thing standing in the way of our usefulness is our own unhappiness about what we have to offer God; we think we could offer him a married life, but not a single one. Or a healthy life, but not one compromised by illness. Yet God can and will be glorified by anything we yield to him to do greater things than we can imagine.

Reflection: What is the difference between merely enduring a situation through gritted teeth and offering it to God as a sacrifice? What attitudes does it require? What practices?

Thought for prayer: Meditate on Romans 12:1–2. Then ask God to help you to make your life a whole burnt offering—a living sacrifice.

December 14

[In dating], act your age. Teenagers generally shouldn't try to awaken emotional and physical desires that can't . . . responsibly find their fulfillment in marriage. However, if you are single and in your thirties, you should recognize that if you insist on trying to continue the entertainment category of dating with others of your age, you will be often playing with people's emotions. The older you are, and the more often you "go out," the quicker both people must be to acknowledge that you are seeking marriage. (Hardcover, p. 209; paperback, p. 239)

SELF-CONTROL. It makes no sense to deliberately arouse sexual desire that, outside of a marriage covenant, will either be frustrated or unrighteously consummated (see November 7). Unless you can embrace lifelong chastity (and most people cannot), then seek a spouse with whom you can exult in the gift of sexuality, and God willing, the creation of new life. If someone gave you a beautiful and expensive car, would you turn it on in the driveway and just rev the engine while remaining in park? That would be terrible for the engine, besides not being what the car was built for. Then, similarly, don't deliberately arouse sexual desire by what you watch, look at, listen to, or fantasize about, unless you are legitimately arousing your spouse for mutual sexual bonding.

Reflection: Unmarried couples, are you being careful to not deliberately arouse strong sexual desire before you are married?

Thought for prayer: Remember before God that self-control is not simply a matter of stoical willpower but of loving the important thing more than the urgent thing. Then ask the Lord to increase in you the spiritual fruit of self-control in every area of your life (2 Timothy 1:7).

December 15

> *Do not allow yourself deep emotional involvement with a nonbelieving person. . . .* The Bible everywhere assumes that Christians should marry other Christians. . . . If your partner doesn't share your Christian faith . . . and if Jesus is central to you, then that means that your partner doesn't truly understand *you.* He or she doesn't understand the mainspring of your life, the ground motive of all you do. . . . [Y]ou will repeatedly make decisions that your partner won't be able to fathom at all. (Hardcover, pp. 209–10; paperback, pp. 239–40)

ONLY MARRY A BELIEVER. I would direct you to a longer treatment of this question called *Don't Take It from Me* by Kathy Keller, easily found on the internet.[140] In that article I wish that I could have filmed or taken statements from all the men and women I have known over the years who have had the sorrows that come with marriage to a nonbeliever (resulting sometimes from ignorance, other times from a postmarriage conversion, or, too often, because of disobedience). Please take the time to read it all. The pronouncements of the happily married often carry little weight with those eager to marry the person of their choice, even if he or she is not a Christian. You need to hear instead from those who have lived with this choice.

Reflection: When you were single and uncommitted to anyone, were you convinced that it is better to remain single than to marry a person who didn't share your faith? Married people, if you are married to a spouse who doesn't share your faith, how are you remaining faithful to your true Bridegroom without wounding your earthly spouse?

Thought for prayer: Ask God to help you as a couple, so you do not merely know each other emotionally, but understand each other spiritually, and are familiar with each other's faith in the Lord, both its strengths and weaknesses.

> If you do marry someone who does not share your faith, then there are
> only two ways to proceed. One is that you will . . . lose your transpar-
> ency. In the normal . . . Christian life, you relate Christ . . . to
> everything. . . . You will base decisions on Christian principles. You
> will think about what you read in the Bible that day. But if you are
> natural and transparent about all of these thoughts, your partner will
> find it at least tedious or annoying and even offensive. . . . You will just
> have to hide it all. (Hardcover, p. 210; paperback, p .241)

HOW TO REALLY WIN. Peter gives advice to women married
to unbelieving husbands in 1 Peter 3:1–4. Modern people may
cringe at the suggestion that women submit to their husbands,
but if the goal of that submission is a life of purity and reverence
that will be so winsome and attractive it might win their spouse
to Christ, very few women would refuse. This is not a suggestion
that women allow themselves to be abused (even though many
want to confuse submission with an invitation to abuse), but
rather a display of a "quiet and gentle spirit." Spouses of either
sex who attempt to nag their husband or wife into belief in Jesus
will find they only create resentment and resistance.

Reflection: Married women, how is that "quiet and gentle spirit"
expressing itself in your marriage? Well, not so well, or not at all?
Married men, when your wife entrusts herself to you, do you
find your heart softening toward her, or becoming resentful?
How do you let her know that you find her kindness attractive?

Thought for prayer: Ask God to increase Christlike qualities
in you primarily to please and honor him, but also to attract
your spouse toward Jesus as well.

December 17

The other, worse possibility is that you simply move Christ out of a central place in your consciousness. You will have to let your heart-ardor for Christ cool. You will have to deliberately *not* think out how your Christian commitment relates to every area of your life. You will demote Christ in your mind and heart, because if you keep him central, you will feel isolated from your spouse. (Hardcover, pp. 210–11; paperback, p. 241)

UNEQUALLY YOKED. The description above can happen in marriages in which one spouse is not a Christian, but also in those where one partner falls far behind the other in spiritual interest and growth. The end result is that the spouse who is "out in front" feels pressure to demote Christ to be less central in the life. No one really believes this will happen. The partner promises the believer that he or she will have freedom to practice and believe as he or she chooses. This may be meant sincerely, but it cannot be implemented. Because marriage creates a one-flesh unity, both partners need to agree on what things are of critical importance in all of life's choices. Since Jesus is Lord in one person's life and not in the other person's, that will be nearly impossible.

Reflection: Answer this question: Is your spouse in any way discouraging you from moving forward in your Christian walk? If so, how? What can be done to change that?

Thought for prayer: Ask God that, whatever the situation in your marriage, he would continue to change you, from one degree to the next, into the likeness of your Savior (2 Corinthians 3:18).

[P]hysical attraction is something that must definitely grow between marriage partners and it will grow (rather than diminishing) as time goes on if you start with . . . "comprehensive attraction." . . . Partly it is being attracted to the person's "character" or spiritual fruit. . . . [Partly it is] a "secret thread" that unites . . . [your] favorite books, music, places, or past-times—[things that] move you [most deeply]. . . . Sometimes you will meet a person who shares to a great degree the same "mythos" thread. . . . "[C]omprehensive" attraction is . . . on the basis of character, mission, future-self, and mythos. (Hardcover, pp. 211–12; paperback, pp. 242–43)

THE NEW CREATION. The term we use in *The Meaning of Marriage*—"comprehensive attraction"—is all but incomprehensible to people today. They only recognize sexual attraction, or separately and distinctly, a chemistry based on political ideals, social causes, and/or hobby enthusiasms. Comprehensive attraction includes the physical and even "common interests," but it recognizes that these things are superficial and the ones most doomed by time and circumstance to change. However, if you are in love with the new creation that God is making in your beloved's life, you will find yourself more and more deeply attracted as that person grows and emerges throughout the years.

Reflection: Couples, married or dating, what do you see in your partner's inner being that attracts you? Can you identify the seeds of what God is doing to make your partner glorious?

Thought for prayer: Think of the ways that you have already seen God change your spouse toward Christlikeness during the time you have known him or her. Praise and thank God for them, and ask him for more of this growth in both of you—so much more.

December 19

Sometimes . . . powerful emotions . . . seem on the surface to be deep love. . . . The fact that these infatuations can become so hostile and bitter so quickly shows that the comprehensive attraction and love was never really there. . . . [To know if] you have moved past the infatuation stage is to ask a set of questions. Have you been through and solved a few sharp conflicts? Have you been through a cycle of repenting and forgiving? Have each of you shown the other you can make changes out of love for the other? (Hardcover, pp. 213–14; paperback, pp. 244–46)

LASTING LOVE. Infatuation and obsession are based on fantasy. They will never survive the reality—sometimes harsh—of life in our fallen world. What kind of love will? It is the kind Jesus gave and that he commanded that his followers show to one another. That kind of love was so radical that a new word had to be used to describe it—*agape* love. C. S. Lewis uses "charity" or the Greek word *agape* in his book *The Four Loves* to describe a self-giving love that was sacrificially committed to the well-being of others.[141] Within marriage it is a deep unitive attachment that is the product of promises, trials faced together, reconciliations, sacrifices, and time.

Reflection: Unmarried couples, are you able to tell whether your feelings for the other person are self-giving and sacrificial, or mainly about how good the other person makes *you* feel? Married couples, think of the sacrifices you have made to keep your feelings alive and warm toward one another. What sacrifices have you made to further your spouse's growth in Christ?

Thought for prayer: Thank God that his love for us is not based on our perfection but on his, and ask him to create in you both a growing *agape* love for one another.

Two kinds of couples answer "no" [to the question of whether they can resolve conflicts well]. The first kind are those who never have any conflicts. It may be they are not past infatuation. The second kind of couple has had a stormy relationship and has the same unresolved fights over and over again. They haven't learned even the rudimentary skills of repentance, forgiveness, and change. Neither of these couples may be ready for marriage. (Hardcover, pp. 214–15; paperback, p. 246)

THE STRING THROUGH EVERYTHING. Malcolm Gladwell famously said that ten thousand hours of practice were needed in order to reach competency. In premarital counseling we were horrified to hear the pastor say that after fifteen years of marriage, his wife and he thought they "might just about be getting the hang of married life." I (Kathy) now think he set the bar too low. The hardness of marriage is due largely to how much we change. Just when you think you have "gotten the hang" of loving someone without children, you have to learn to love someone with them. But remember Lewis Smedes (June 17) who said, "My wife has been married to five men, and they have all been me." The string that unites all the different "selves" and situations is your marriage promise to be loving no matter what.

Reflection: How do you prepare for the changes that will occur in your marriage and yourself over the course of a marriage? Does your covenantal vow offer you support?

Thought for prayer: Ask God to help you see that your spouse's changes are part of his plan for him or her, so you won't be either too afraid or too angry. Then ask him for help in loving your spouse as is needed now.

December 21

Get and submit to lots of community input. . . . Marriage should not be a strictly individual, unilateral decision. It is too important, and our personal perspective is too easily skewed. The community has many married people in it who have much wisdom for single people to hear. Singles should get community input at every step of the way when seeking marriage. (Hardcover, p. 217; paperback, p. 248)

SPLENDOR IN THE ORDINARY. Once you are married and full sexual expression is not only allowable, but deeply nourishing, how does one avoid sex becoming routine and dull? By going back to the same expressions and caresses and imbuing them with new tenderness and new meaning, based on better understanding and insight into your partner. When I hold Tim's hand now, it means much more than when we first held hands. And if you are an unmarried couple, why not start now, before marriage, by imbuing those expressions of longing and tenderness that are wise and prudent ("do not stir up love until its time") with ever-new meaning, rather than trying to get a new thrill by pushing the envelope just a little further out?

Reflection: Unmarried couples, are you trying to walk as close to "the line" as you can without actually falling into sin? Or, knowing your own heart, are you giving yourself a wide margin for error? Married couples, how well have you done in adding new levels of loving tenderness into your love-making over the years? How could you do even better?

Thought for prayer: Meditate on Ephesians 5:19–20. We are to go through ordinary daily life "singing" thankfully in our hearts to the Lord. So ask God to give you that same spirit and ability to go through the day thanking him often for your spouse and your marriage until your heart sings.

According to Paul, sex with a prostitute is wrong because *every* sex act is supposed to be a *uniting act*. Paul insists it is radically dissonant to give your body to someone to whom you will not also commit your whole life. C. S. Lewis likened sex without marriage to tasting food without swallowing and digesting. The analogy is apt. . . . Paul, then, is decrying the monstrosity of physical oneness without all the other kinds of oneness that every sex act should mirror. (Hardcover, p. 225; paperback, pp. 258–59)

HOW TO MEASURE LOVE. It is typical in our culture to make a distinction between a mere hookup for sexual pleasure and two people who sleep together because they "really love each other." But surely even a hookup ordinarily happens because they are feeling attraction—isn't that love? The problem comes when we define love as simply an emotional intensity of feeling. The fact is that such a feeling can be a function of your desire to possess and experience the other person's affirmation more than a desire for the good and happiness of the other person. How can we measure real love, then? A good test is this: Do you love the other person enough to marry them? To give away your independence in order to be with them? If you can't do that, don't talk of loving someone enough to sleep with them.

Reflection: Unmarried couples, are you willing to assess your love with this test and refrain from sex until you have made the marriage promise? Married couples, can you take comfort that, when your feelings are up and down, your faithfulness to your marriage promise is still a steady, sustaining way to love each other?

Thought for prayer: Thank God that he saved us through a promise, a promise to redeem us even at the greatest cost (Genesis 15 and Galatians 3:10–14). Then ask him to enable you both to continue to love each other through being faithful to your promise.

Unless your marital relationship is in a good condition, sex doesn't work. So be very careful to look beneath the surface. A lack of "sexual compatibility" might not really be a lack of love-making skill at all. It may be a sign of deeper problems in the relationship. It is often the case that, if the problems are addressed, the sexual intimacy improves. (Hardcover, p. 235; paperback, p. 270)

SEX AS TEST. We have seen that sex is in a sense a "marriage renewal ceremony," in which you give yourself to each other afresh as you did at the first. Your bodily union is at the same moment a way to bear witness to the whole-life giving of the past as well as a way to deepen the emotional spiritual bond at that moment. No wonder, then, that if anything is wrong anywhere else in the marriage it will have an effect on sex. It will "show up in bed." Sex is therefore a test. A loss of sexual intimacy is usually a sign not that the chemistry has mysteriously vanished, but in some part of your marriage you are failing to love each other as you ought.

Reflection: Together, look back at your past and see if, as it were, problems outside of bed showed up in bed. Is that happening now?

Thought for prayer: Meditate on Psalm 139:23–24. Then apply this to your marriage. Ask God to show you hidden stresses, or ways you are failing each other to which you may be blind. Then ask for help to love each other more skillfully.

While the first view sees sex as an unavoidable drive and the second as a necessary evil, the last view sees sex as a critical form for self-expression, a way to "be yourself" and "find yourself." . . . Sex is there primarily for an individual's fulfillment and self-realization. . . . The Biblical attitude toward sex is popularly thought to be the second view—sex as demeaning and dirty. But it is most definitely not. It differs quite radically from each of these other understandings. (Hardcover, p. 220; paperback, p. 252)

THE MOST POSITIVE VIEW. In the ancient Greco-Roman world, sex was either seen as just a physical appetite or as a defiling distraction from higher, more spiritual goals. Our own modern culture has a much more positive view of sex than the ancients did, which some scholars argue is credited to Christianity.[142] Yet even today sex is seen as an emotional appetite for intimacy that we must gratify. Both the ancient and the modern say the purpose of sex is to meet your own needs. Christianity rejects both of these views, proclaiming that sex is a way to serve the other, to build community, and to image God and his saving love. Don't settle for any view lower than this one.

Reflection: In the popular mind, what is the Christian view of sex? Why is that the view?

Thought for prayer: Meditate on Matthew 5:13–16, on being both "salt" and "light" in society. Ask God to help you be both.

Sin, which is first and foremost a disorder of the heart . . . has a big impact on sex. Our passions and desires for sex now are very distorted. Sex is for whole-life self-giving. However, the sinful heart wants to use sex for selfish reasons, not self-giving, and therefore the Bible puts many rules around it to direct us to use it in the right way. The Christian sex ethic can be summarized like this: sex is for use within marriage between a man and woman. (Hardcover, pp. 220–21; paperback, p. 253)

GIFT GIVING. God so loved the world that he gave himself to us in Jesus Christ (John 3:16). Christmas is all about gift-giving and that is appropriate. The incarnation, in which God became human and lost his glory and invulnerability, is the great act of self-giving. Where Christianity differs from our society regarding marriage is at this very point. Many want love, sex, and intimacy but they don't want to give away their independence through marriage. But Jesus lost independence when he gave himself to us, and we lose ours when we give ourselves to him—yet in that mutual self-giving comes glory and freedom. Marital union should be an image of our union with Christ (Ephesians 5:25ff.) and it brings freedom-through-giving in the same way.

Reflection: Some say that Christianity has so many rules about sex because it has such a negative view of it. Make an argument that the rules reflect a *higher* view, not a lower view of sex.

Thought for prayer: On this Christmas Day, thank God for his gift of marriage and of your marriage, even with all of its ups and downs and challenges.

December 26

Biblical Christianity may be the most body-positive religion in the world. It teaches that God made matter and physical bodies and saw that it was all good (Genesis 1:31) . . . that in Jesus Christ God himself actually took on a human body . . . and that someday he is going to give us all perfect, resurrected bodies. It says that God created sexuality and gave a woman and man to each other in the beginning. (Hardcover, p. 221; paperback, p. 253)

PRUDISHNESS IS BAD THEOLOGY. Modern people think of Christianity as being negative toward the physical body, but that is not true. Historians have shown that the idea of the goodness and reality of the body and of physical creation was given to Western culture by Christianity.[143] God made the physical world and it was "good." When the God of the Bible comes into the world he takes on a human body. He is so committed to restoring his physical creation to its original beauty and brilliance that he atoned for sin and rose in a new resurrection body, something that all believers will someday receive. The goodness of sex is an implication of all this. Christians should be the last to be prudish.

Reflection: Think of other implications of this doctrine of creation—that the physical world is good—for other aspects of your life.

Thought for prayer: Spend some time thanking God for the gift of your body—for all the pleasures and sensations of which it is capable—and for his commitment to redeem our bodies (Romans 8:23), a prospect wonderful beyond our imaginings.

God not only allows sex within marriage but strongly commands it (1 Corinthians 7:3–5). In the book of Proverbs, husbands are encouraged to let their wives' breasts fill them with delight and be intoxicated by their sexual love (Proverbs 5:19; cf. Deuteronomy 24:5). The book Song of Solomon does much barefaced rejoicing in the delights of sexual love in marriage. . . . The Bible is a very uncomfortable book for the prudish! (Hardcover, pp. 221–22; paperback, p. 254)

A HIGH VIEW OF SEX. There is a paradox in the biblical attitude toward sex. Paul says that "sexual immorality, or any kind of impurity . . . should not even be named among you"[144] (Ephesians 5:3), and we should "flee sexual immorality" (1 Corinthians 6:18). Yet in the texts cited above (and December 3) the language regarding sex is unashamedly celebratory. How do we explain this? The answer is that the uniquely lofty view of sex in the Bible—that it is a signpost and participation in God's restoration of the world—accounts for both emphases. If our view of sex is lower, we might be uptight about sex *or* we might be casual about it. For Christians, because it is such an incredible good, it must not be indulged in lightly.

Reflection: What attitudes toward sex have you had in your background? How do they affect you now? What part of the Christian teaching on this do you need to keep most in mind?

Thought for prayer: Remember that the early Christians' unique vision toward sex was an important part of their witness to the world (see September 1–7 and October 1–7). Ask God to give you such an appropriate attitude toward sex that it is a sign to others of the kingdom.

December 28

[When Jane Eyre is tempted] she *ignores* what her heart says and looks to what God says. The moral laws of God at that very moment made no sense to her heart and mind at all. . . . But, she says, if she could break them when they appear inconvenient to her, of what would be their worth? . . . God's law is *for* times of temptation, when "body and soul rise in mutiny against their rigor." On God's Word then, not her feelings and passions, she plants her foot. (Hardcover, p. 231; paperback, p. 265)

TRUE SELF-RESPECT. Jane Eyre's internal speech comes when Mr. Rochester is asking her to live with him though he is still legally married. Jane turns him down, saying: "The more solitary, the more friendless, the more unsustained I am, the more I will respect myself. I will keep the law given by God."[145] Modern people would say self-respect means following your heart and desires rather than anything else. But Jane knows that if she does *not* obey God's law, she is not really following her heart but rather Mr. Rochester's agenda for her. In the same way, if we think we are following our heart when we have sex outside of marriage, we are really just a pawn of our culture, which has defined an "authentic life" for us. Obey God and respect yourself.

Reflection: Think of some other ways that obeying God despite your desires can be a way of respecting yourself.

Thought for prayer: Ask God to show you all the ways that our culture's agendas may have burrowed into your mind and heart all the while claiming they were really *your* desires and needs. Ask the Lord to save you from worldliness (1 John 2:15–17).

Is sex, however, primarily a means of individual happiness and fulfillment? No, but that doesn't mean that sex is not about joy and only about duty. The Christian teaching is that sex is primarily a way to know God and build community, and, if you use it for those things *rather* than your own personal satisfaction, it will lead to greater fulfillment than you can imagine. (Hardcover, p. 222; paperback, p. 255)

HAVING IT ALL. This is another version of a profound Christian principle, formulated in C. S. Lewis's phrase "Aim at heaven and get earth thrown in; aim at earth and you will get neither." Look at sex as something you do not do for yourself. That means first that you don't do it outside of marriage. Second, it means within marriage you do it often when you don't especially feel like it but as a way to celebrate and love your spouse. And yet, in order to truly meet the needs of your spouse in this way, you *do* need to have sex joyfully, to learn how to make love in ways that delight both of you. So aim for self-giving in sex, not self-fulfilling, and you get both thrown in.

Reflection: What can you learn practically from this way of looking at sex for your own marriage? What difference could this concept make to you?

Thought for prayer: It is not easy, in our culture, to believe that prioritizing holiness over happiness will bring you both, but putting happiness first gets neither. Ask God to burn this truth into your consciousness and heart so you can live in accordance with it—and flourish.

December 30

> To call the marriage "one flesh," then, means that sex is understood as both a sign of that personal, legal union and a means to accomplish it. The Bible says don't unite with someone physically unless you are also willing to unite with the person emotionally, personally, socially, economically, and legally. Don't become physically naked and vulnerable to the other person without becoming vulnerable in every other way, because you have given up your freedom and bound yourself in marriage. (Hardcover, p. 223; paperback, p. 256)

LOVE AND FREEDOM. The final phrase above, "you have given up your freedom and bound yourself in marriage," uses the word *freedom* in the modern sense. Today we define it as independence, the absence of any restraints on our choices. But Jesus says that the more we submit to his truth, the more that "truth will set you free" (John 8:32; cf. Psalm 119:45). Just as a fish is not free when it is flopping on the beach but when it is confined to the water for which it was designed, so humans are only truly free to be themselves when they are obeying the God who designed them. The modern definition of freedom is antithetical to love, because to love is to give the loved one say in your life. But the biblical view fits it perfectly. Give up your independence to love your spouse and you will learn greater freedom.

Reflection: Have you chafed under the loss of independence that marriage brings? How can this principle help you?

Thought for prayer: Meditate on Psalm 119:45. Then ask God to give you that deeper freedom that lies on the far side of promise-keeping, obedience, and self-discipline.

In the Old Testament . . . [God] directed that . . . there be an opportunity to have [people] remember the terms of the covenant . . . and then recommitting themselves to it. [So sex is the way for] husband and a wife . . . to do that. . . . Sex is God's appointed way for two people to reciprocally say to one another, "I belong completely, permanently, and exclusively to you." You must not use sex to say anything less. [Therefore] a covenant is necessary for sex . . . [to create] a place of security for vulnerability and intimacy. (Hardcover, pp. 223–24; paperback, pp. 256–57)

SECURITY AND INTIMACY. The relationship between the marriage covenant and sex is an interdependent, symbiotic one. Each member of an unmarried couple knows that the other person can walk away at any time with a minimum of trouble. There has been no promise or bond. But a marriage covenant creates a far greater cradle of security in which we can reveal ourselves to each other. There is no greater intimacy than vulnerable transparency, and that translates readily into sexual tenderness and delight in one another. Physical union then leads to a much greater sense of emotional and personal union. So the covenant gives us sex in a new depth and dimension, and sex strengthens and renews the vital strength of the covenant.

Reflection: Discuss the principle that "transparency translates into sexual intimacy." Have you seen this in your own marriage?

Thought for prayer: Thank God for what you have learned through this volume about marriage this year, and ask him for help implementing those lessons with wisdom, love, and grace.

ACKNOWLEDGMENTS

Thanks must go to Ray and Gill Lane who gave us exceptional support while writing this volume. They provided space to work, cooked us great meals, and gave us constant encouragement. They did this for us in one of the most beautiful parts of the world—the Lake District of England. We can think of no better setting for any writers to work. Great appreciation goes also to our editor at Viking, Brian Tart, and our literary agent David McCormick. Both of these men have been our friends and partners since 2007, a remarkable record in a world of fragile and transactional relationships. Brian and David have been indefatigable in their commitment and unfailingly wise in their work with us. We have dedicated this book to our sons and their wives—David and Jennifer, Michael and Sara, Jonathan and Ann-Marie. We have watched with admiration and respect as they have done whatever it has taken to nurture their marriages.

NOTES

1. Gerhard Von Rad, *Genesis*, trans. John H. Marks (Philadelphia: The Westminster Press, 1961), 82.
2. The Bible does allow for divorce in some situations, as we will see. Genesis, of course, does not address that, but it does show that divorce is unnatural and that marriage should be entered into with the full intention and expectation that it will be permanent.
3. Marissa Hermanson, "How Millennials Are Redefining Marriage," *The Gottmann Institute*, July 3, 2018, https://www.gottman.com/blog/millennials-redefining-marriage/.
4. Mervyn Cadwallader, "Marriage as a Wretched Institution," *The Atlantic*, November 1966.
5. C. S. Lewis, *Mere Christianity* (New York: Macmillan Company, 1958), 105–6.
6. See "Omiai: The Culture of Arranged Marriage in Japan," *Japan Info*, December 11, 2015, https://jpninfo.com/36254.
7. See Timothy Keller with Kathy Keller, *The Meaning of Marriage* (New York: Dutton, 2011), 26.
8. Wendy Wang and Kim Parker, "Record Share of Americans Have Never Married," Pew Research Center, September 24, 2014, https://www.pewsocialtrends.org/2014/09/24/record-share-of-americans-have-never-married/.
9. "Marriage Falls Out of Favour for Young Europeans," *The Guardian*, July 25, 2014, https://www.theguardian.com/lifeandstyle/2014/jul/25/marriage-young-europeans-austerity.

10. Wang and Parker, "Record Share of Americans Have Never Married," Pew Research Center.

11. There are too many studies to cite that support this. Just one example is W. Bradford Wilcox and Alysse El Hage, "The Wealth of Nations Begins at Home," Institute for Family Studies, November 8, 2018, https://ifstud ies.org/blog/the-wealth-of-nations-begins-at-home.

12. Charlotte Brontë, *Jane Eyre* (New York: Macmillan, 2017), 450–51.

13. Derek Kidner, *Genesis: An Introduction and Commentary* (Downers Grove, IL: InterVarsity Press, 1972), 66.

14. David Atkinson, *The Message of Genesis 1–11*, The Bible Speaks Today (Downers Grove, IL: InterVarsity Press, 1990), 79.

15. "Who's More Interested in Marrying—Men or Women?," Relationships inAmerica.com, n.d., http://relationshipsinamerica.com/marriage-and -divorce/whos-more-interested-in-marrying-men-or-women.

16. Christian Jarrett, "Do Men and Women Really Have Different Person-alities," BBC.com, October 12, 2016, http://www.bbc.com/future/story /20161011-do-men-and-women-really-have-different-personalities.

17. Wendy Wang, "Who Cheats More? The Demographics of Infidelity in America," Institute for Family Studies, January 10, 2018, https://ifstudies .org/blog/who-cheats-more-the-demographics-of-cheating-in-america.

18. Hermanson, "How Millennials Are Redefining Marriage," The Gottman Institute.

19. Hermanson, "How Millennials Are Redefining Marriage," especially "Millennials have a strong sense of identity."

20. Hermanson, "How Millennials Are Redefining Marriage," especially "Millennials question the institution of marriage."

21. Neil Postman, "Thy Typographical Mind" in *Amusing Ourselves to Death: Public Discourse in the Age of Show Business, anniversary edition* (New York: Penguin Books, 2005), 44–48.

22. Hermanson, "How Millennials Are Redefining Marriage."

23. C. S. Lewis, *The Four Loves* (New York: Harcourt, 1960), 123.

24. Stanley Hauerwas, "Sex and Politics: Bertrand Russell and 'Human Sex-uality,'" *Christian Century*, April 19, 1978, 417–22.

25. "All those eyes intent on me. Devouring me. What? Only two of you? I thought there were more; many more. So this is hell. I'd never have believed it. You remember all we were told about the torture-chambers, the fire and brimstone, the 'burning marl.' Old wives' tales! There's no need for red-hot pokers. Hell is—other people!" from Jean-Paul Sartre, *No Exit and Three Other Plays*, reissue edition (New York: Vintage, 1989), 45.

26. Stanley Hauerwas, *A Community of Character* (South Bend, IN: University of Notre Dame Press, 1981), 172.

27. Denis de Rougemont, *Love in the Western World* (New York: Harper and Row, 1956), 300, quoted in Diogenes Allen, *Love: Christian Romance, Marriage, Friendship* (Eugene, OR: Wipf and Stock, 2006), 96.

28. Ernest Becker, *The Denial of Death* (New York: Free Press, 1973), 160, 167.

29. Wang and Parker, "Record Share of Americans Have Never Married," Pew Research Center.

30. See Jonathan Edwards, "Sermon Fifteen: Heaven Is a World of Love" in *The Works of Jonathan Edwards*, WJE Online, Jonathan Edwards Center, Yale University, http://edwards.yale.edu/archive?path=aHR0cDovL2Vkd 2FyZHMueWFsZS5lZHUvY2dpLWJpbi9uZXXdwaGlssby9nZXRvYmplY 3QucGw/Yy43430jQ6MTUud2plbw==.

31. Thomas Watson, *A Body of Divinity* (Passmore and Alabaster, 1890; reprint, Ada, MI: Baker Books, 1979), 334.

32. Derek Kidner, *Proverbs: An Introduction and Commentary*, vol. 17, Tyndale Old Testament Commentaries (Downers Grove, IL: InterVarsity Press, 1964), 51.

33. Leon Morris, *The Gospel According to Matthew*, The Pillar New Testament Commentary (Grand Rapids, MI: Eerdmans Publishing Co., 1992), 117.

34. See especially Dietrich Bonhoeffer's unsurpassed *Life Together* (New York: Harper & Row, 1954).

35. See Kyle Harper, *From Shame to Sin: The Christian Transformation of Sexual Morality in Late Antiquity* (Cambridge, MA: Harvard University Press, 2016). The sex ethic in the Roman world dictated that wives had to be virgins when married and could only have sex with their husbands, while men before and after marriage were expected to have sex with prostitutes, servants, and anyone beneath them in the social order.

36. This idea of the church as the "Second Eve" to Christ's "Second Adam" comes from Eowyn Jones Stoddard, in correspondence.

37. The quote within *The Meaning of Marriage* is from Robert Letham, *The Holy Trinity: In Scripture, History, Theology, and Worship* (Phillipsburg, NJ: Presbyterian and Reformed, 2004), 456.

38. C. S. Lewis, *Mere Christianity* (New York: HarperCollins, 2001), 174–76.

39. For a taste, see the coronation scene in C. S. Lewis's novel *Perelandra: A Novel* (New York: The Macmillan Company, 1965), 195–222.

40. See Philippians 2:6: "Who, being in very nature God . . . he made himself nothing by taking the very form of a servant." If we say, "Being a kind man, he lent him the money," the first clause is the cause of the second

clause's action. So here the Bible indicates that Jesus gave up his power and became a servant because it was his nature as God to do so.

41. There are too many articles and studies to cite here. Here is one example: "Millennials in Adulthood: Detached from Institutions, Networked with Friends," Pew Research Center, March 7, 2014, https://www.pew socialtrends.org/2014/03/07/millennials-in-adulthood/.

42. "Love (III)", in Helen Wilcox, ed., *The English Poems of George Herbert* (Cambridge, UK: Cambridge University Press, 2007), 661.

43. Simone Weil, *Waiting for God* (New York: Harper, 2009), 27.

44. For a look at the power of the Scriptures as a means of life transformation and of communion with God, see our treatment of Psalm 119 in Timothy and Kathy Keller, *The Songs of Jesus: A Year of Devotions in the Psalms* (New York: Viking Penguin, 2010), 304–25.

45. See the June 11 devotional in Timothy and Kathy Keller, *God's Wisdom for Navigating Life: A Year of Devotions in the Book of Proverbs* (New York: Viking Penguin, 2017), 162.

46. English Standard Version translation.

47. Judith Viorst quoted in "How to Stay Happily Married," Penelope Green, *The New York Times*, May 4, 2019, https://www.nytimes.com/2019/05/04/style/judith-viorst-poems.html.

48. Lewis, *Perelandra*, 17.

49. John Newton, "Glorious Things of Thee Are Spoken" (1779).

50. C. T. Studd (1860–1931), "Only One Life," public domain.

51. C. S. Lewis, *Mere Christianity* (Macmillan, 1960), 190.

52. We are "free to choose or change spouses . . . to choose or change careers. But we can never choose or change [who are] our children. They are the last binding obligation in a culture that asks for almost no other permanent commitments at all." Jennifer Senior, *All Joy and No Fun: The Paradox of Modern Parenthood* (New York: HarperCollins, 2014), 44.

53. English Standard Version translation.

54. Joyce G. Baldwin, *Haggai, Zechariah and Malachi: An Introduction and Commentary*, vol. 28, Tyndale Old Testament Commentaries (Downers Grove, IL: InterVarsity Press, 1972), 260–61.

55. Baldwin, *Haggai, Zechariah and Malachi*, 260–61.

56. W. Bradford Wilcox, "The Evolution of Divorce" in *National Affairs*, Spring 2009.

57. Pieter A. Verhoef, *The Books of Haggai and Malachi*, The New International Commentary on the Old Testament (Grand Rapids, MI: Eerdmans Publishing Co., 1987), 281.

58. R. T. France, *The Gospel of Matthew*, The New International Commentary on the New Testament (Grand Rapids, MI: Eerdmans Publishing Co., 2007), 721. See also the article by John Murray, "Divorce and Remarriage," available at https://www.the-highway.com/divorce_Murray.html.

59. See the Westminster Confession of Faith, Chapter 24, "Of Marriage and Divorce,"which reads "nothing but adultery, or such willful desertion as can no way be remedied by the Church, or civil magistrate, is cause sufficient of dissolving the bond of marriage" (Matt. 19:8–9; 1 Cor. 7:15; Matt. 19:6).

60. See the "The Westminster Divines on Divorce for Physical Abuse." This paper examines whether physical abuse of a spouse could be seen as a form of "willful desertion." With a number of qualifications, it concludes that it can. See https://docs.google.com/viewer?url=http%3A%2F%2Fwww.pcahistory.org%2Fpca%2F2-267.doc.

61. David Itzkoff, "'Avengers: Endgame': The Screenwriters Answer Every Question You Might Have," *The New York Times*, April 29, 2019, https://www.nytimes.com/2019/04/29/movies/avengers-endgame-questions-and-answers.html.

62. See also Psalms 42:5–6, 11; 43:5; 103:1, 22; 104:1, 35; 116:7; 146:1.

63. Alexander Schmemann, "Worship in a Secular Age," a chapter in *For the Life of the World: Sacraments and Orthodoxy* (Crestwood, NY: St. Vladimir's Press, 1970), http://jean.square7.ch/wolfcms/public/SyndesmosTexts/Text_34_Schmemann-Secular%20Age.pdf.

64. The Wallace address can be found at https://web.ics.purdue.edu/~drkelly/DFWKenyonAddress2005.pdf.

65. Thomas Chalmers (1780–1847), "The Expulsive Power of a New Affection," https://www.monergism.com/thethreshold/sdg/Chalmers,%20Thomas%20-%20The%20Exlpulsive%20Power%20of%20a%20New%20Af.pdf.

66. This is based on the first line of the hymn by Charlotte Elliott (1780–1871): "O Jesus make Thyself to me/ A living, bright reality/ More present to faith's vision keen/ Than any earthly object seen/ More dear, more intimately nigh/ Than e'en the closest earthly tie."

67. I'm speaking here of Western marriages, not arranged marriages, which can work in the opposite direction, the service-love leading to pleasure-love. See the devotional for January 24.

68. See Edwards, "Sermon Fifteen: Heaven Is a World of Love," part V.

69. For further reflections on this week's Bible verses see Keller, *God's Wisdom for Navigating Life*, 247, 251.

70. This is the verse Psalm 86:11 in the English Standard Version, paraphrased into a plural form.

71. Bruce Waltke, *The Book of Proverbs: Chapters 15–31*, New International Commentary on the Old Testament (Grand Rapids, MI: Eerdmans Publishing Co., 2004), 529, 532.

72. Waltke, *The Book of Proverbs*, 521.

73. Christopher Wright, *Deuteronomy* (Peabody, MA: Hendrickson Publishers, 1996), 256.

74. See Edwards, "Sermon Fifteen: Heaven Is a World of Love," part V.

75. Respectively, "I Will Always Be with You" by Sheena Easton, "I'll Be Loving You Eternally" by Petula Clark, "Longer Than" by Dan Fogelberg, and "I Will Love You Forever" by Demis Roussos.

76. See the third installment of the instructional film *The Trumpet* by Rafael Mendez, https://www.youtube.com/watch?v=gUij8FCg0z8.

77. D. M. Lloyd-Jones, *Spiritual Depression: Its Causes and Cure* (Grand Rapids, MI: Eerdmans Publishing Co., 1965), 20–21.

78. "We conclude that it constituted a physical sign in the public domain of respect, affection, and reconciliation within the Christian community, and that its distinctive use among fellow believers underlined and nurtured the mutuality, reciprocity, and oneness of status and identity which all Christians share across divisions of race, class, and gender." Anthony C. Thiselton, *The First Epistle to the Corinthians: A Commentary on the Greek Text*, New International Greek Testament Commentary (Grand Rapids, MI: Eerdmans Publishing Co., 2000), 1346.

79. English Standard Version translation.

80. English Standard Version translation.

81. Lewis, *Mere Christianity*, 117.

82. Edmund Morgan, *American Slavery, American Freedom* (New York: W. W. Norton, 1975), 328.

83. Robert Bellah et al., *Habits of the Heart*, 2nd ed. (Berkeley and Los Angeles: University of California Press, 1996), 333.

84. Aristotle, *Nicomachean Ethics*, trans. W. D. Ross, Book II:1, http://classics.mit.edu/Aristotle/nicomachaen.2.ii.html.

85. For more on meditation as a means of grace somewhat distinct from Bible reading and prayer, see "As Conversation: Meditating on His Word" in Timothy Keller, *Prayer: Experiencing Awe and Intimacy with God* (New York: Penguin Books, 2014), 145–64.

86. These four are taken from Kidner, *Proverbs*, 45.

87. English Standard Version translation.

88. Lewis, *Mere Christianity*, 134.

89. "Ten thousand (*myria*, hence our 'myriad') is the largest numeral for which a Greek term exists, and the talent is the largest known amount

of money. When the two are combined the effect is like our 'zillions.' What God has forgiven his people is beyond human calculation." R. T. France, *The Gospel of Matthew*, The New International Commentary on the New Testament (Grand Rapids, MI: Eerdmans Publishing Co., 2007), 706.

90. There are boundaries. Romans 12:9, "Love must be sincere. Hate what is evil; cling to what is good," reminds us that we are not loving wisely or truly when we enable someone to sin or sin against us. It is not loving someone to allow them to abuse or to make it easy for them to do so. See Part Three of Dan B. Allender and Tremper Longman, *Bold Love* (Colorado Springs, CO: NavPress, 1992), 229–310, which distinguishes between loving an "evil person," a very "foolish person," and a "normal sinner."

91. Bonhoeffer, *Life Together*, 110–11.

92. Bonhoeffer, *Life Together*, 120.

93. Aelred of Rievaulx, *Spiritual Friendship* (Trappist, KY: Cistercian Publications, 2010).

94. Mine is, writes Tim.

95. Harper, *From Shame to Sin*, 87.

96. Harper, *From Shame to Sin*, 87–88.

97. "[Christians pulled off a] transformation in the deep logic of sexual morality. Even where the rules of conduct remained the same (such as the nearly unchanging expectations placed on respectable women) the moral sanctions [deep logic] changed. Christian sexual morality marked a paradigm shift, a quantum leap to a new foundational logic of sexual ethics, in which the cosmos [God] replaced the city [polis—social order] as the framework for morality. . . . For the Greeks and Romans, public sexual ideology was an organic expression of a social system. . . . Even pagan philosophy tended, at its deepest level, to offer a duty-based sexual ethics that accepted the logic of social reproduction while devaluing pleasure as such. But . . . Christianity broke sexual morality free from its social moorings. The . . . new model of moral agency centered around an absolutely free individual whose actions bore an eternal and cosmic significance. . . . Into this . . . cityscape of tremulous paganism crept a missionary [St. Paul] with a startling message: 'Do you not know that your body is a temple of the Holy Spirit within you?'" Kyle Harper, "The First Sexual Revolution: How Christianity Transformed the Ancient World," *First Things*, January 2018, https://www.firstthings.com/article/2018/01/the-first-sexual-revolution.

98. See entry on *"symphero"* in Johan Lust et al., *A Greek-English Lexicon of the Septuagint, Revised Edition* (Peabody, MA: Hendrickson Publishing, 2008).

99. Wendell Berry, *Sex, Economy, Freedom, and Community* (New York: Pantheon, 1994), 119–20. See the endnote about this in Keller, *The Meaning of Marriage*, 277n172.

100. See Thiselton, *The First Epistle to the Corinthians*, 462.

101. See the Second Collect for Peace in "The Order for Morning Prayer Daily throughout the Year" in the Book of Common Prayer.

102. "Paul will argue in the next few verses that being-in-Christ entails a bonding and binding (κολλάω) which is threatened with a wrenching apart if the body (τὸ σῶμα) is 'bonded' with that which contradicts the Christ bonding, or pulls in a different direction." Thiselton, *The First Epistle to the Corinthians*, 464.

103. D. S. Bailey, *The Man-Woman Relation in Christian Thought* (London: Longmans, 1959), 10.

104. Harper, "The First Sexual Revolution."

105. "[I]n the context equally of union with Christ and of physical union the issue becomes one of fully 'giving' oneself to the one to whom one belongs." Thiselton, *The First Epistle to the Corinthians*, 474.

106. Harper, "The First Sexual Revolution."

107. *"Porneia*, fornication, went from being a cipher for sexual sin in general to a sign for all sex beyond the marriage bed, and . . . [for] same sex love, regardless of age, status, or role [which] was forbidden without qualification. . . . The code of sexual rules that came to prevail in the early Christian church was highly distinctive. It came to mark the great divide between Christians and the world. Its moral logic was more innovative still." Harper, *From Shame to Sin*, 85.

108. English Standard Version translation.

109. "[Walter] Brueggemann argues that the phrase "my/your bone and flesh" is actually a covenant formula. . . . Thus when representatives of the northern tribes visit David at Hebron and say to him, 'we are your bone and flesh' (2 Sam. 5:1), this is not a statement of relationship ('we have the same roots') but a pledge of loyalty ('we will support you in all kinds of circumstances'). Taken this way, the man's *this one, this time, is bone of my bones and flesh of my flesh* becomes a covenantal statement of his commitment to her." Victor P. Hamilton, *The Book of Genesis: Chapters 1–17*, The New International Commentary on the Old Testament (Grand Rapids, MI: Eerdmans Publishing Co., 1990), 179–80.

110. See Ed Wheat and Gloria Okes Perkins, *Love Life for Every Married Couple: How to Fall in Love, Stay in Love* (Grand Rapids, MI: Zondervan), 256.

111. Judson Swihart, *How Do You Say "I Love You"?* (Downers Grove, IL: InterVarsity Press, 1977).

112. Don Carson, *Love in Hard Places* (Wheaton, IL: Crossway, 2002), 83.

113. "Most scholars believe that some in Corinth were saying that 'it is good for a man not to have (any) sexual relations with a woman' (7:1) and were consequently advocating celibacy in marriage, divorce from unbelieving partners, and remaining single if you were a 'virgin' or a widow. In other words, they were promoting celibacy as a rule or norm and considered sex to be a sin (cf. 'sin' in 7:28, 36)." Roy E. Ciampa and Brian S. Rosner, *The First Letter to the Corinthians*, The Pillar New Testament Commentary (Grand Rapids, MI: Eerdmans Publishing Co., 2010), 267.

114. ". . . a low view of the body, which was rife in Greek and Roman thought, may have impacted the Corinthians . . . to their movement in an ascetic direction. Stoic and Cynic philosophy taught that the unmarried may have an advantage in the pursuit of wisdom. Similarly, Greek popular piety viewed virginity as a means to religious power, as, for example, with the priestesses of the Oracle at Delphi. Thus, some in Corinth may have taken the irrelevance of the body to things of the spirit (cf. 'body and spirit' in 7:34) to imply license and libertinism in sexual matters (see 6:12–20), while others took it as an encouragement to celibacy and denial of bodily pleasures (see 7:1–40)." Ciampi and Rosner, *The First Letter to the Corinthians*, 267.

115. See Harper, *From Shame to Sin*, 182–85. The Christian emperor Theodosius II in 428 A.D. passed a law that said men could not force daughters or slaves or other women with less social status into sex. It was a remarkable first step toward the idea that sex had to be consensual, and it was also a major bulwark against the exploitation of women.

116. Courtney Sender, "He Asked Permission to Touch, but Not to Ghost," *The New York Times*, September 7, 2018.

117. See Matthew 15:19; Mark 7:21; Acts 15:20; Romans 1:29; 1 Corinthians, 6:9–10, 18; Galatians 5:19; Ephesians 5:3–5; Colossians 3:5; 1 Thessalonians 4:3; 1 Timothy 1:10; and Hebrews 13:4.

118. "One . . . clear difference between Christianity and Judaism [and all other traditional religions] is the former's entertainment of the idea of singleness as the paradigm way of life for its followers." Hauerwas, *A Community of Character*, 174.

119. Hauerwas, *A Community of Character*, 191.

120. From John Newton, "I asked the Lord that I might grow" in *Olney Hymns*, https://hymnary.org/text/i_asked_the_lord_that_i_might_grow.

121. Genesis 3:16 says that one of the results of sin is that the husband will "rule over" his wife. In the context it is the consensus of interpreters, regardless of their view of roles in marriage, that this is speaking not about loving authority but tyranny.

122. Patrick O'Brian, *Post Captain* (New York: W. W. Norton, 1990), 249.

123. "Applied to Genesis 3:16, the desire of the woman for her husband is akin to the desire of sin that lies poised ready to leap at Cain. It means a desire to break the relationship of equality and turn it into a relationship of servitude and domination. The sinful husband will try to be a tyrant over his wife." Hamilton, *The Book of Genesis*, 202.

124. This is referring to Paul and Linda McCartney's "Silly Love Songs," which appears in the 1976 album *Wings at the Speed of Sound*.

125. Iain M. Duguid, *The Song of Songs: An Introduction and Commentary*, Tyndale Old Testament Commentaries (Downers Grove, IL: IVP Academic, 2015), 40.

126. Duguid, *The Song of Songs*, 82–83.

127. Duguid, *The Song of Songs*, 93.

128. Duguid, *The Song of Songs*, 87.

129. Duguid, *The Song of Songs*, 92–93.

130. Duguid, *The Song of Songs*, 96.

131. Elisabeth Elliot, *The Savage My Kinsman. 40th anniversary edition* (Ventura, CA: Regal Books, 1996).

132. The article is found several places on the internet. Here is one: wstatic .pcpc.org/articles/singles/singledout.pdf.

133. Duguid, *The Song of Songs*, 116.

134. Duguid, *The Song of Songs*, 116.

135. Duguid, *The Song of Songs*, 117.

136. Duguid, *The Song of Songs*, 117.

137. Duguid, *The Song of Songs*, 46.

138. Dan Allendar and Tremper Longman, *Intimate Allies: Rediscovering God's Design for Marriage and Becoming Soul Mates for Life* (Wheaton, IL: Tyndale House Publishers, 1999), 254.

139. Duguid, *The Song of Songs*, 156.

140. Kathy Keller, "Don't Take It from Me: Reasons You Should Not Marry an Unbeliever," The Gospel Coalition, January 22, 2012, https://www .thegospelcoalition.org/article/dont-take-it-from-me-reasons-you -should-not-marry-an-unbeliever/.

141. The Greek word *agape* is used widely in the New Testament and it often denotes God's gracious love for us, something like the Hebrew word

chesedh that means God's covenantal, steadfast love. However, the Greek word does not always mean 'unconditional love' in the New Testament as a technical term whenever it is used, as is commonly thought. For more on this, see the article by Mark Ward, "What Agape Really Means," Logos Talk, November 4, 2015 found at https://blog.logos.com /2015/11/how-to-pronounce-logos-and-what-agape-really-means/.

142. Harper, "The First Sexual Revolution."

143. For example, see Charles Taylor, *A Secular Age* (Cambridge, MA: Harvard University Press, 2018), 276–79.

144. English Standard Version translation.

145. Brontë, *Jane Eyre*, 450–51.